MACHIAVELLI

Giuseppe Prezzolini

MACHIAVELLI

ROBERT HALE LIMITED · LONDON

Translated by Gioconda Savini from
the Italian, *Machiavelli anticristo*, published
by Gherardo Casini Editore, Rome

PRINTED IN GREAT BRITAIN
BY EBENEZER BAYLIS AND SON, LTD.
THE TRINITY PRESS, WORCESTER, AND LONDON

AUTHOR'S NOTE

The present work, which served originally as the basis for several courses given by the author at Columbia University between 1930 and 1950, is based on the concept that Machiavelli's thought cannot be adequately understood solely through a study of his works. It must also be interpreted through the writings it has inspired in the course of history. The true history of a thinker begins at the point where his thought has been developed, modified and enriched by others. Therefore the explanation of a particular theory is not to be found in the historical circumstances of the author's own time alone, but in its potential adaptability to new circumstances, events, criticism and opposition. The power of Machiavelli's thought is found in Machiavellianism. Centuries after Machiavelli's death, Machiavellianism is still in force. It has had its greatest influence since the nineteenth century, when awareness of its validity became explicit and it was universally accepted.

The kernel of Machiavelli's thought is that politics is a human activity incompatible with Christian morality. He advocated the ideal of the Roman State, the great political creation which he believed was weakened and destroyed by Christianity. Machiavelli's thought has stung to the quick all political writers from his time on. It is alive today because his propositions have stood up in the face of condemnation, misunderstanding, and false interpretation.

This edition is a translation of a book of 477 pages published in

Italy under the title *Machiavelli anticristo* (Rome, 1954). It is the only modern work available at present that considers both the thought of Machiavelli and of his adversaries, followers, interpreters and appropriators. The two volumes of Oreste Tommasini (1844–1919), *La vita e gli scritti di N. Machiavelli nella loro relazione col Machiavellismo*, are not only antiquated and badly organized, but out of print; moreover, they were never translated into English.

This condensation of the original work was made by the author himself; the passages omitted either concern certain peculiarities of Machiavelli's style and are of no interest to those who do not read Italian, or deal with secondary circumstances and movements of marginal thought. A few passages have been added to bring the work up to date. Nothing essential has been omitted in this translation made by the author's wife, Gioconda Savini, under his supervision and direction.

The author is grateful to Professor Allan H. Gilbert of Duke University, whose translations of Machiavelli's letters have been used. He is also indebted to Joseph Tusiani, who very kindly translated the poems for this edition of the book.

GIUSEPPE PREZZOLINI

June, 1966

CONTENTS

Author's Note

page
I THE DOCTRINE   15

  1 The repugnance of Machiavelli's ideas

  2 His ideas misinterpreted

  3 Machiavelli, founder of political science

  4 Machiavelli and Galileo

  5 His awareness of being an innovator

  6 The new concept of the state

  7 The state and the individual

  8 The state must combat foreign powers

  9 The state is might and only might

 10 Recourse to evil is necessary in politics

 11 The pessimism of Machiavelli

 12 *Virtù* in Machiavelli

 13 The most anti-Christian thinker of his time

 14 His intellectuality

 15 Religion at the service of the state

 16 His criticism of the Church of Rome

 17 Modern states have adopted his ideas of religion

7

18 His religiosity

19 The relativity of forms of government

20 The state as form imposed on the people

21 The state as an end in itself

22 The end and the means

23 The "one man" or redeemer

24 The return of the state to first principles

25 Human nature and education

26 Necessity and liberty

27 Liberty

28 Idleness and action

29 Fortune

30 The national state

31 Love of country above all else

32 The forms of government

33 Machiavelli and the Renaissance

34 Breaking away from the Middle Ages

35 Motives in history

36 Machiavelli's political formula

37 His dialectics

II MACHIAVELLI'S PRECURSORS   87

1 Plato

2 The Sophists

3 Euripides

4 Thucydides

5 Aristotle

6 Polybius

7 Plutarch

8 Carneades

9 The Romans: Cicero
10 St. Augustine
11 Dante
12 The Humanists

III HIS WORK   109

1 Report on the Pistoia Factions
2 Method used by Duke Valentine
3 On Providing Money
4 On Dealing with the Valdichiana Rebels
5 Annals of Italy
6 The Prince
7 Discourses
8 *The Comedies*
9 The Art of War
10 The Life of Castruccio Castracani
11 Florentine Histories
12 Reforming the State of Florence
13 The Golden Ass
14 The Capitoli
15 Dialogue on Language
16 *The Letters*

IV HIS LIFE   141

1 *First period:* Early years, 1469–98
2 *Second period:* To his dismissal by the Medici,
   1498–1512
3 *Third period:* To his death, 1512–27

V HIS FRIENDS AND CONTEMPORARIES 167

   1 Buonaccorsi
   2 Savonarola
   3 Francesco Vettori
   4 Alamanni
   5 Leonardo da Vinci
   6 Fregoso
   7 Francesco Guicciardini
   8 Brucioli and Luigi Guicciardini
   9 Bandello

VI MACHIAVELLIANISM 181

   1 The real life of Machiavelli: Machiavellianism
   2 Universal hatred of Machiavelli *and* its origin
   3 The first enemy, Cardinal Reginald Pole
   4 Gentillet
   5 Busini
   6 The Florentine Historians
   7 Writers and Literati
   8 Giovio
   9 The Plagiarists
  10 The purge and the Tuscans
  11 The Jesuits
  12 Paolo Paruta
  13 Botero, Boccalini, Sarpi and others
  14 The Utopians

MACHIAVELLI AND THE PHILOSOPHERS 217

   1 Francis Bacon
   2 Descartes

3 Thomas Hobbes

4 Spinoza

5 Vanini

6 Leibnitz

MACHIAVELLI AND THE EIGHTEENTH CENTURY   224

1 Alfieri

2 Baretti

MACHIAVELLI IN FRANCE   226

1 Corbinelli

2 Hostility of the French

3 Montesquieu

4 The French translators

5 Richelieu

MACHIAVELLI IN ENGLAND   232

1 The diabolic legend

2 Edmund Spenser

3 Walter Raleigh

4 The dramatists

5 David Hume

6 Milton

7 The romantics

8 The moderns

MACHIAVELLI IN SPAIN   242

1 A positive anti-Machiavellianism

2 Juan de Mariana, S.J.

3 The Machiavellists: Barrientos

4 Setanti
5 Gracian

MACHIAVELLI IN GERMANY   254

    1 Acceptance by the Germans
    2 Lipsius and Schoppe
    3 Conring, Althusius, Christ
    4 Herder
    5 Fichte and Hegel
    6 The historians
    7 The diabolic in politics

PERIODIC REBIRTH OF MACHIAVELLI   265

    1 Ferrari, Joly and others
    2 G. B. Vico

MACHIAVELLI AND THE ENCYCLOPAEDISTS   274

    1 Bayle
    2 Voltaire and Frederick II
    3 Diderot
    4 Rousseau
    5 Helvétius, Condillac and others
    6 Galiani

MACHIAVELLI AND THE RISORGIMENTO   285

    1 Machiavelli's reduced stature
    2 Cuoco
    3 Leopardi
    4 Balbo
    5 Gioberti

6 Manzoni

7 Mazzini

8 De Sanctis

9 Giuseppe Ferrari

10 The Romantics

VII MACHIAVELLI, OUR CONTEMPORARY 299

1 Machiavelli in the twentieth century

2 Machiavelli in Russia

3 Machiavelli in America

4 Machiavelli, our contemporary

Sources 329

Index 339

I

THE DOCTRINE

1 The repugnance of Machiavelli's ideas

The most serious obstacle to an understanding of Machiavelli is his thought itself, even when it is clearly expressed. People seldom believe what seems reasonable nor do they always willingly accept what is expressed clearly, because logic and clarity have a weaker hold than imagination and mystery. Propositions that run counter to common morality do not create a desire for discussion or even contradiction but rather an urge to sidestep, ignore, or misinterpret. Life, which is full of such blindness to the most clearly expressed ideas, is ruled not by intellect but by desire and pride. Men want to live, not to understand; and they want to live in their own way. If an idea seems to contradict what they want to believe, they refuse to accept it. If they really understand it, they either suppress it or avert their gaze in order not to see it.

Machiavelli's message, as we shall see, is profoundly pessimistic. He repudiates the relevance of Christian morality, the basis upon which the Western world was founded. And he even denies the values of life, except for pride, and presents a vast universal panorama that offers no reward to valour, no justice to innocent victims, and only partial victory over adverse forces to those who know how to make use of guile and power. Machiavelli conceives of the destiny of humanity as a compulsive sequence of events in which the individual participates for no particular reason, and in which he is capable of living in peace with others. Again and again Machiavelli says that "men tire of evil, and of good they sicken", and that they move from one thing to another as though driven by some diabolic force. All this is deeply significant in Machiavelli. It is far from pleasant because men like to be pictured as noble, honest, idealistic; they want to be assured of receiving a reward for their virtue not only in the hereafter, but in this life.

2   His ideas misinterpreted

It is completely understandable that Machiavelli should be one of the most condemned and, above all, the most misinterpreted thinkers in the world. His ideas seem to inspire fabrication, modification, distortion and substitution, rather than actual confutation. However, he continues to be read and discussed. Virtually every year he is laid to rest only to rise again from his uneasy grave.

Though political and religious bias and distrust of pessimistic theories are largely responsible for the blindness and prejudice surrounding him, Machiavelli himself is partly to blame for the misinterpretation of his thought: he never bothered to express it in a systematic form or in consistent terms. His style is often cited for its lucidity, simplicity, and absence of rhetoric, but it is never recommended for its consistency. True, there are writers who are difficult to understand but to some degree they employ a fairly consistent vocabulary. Machiavelli, however, employs the same words for different concepts and expresses the same concepts in different words. This is one of the chief obstacles to understanding him.

The word *state* can be taken as typical. It was used for the first time by Machiavelli in the sense that it possesses today, of a political entity enduring beyond the lifetime of single individuals and ruled by different governments. Thus Russia is the same *state* whether under the government of the Tsars or the Soviets. Machiavelli, however, also uses this word to signify *politics*[*][1]; *territory*[2]; *continuity of time*[3]; *the opposing party*[4]; *might* or *authority*[5]; *form of government* or *constitution*[6]; and even *province*[7]. Ercole[†] was

[*] Sources for citations are given in the appendix, starting on page 329.
[†] Prof. Francesco Ercole, *La politica di Machiavelli*, Rome, 1926.

the first writer to note that other expressions were used by Machiavelli for the concept "state", such as *political life, civil life, communal life*. The term *public liberty*[8] even has this meaning, and it should not be forgotten that Machiavelli often translated *res publica* as "state".

Moreover, Machiavelli did not write with the express purpose of setting forth an organic system of political philosophy but to illustrate special circumstances; this undoubtedly exerted an influence on his manner of presenting and connecting his ideas. Unlike some writers, he did not attempt to found an actual system and did not feel called upon to develop the consequences of his thought, nor to explain actual or apparent contradictions. He made use of concepts for practical purposes, at times citing examples from Italian or Florentine history, and at other times from his own personal experience. This too is characteristic of his manner of expression. But when he made a profound study of a problem, he never hesitated to express his findings. His complete honesty is one of the reasons why he is not popular. People are generally afraid of the truth, whether revealed by Christ or Machiavelli.

Meinecke* starts his history of the *raison d'état* with Machiavelli, although he observes that the phrase, "reasons of state", is not found in his writings. Rightly he adds:

> What matters is the substance of the thing, not the word . . . Machiavelli did not compress into a single term his concepts about the *raison d'état;* and as fond as he was of strong and synthetic expressions—he coined more than one—he felt no need of a verbal expression for the concepts that moved him, when they seemed obvious and entirely pervaded his thought.[9]

As a matter of fact, the essential concept of the *raison d'état* is well expressed by Machiavelli in these words:

> I answered that a state and a people are governed differently from a private individual.[10]
> Private enemies are to be preferred to enemies of the state.[11]

* F. Meinecke, *Die Idee der Staatsräson in der Neueren Geschichte*, 1924.

In addition to using different terms to express the same concepts and identical terms to express different concepts, we also find in Machiavelli a sequence of ideas not expressed in any precise terms, forming the real kernel of his thought.

3   Machiavelli, founder of political science

Machiavelli's principal contribution to the history of philosophy and of political doctrine is in having fundamentally renovated the concept of politics—in basing his generalizations on the direct observation of events. There were treatises on politics before Machiavelli, but they only sought to determine which was the best state. Machiavelli upset these attempts to define an ideal state in order to discover the real nature of states and how they functioned. The difference between Plato and Aristotle, on the one hand, and Machiavelli on the other is the same difference that exists between a student of anatomy who uses a statue for a model and one who uses a living body: the statue may be perfect aesthetically, but it is not realistic.

From our Giuseppe Ferrari to Dunning, from Höffding to Windelband, from Burckhardt to Dilthey, from Treitschke to Pareto, down to the recent political manual of Enrico Leone, historians of philosophy and of political doctrines, and essayists on these sciences, are all in agreement that Machiavelli was the renovator of modern political science and, to use an apt expression of Gioberti, that Machiavelli was the "Galileo of politics".[12]

4   Machiavelli and Galileo

The comparison of Machiavelli to a scientist like Galileo dates back to the eighteenth century, to Algarotti, who compared Machiavelli to Kepler. This comparison is substantially valid, even in detail. Indeed the greatness of a scientist like Galileo stems from the fact that he laid the foundations of modern science, tying it in with the Greek thought of Archimedes and Apollodorus, just as Machiavelli tied his in with Polybius. Through them humanity learned that the universe—the solar system for Galileo, and history for Machiavelli—was indifferent to the desires and destinies of the individual. Before Galileo, man believed that the universe was created expressly for him, that the stars influenced his destiny and, in a certain sense, were involved in his fate. With Machiavelli history is seen as a conflict among the forces that envelop man. It unfolds with an inexorable rhythm in which only for a short period can man exert a limited influence, and then only if he subscribes and adheres to the laws of history. With Galileo the starry world ceased to be Christian; with Machiavelli history ceased to be Christian. When he quotes examples from pagan and Christian history, Machiavelli gives no sign of believing in revelation.

5   His awareness of being an innovator

Machiavelli was fully aware of presenting a new method and of taking a different stand from those who had preceded him. He says:

> And as I know that many have written of this, I fear that my writing about it may be deemed presumptuous, differing as I do, especially in this matter, from the opinions of others. But my intention being to write something of use to those who understand, it appears to me more proper to go to the real truth of the matter than to its imagined ideal; and many have imagined republics and principalities which have never been seen or known to exist in reality.[13]

In this new political doctrine, *verità effettuale,* he knows he has made great strides:

Though the enterprise is difficult, yet . . . I think I can carry it out in such a way that there shall remain but a short road for another to travel in order to reach the proper destination.[14]

The proper destination which Machiavelli hoped to attain was in the sphere of action—although he realized that he himself could never reach the goal because of the modest social position he occupied. He hoped that the knowledge which he possessed would serve Italy as a weapon to recapture her past greatness.

At the end of the preface to the second book of his "lectures" to Florentine youths, Machiavelli says:

I shall make so bold as to declare plainly what I think of those days and of our own, so that the minds of young men who read what I have written may turn from the one and prepare to imitate the other, whenever fortune provides them with occasion for so doing. For it is the duty of a good man to point out to others what is well done, even though the malignity of the times or of fortune has not permitted him to do it for himself, to the end that of those who have the capacity one more beloved of heaven may be able to do it.[15]

6   The new concept of the state

Central to Machiavelli's teaching is a clearly formulated concept of the state—although never openly defined as such—as an organization that unites its component parts into a composite whole, and whose aims transcend those of the individual. Religions are also such organizations. The state is a living being, composed of individuals—a mixed body, as he calls it, that complies with the general laws of life and history. Like any other organism, it is born, lives, changes, becomes corrupt, sickens, can be healed or renewed by a return to its principles, may be absorbed by other organisms, wages war, dies.

It is a well-established fact that the life of all mundane things is of finite duration. But things which complete the whole of the course appointed them by heaven are in general those bodies which do not disintegrate, but maintain themselves in orderly fashion either without change or, if there be, these changes tend rather to their conservation than to their destruction. Here I am concerned with composite bodies, such as states and religious institutions; in their regard I affirm that those changes make for conservation which lead them back to their start. Hence those are better constituted and have a longer life whose institutions make frequent renovations possible, or which can be brought to renovation by some event which has nothing to do with their constitution. For it is clearer than daylight that, without renovation, these bodies do not last.[16]

This is one passage among many which clearly expresses a naturalistic and organic concept of the state. The state is not eternal, but is a natural organism; even the Roman state, one of the greatest expressions of human political strength, came to an end.

The principal aim of the state is to survive. And it must submit to the laws of survival, and be continuously renewed in order not to expire within a short time. Every state will eventually come to an end—this is the law of life—but intelligence and science can prolong its lifetime, while ignorance can destroy it. Machiavelli's discourse to his fellow citizens is similar to the advice that a modern doctor—one who does not promise immortality but who recommends hygiene and a change of habits—gives to his patients. Machiavelli makes constant use of contemporary medical terms—a legacy from his Roman and Greek schooling, and a common practice at that time. His is the role of a "political doctor" of states, those strange composite beings as he calls them, which are subject to the same laws as other creatures.

If there were a man who could put down political disorders and by his ability cure them, think how much credit he would have with God and men.[17]

In every large city there inevitably occur unfortunate incidents which call for the physician, and the more serious the incidents the wiser should be the physician one looks for.[18]

The analogy that Machiavelli draws between the state and the human body is not only metaphorical. He is firmly convinced that there is a profound similarity between the two natural realities. The state, as he often repeats, is a mixed body made up of individuals. He says:

> I am concerned here with composite bodies like states and religious institutions.[19]
> Cities [as in the word *polis,* in the sense of state] ... are mixed bodies.[20]

And he demonstrates, by means of detailed examples:

> For it is the heart and the vital parts of the body that have to be strengthened, not the extremities, since without them the body can survive, but if the former be injured, it dies; yet such states keep the heart disarmed but arm the hands and feet.[21]

To sum up, the state like any organic society is made up of various parts, some central and important, others secondary and subordinate. Since survival is the prime function of a state, the less important parts may be sacrificed to the welfare of the whole state. (Lincoln agreed with Machiavelli on this point, when he was defending himself against the accusation of having overridden the Constitution. "Was it possible to lose the nation and yet preserve the Constitution? By general law, life and limb must be protected, yet often a limb must be amputated to save a life, but a life is never wisely given to save a limb. I felt that measures, otherwise unconstitutional might become lawful by becoming indispensable to the preservation of the Constitution through the preservation of the nation.") The healthy state is not concerned with the good of its single components; nor does it need to strive for a superior or ulterior good, only if this good is a condition of survival. Never in Machiavelli's works does he speak of a state sacrificing itself for ends that transcend those of its own survival or the good of a single individual. If Machiavelli could have imagined a state that would sacrifice itself for a reason other than for its own existence, he would probably have reverted to his medical analogy and called that state mentally sick—an insane state. Naturally, this viewpoint is in direct contrast to the one widely held in our time by those who profess that the state is merely an agency for the benefit of individuals.

7 The state and the individual

It is not precisely in these terms—which became popular much later, in the nineteenth century—but in his thought that Machiavelli is fully aware that a conflict of interest often exists between the individual and the state. However, for Machiavelli, each time the interests of the individual take precedence over those of the state, the state suffers. The common good is the highest good that man can attain, and whatever tends to establish the state and save it is to be accepted, even if recourse is taken to violent measures, including fratricide. He says:

> Wherefore the prudent organizer of a state whose intention it is to govern not in his own interests but for the common good, and not in the interests of his successors but for the sake of that fatherland which is common to all, should contrive to be alone in his authority. Nor will any reasonable man blame him for taking any action, however extraordinary, which may be of service in the organizing of a kingdom or the constituting of a republic. It is a sound maxim that reprehensible actions may be justified by their effects, and that when the effect is good, as it was in the case of Romulus, it always justifies the action. For it is the man who uses violence to spoil things who is blameworthy, not the man who uses it to mend them.[22]

In sketching his own idealistic "programme" where the head of a state "introduces a new culture into a state which still possesses something good," Machiavelli urges "forcing the citizens ... to think less of their own interests than of the common good."[23]

When war, carried on by mercenary troops, becomes an instrument for the personal gain of the captains, he calls it dishonest (*The Art of War*, I, 270a); when he speaks of political economy, he favours regulations that contribute to enriching the state even, if necessary, at the risk of impoverishing private citizens. And he considers a good citizen to be one who sacrifices everything for the state without seeking anything in return, and who does not even rebel against the ingratitude of his country.

8 The state must combat foreign powers

This thought prompts him to jeer at unarmed prophets and theocratic principalities. And it also explains his accepting as true princes those country tyrants—whether from the backwoods or from the merchant class—or those rebels and fugitives who formed a Commune and successfully took up arms against their Emperor. However, he denounced them for not having the courage, as he would have had, to declare their independence, and for continuing to pay tribute—only a formal tribute, but sometimes a substantial one—to their former but now vanquished masters.

The state uses might against internal disorders, which Machiavelli, again using a medical term, occasionally calls *"omori"*, an indeterminate source of disease resembling the present-day virus. The state also uses might against other states, which are always potential enemies even when they pretend to be allies, because they are ready to become overt enemies as soon as the balance of power shifts. Although Machiavelli distinguishes between the divisions of Rome which brought good to that city and those of Florence which brought ruin on it; in general he condemns "parties" or "sects". In the speech of a Florentine citizen, in whose mouth he puts his own words, he says they are the first cause of the ills of Italy:

> The universal corruption of all the Italian cities has infected and continues to infect our city also. Her towns, for want of any controlling power to restrain them, have ordered their rule and govern-

ment on a footing not of freedom, but of factious division. Thence spring all the other evils and disorders from which these cities suffer; hence the avarice we note among our citizens, and ambition, not for true glory but for discreditable honours, that in their turn give rise to hatreds, jealousies, and dissensions, feuds that bring with them death, exile, oppression of the good, and exaltation of the worthless.[24]

On the other hand, he exalts unity as a product of good government, and on this he bases his defence of the government of Borgia in Romagna, which by means of acts of terror "in a short time was highly successful in making the country orderly and united."[25]

9   The state is might and only might

Without stating it in such explicit terms, Machiavelli more than any other political writer believes that there can be no government without might.

For government consists in nothing else but so controlling subjects that they shall neither be able to, nor have cause to, do you harm; which may be done either by making quite sure of them by depriving them of all means of doing you harm, or by treating them so well that it would be unreasonable for them to desire a change of fortune.[26]

This implies a calculated ratio of might. Whoever commands must be sure of being obeyed.

It has been said by a wise man that, if one is to hold a state by violent means, the force employed should be proportionate to the resistance offered. So long as this proportion obtains, it is to be expected that the violence will last; but should the violated be stronger than the violator, it is probable that the violence will some day cease.[27]

And in the celebrated eighteenth chapter of *The Prince*, he expresses his own personal appreciation for and his philosophical conviction of a contrast that will be seen as a recurrent motif throughout his works:

How laudable it is for a prince to keep good faith, live with integrity, and not with cleverness, everyone knows. Still the experience of our times shows those princes to have done great things who have had little regard for good faith, and have been able by cleverness to confuse men and ultimately overcome those who have made loyalty their foundation.[28]

The emotional charge of that word "still" (*nondimanco*) expresses Machiavelli's sorrow that the world is not as it should be. His bitter message to men should not be overlooked. The forces that politics makes use of are love as well as fear, generosity as well as avarice, pity as well as cruelty, chastity as well as wantonness (a list can be found in Chapter 15 of *The Prince*), but it must be seen how they function. In politics everything is judged by its effect. Looking at these attributes from this point of view, vice and virtue are found to be on the same plane and are to be judged only by their ability to get results. It is true that vices are condemned by the majority of men and the immoral prince may lose the state because "reputation governs the world",[29] but it is also true that:

It is easy for strength to acquire a reputation but not for a reputation to acquire strength.[30]

At worst, the prince (that is, the head of a state, whatever form of government that state has) must only pretend to possess all those qualities which men call virtue, without having them. At any rate, he must be prepared to abandon them when the good of the state so requires.

It is not, therefore, necessary for a prince to have all the above-mentioned qualities, but it is very necessary to seem to have them. I would even be so bold as to say that to possess them and always to practise them is dangerous, but to appear to possess them is useful. Thus it is well to seem merciful, faithful, humane, sincere, religious, and also to be so; but you must have your mind so disposed that, when it is needful to be otherwise, you can change to the opposite qualities.[31]

10   Recourse to evil is necessary in politics

With this we come to another central point of Machiavellian thought, the distinction between politics and Christian ethics. What does this proposition mean? It means that a person would not dream of doing as a private individual what he is obliged to do as head of a government. If for personal gain he lied, broke his word and cheated, he should be filled with remorse. However, once he assumes the responsibility as the leader of his country, he abandons the moral criteria he held as a private individual without a twinge of conscience. His prime concern is the good of the state. The head of a state is like the captain of a boat who subordinates everything to his principal duty, to bring his ship safely into port. He does not hesitate a moment to lie or to use force against a passenger or a member of his crew when the safety of the ship is threatened. The Romans with their economy of style called this principle *salus reipublicae;* the safety of the state is the supreme law. And in his time Machiavelli and others were so convinced of the validity of this principle that they often repeated Cosimo de' Medici's motto—"states are not maintained by reciting the rosary or the Lord's Prayer"—without feeling the necessity to comment on it or to defend it. Machiavelli invented nothing new but he was the first to express a scientific awareness of this practice of statesmen.

Of him [Philip of Macedon] a writer says that he moved men from province to province as shepherds move their sheep. Such methods are exceedingly cruel and repugnant to any community, not only to a Christian one, but to any composed of men. It therefore behooves every man to shun them, and to prefer rather to live as a private citizen than as a king with such ruination of men to his score. Nonetheless, for the sort of man who is unwilling to take up this best course, it is expedient if he wishes to hold what he has to enter on the path of wrongdoing.[32]

It is to be noted that Machiavelli never fails to say that only the evil committed to create and maintain a state and to continue its existence is justified. He never says this of evil committed for personal gain; almost always, by means of a telling adjective, adverb, or a deprecatory phrase, as Croce aptly pointed out, he lets his sorrow be known that men are made as they are, and the state can only survive in this manner.

> For how we live is so far removed from how we ought to live that he who abandons what is done for what ought to be done will rather learn to bring about his own ruin than his preservation. A man who wishes to make a profession of goodness in everything must necessarily come to grief among so many who are not good.[33]

11   The pessimism of Machiavelli

The only reason that Machiavelli adduces what I would call "the necessity for evil" in political activity is that human nature is made in such a way that without force or trickery it would be impossible to maintain a "civil life" among men.

The first postulate of Machiavelli is that human nature in all times and in all places is always the same. There is no difference between the material world and the human world. As Machiavelli observes:

> The sky, the sun, the elements and men have not changed in any way from the way they were in antiquity.[34]
>
> Men are born and live and die in an order which remains ever the same.[35]
>
> Men have, and always have had, the same passions, whence it necessarily comes about that the same effects are produced.[36]

This animal species, immutable and unalterable, is condemned to undergo a continuous change of institutions because of its perpetual dissatisfaction.

Men are so created by Nature that they can desire all things but they cannot acquire all things.[37]

Men are never satisfied; when they have a thing, they are not happy with it but desire something else.[38]

Men are wont to get annoyed with adversity and fed up with prosperity.[39]

Machiavelli's verses, his comedies, his private correspondence, his writings, his reports to the Republic of Florence are filled with expressions of condemnation of men because of their wickedness, cowardice, and avidity.

For it may be said of men in general that they are ungrateful, voluble, dissembling, anxious to avoid danger, and covetous of gain. As long as you benefit them, they are entirely yours; they offer you their blood, their goods, their life, and their children, as I have said before, when the necessity is remote; but when it approaches, they revolt.[40]

And often his disdain is expressed in characteristic couplec antitheses:

In prosperity men are insolent, and in adversity abject and humble.[41]

How blind men are to the things in which they sin, and what sharp persecutors they are of the vices they do not have.[42]

But what seems to irritate Machiavelli above all is the "mediocrity of mankind". As he repeats, "They know not how to be wholly good, nor yet wholly bad."[43] It is not so extraordinary then if "in constituting and legislating for a Commonwealth, it must be taken for granted that all men are wicked."[44]

Machiavelli never seems to realize what he has in common with, nor what separates him from, Christian thought. His thought can be equated with the idea of "fallen human nature" and he seems to agree with St. Augustine's definition of man: *homo expoliatus supernaturalibus, vulneratus in naturalibus* ("Deprived of the supernatural, man is by nature corrupt"). The two thinkers agree on the nature of man except for the idea of grace, which is absent in Machiavelli. However, Machiavelli considers Nature a necessity, and a model in the then accepted meaning of the word, without implying derogatory judgment of corruption.

And this way of proceeding [sensual], if to some it may appear censurable, to me seems praiseworthy because we are imitating Nature, who is variable; and he who imitates her cannot be blamed.[45]

This irreproachable Nature, to be imitated as an ideal, is assuredly not the "corrupt nature" of the Christians. This idea alone should suffice to show how baseless is the view held by those who have tried to reconcile Machiavelli's thought with either Catholic or Protestant Christianity, even when the attempts were cleverly made (see the works of Alterisio and Von Muralt). There is really nothing Christian about Machiavelli, but it can be said of him, as of most modern philosophers, that his system seems like an imitation of and at the same time a substitution for Christian theology.

What then saves men from the damnation to which the "fallen nature" of Christianity, the penalty of original sin, leads them? Christians—some of them at least—are saved by "divine grace". According to Machiavelli, what saves certain men, those who are evil not because of corruption but because of their own character, is *virtù*, which for him is a substitute for grace.

12 Virtù *in Machiavelli*

Machiavelli's translators were at a loss to render the word *virtù*. Those who translated his works into Latin met the challenge by merely reproducing the Latin cognate, *virtus*. Realizing that it had a special value and various meanings (besides the most obvious one, corresponding to the Latin term for individual courage), his translators rendered it with many words. Perhaps the first one to study the problem was Mayer, who used it in opposition to the word *fortuna* and maintained that in Machiavelli *virtù* means above all man's will-power to overcome the natural obstacles which fortune has placed in his way. This meaning was accepted by Gentile, who used the word in this sense to expound his original interpretation of the Renaissance. He exalts the idea prevailing in this period, when man felt capable of carving out his own destiny, over the Greek concept of a destiny that crushes mankind, and the medieval idea of the will of God. During the Renaissance man thought highly of himself. He saw himself as strong, intelligent, and capable of creating his own world. It is in this sense of his own times that Machiavelli places *virtù* in opposition to *fortuna,* which limits man's infinite powers:

> *Her natural might spurs every man on earth,*
> *and always violent her kingdom is*
> *unless it is checked by* virtù's *worth.*[46]
> (*Translated by Joseph Tusiani*)

Virtù enables man to overcome ill fortune:

How much more *virtù* helped the Romans to acquire their empire than did *fortune.*[47]

What then is this *virtù?* It is force and ability, daring and prudence, efficiency, energy, *dynamis,* the combination of force and talent (Burckhardt), capacity, ability or power. Ercole gives a longer and more complicated definition:

It is the concrete exercise of liberty typical of a man of energetic and conscious will-power not to stop or control, but to mould the course of action in which he lives in order to stamp it with his own imprint, for the purpose not only of setting a goal but of translating action into reality.[48]

English translators of Machiavelli have rendered the word *virtù* as vertue, vertuous actions, powers, force, conduct, valour and conduct; preparation, virtue and industry; virtue and power; virtue and excellence; ability, powers of mind, strength, valour, qualities, worth. It is seen that the early translators, like Dacres and the Elizabethans, preferred a two-fold expression, like fortune-valour or fortune-vertue; later ones were aware of the difficulties and used various words according to the position of the word in the sentence. Gilbert in the same sentence uses ability and strength; Detmold uses virtue, ability, valour and ability, high qualities, great qualities, and great courage.

One thing is certain—but this is a negative attribute—the word *virtù* as used by Machiavelli, does not correspond to the four virtues of Plato and of the Stoics which became the cardinal virtues of Christians. Machiavelli uses it more in the sense of *dynamis* (virtue of power) than in the sense of *areté* (ethical virtue). It may be natural to wonder if in Machiavelli's description of Hannibal's character,[49] his "inhuman cruelty" should be placed among his virtues. But no one can question this passage:

> If amongst those who died ordinary deaths there was a wicked man like Severus, this must be attributed to his great good luck and to his "virtue", of which two things few men enjoy both.[50]

In Machiavelli's writings, *virtù* appears as opposite to indolence, corruption and idleness (but this was interpreted in the Christian sense). *Virtù* is assuredly an action-provoking quality, as can easily be inferred from the context. A contemplative, quietistic or effeminate attitude towards life is never called "virtuous". It is the opposite of sumptuousness, lasciviousness, licence and, in general, *dolce vita* or the easy life, that is, civilization as we know it today. It is also the opposite of simple barbaric *furor* and insolence. The *virtù* of the ancients is contrasted with the vice of Machiavelli's day. It is sometimes linked with prudence, and it is accompanied by generosity. While it can be evil, it is not necessarily so.

> It cannot be called *virtù* to kill one's fellow citizens, betray one's friends, be without faith, without pity, and without religion.[51]

We can conclude from these quotations that for Machiavelli there can be *virtù* without goodness, but never goodness without *virtù*. Goodness without *virtù* would lack the strength to function.

The *virtù* of Machiavelli is universal and is not bounded in time. The Romans possessed it, but it was also in existence during Machiavelli's day. He felt that he himself was endowed with it. Clearly, it was not necessary to be a Christian to possess it: *virtù* was responsible for Saladin winning over the disunited Christians. Machiavelli alludes to a natural and warlike origin of *virtù*:

> For the whole city, nobles and commons alike taking part in her wars, there were always found in Rome at every stage of her history many valiant and successful soldiers.[52]

Even *virtù* is subject to motion, change and corruption, concept which lies at the root of Machiavelli's thought.

> *Valor it is that quiets regions down:*
> *And then from quiet laziness derives,*
> *And laziness soon burns each land and town.*
>
> *Then once a nation has long had its share*
> *Of black disorder, valor once again*
> *Is born and back it goes to dwell right there.*[53]
> (*Translated by Joseph Tusiani*)

From this idea stems Machiavelli's theory of the migration of *virtù* among people as a veritable march from east to west, an idea for which he has been cited as among the precursors of Spengler, who between the two World Wars foretold the movement of power from Europe to the United States. The passage from which I am going to quote is the longest in Machiavelli and the one in which he is the most committed in respect to the problem of *virtù*. In it he attempts to subject this energy to a law of conservation—a law such as physicists before the discovery of radioactive substances thought would serve for the natural world:

> When I consider how this happens, I am persuaded that the world, remaining continually the same, has in it a constant quantity of good and evil; but that this good and this evil shift about from one country to another, for we know that in ancient times empires shifted from one nation to another according as the manners of these nations changed, the world as a whole continuing as before, the only

difference being that, whereas at first Assyria was made the seat of its excellence, this was afterwards placed in Media, then in Persia, until at last it was transferred to Italy and Rome. And although after the Roman Empire, none has followed which has endured or in which the world has centred its whole excellence, we nevertheless find this excellence diffused among many valiant nations.[54]

Virtù is therefore a kind of vital spirit—as everyone would have called it in Machiavelli's time—which is always maintained quantitatively equal to itself, but is distributed variously over the face of the earth, following a sort of curve or cycle. Obviously, it is not Providence that moves it but its own constitution. Like Christian grace, it breathes on certain individuals and on certain peoples not in order to inspire Christian virtues but political ones, which are energies without moral qualification. They are good and bad not in themselves but only to the degree that they maintain the value of the state and lead it to victory. Even in the event of defeat, *virtù* at least encourages an attempt to accomplish great things. For Machiavelli, a great crime is no longer a crime but an action that brings glory. There is no immortality for men, people or states endowed with *virtù,* because there is an end to all things, but as recompense there is glory.

Reproving Giampaolo Baglioni, who allowed the Pope and the unarmed Cardinals to enter Perugia, whereas he could have "destroyed them and their easy life", he says that Baglioni could have accomplished something "which would have displayed a greatness far transcending any infamy or danger that could attach to it".[55]

Here it might be said that Machiavelli seems like a relativist in moral matters. The moment an action is performed on a large scale, the dimensions of Christian morality no longer apply to it. In a world of curves, a straight line is no longer a straight line but a curve. To him the same transformation occurs when an action passes from the domain of personal interest to the public interest. It is, then, legitimate for a statesman to do things that would be considered dishonourable when done by a private individual.

13   The most anti-Christian thinker of his time

There have been many thinkers who have combated Christianity because of its dogma or its political activity. Except for Machiavelli, no one until Nietzsche in the nineteenth century opposed it for its ethics. In general, sceptics and unbelievers took exception to certain Christian doctrines like the Incarnation or the Trinity, but there have been very few who have not considered Christian morality as the highest expression of moral conduct ever attained by man. Among the few is Machiavelli. Let us for the time being pass over his political anticlericalism, his gibes at papal excommunications. These are also found in many Italian writers who were believers, like Dante and Petrarch. The fundamental point about Machiavelli is the absence of any Christian spirit in his interpretation of history.

In his writings there is no trace of a sense of sin, or of charity, or of love of neighbour. His motivations are always practical, realistic, earthy. His history unfolds independently of the coming of Christ on earth. He holds Christianity indirectly responsible for the weakening of the human spirit and for the fall of the Roman Empire. For Machiavelli, paganism and Christianity are on an equal footing; they are two religions which serve the state. His studies are based on the inapplicability of Christian morality to political life. For Machiavelli, political life is the highest and the most worthwhile activity of man, the way to attain a limited terrestrial immortality. Christian morality, which draws men away from this earth, is defined more or less openly as "lazy ambition". No comment is needed on such a statement when it is remembered how he glorifies action.

This I persuade myself is due not so much to the feebleness to which the present religion has brought the world, or the injury which a pervading apathy has wrought in many provinces and cities of Christendom, as to the want of a right intelligence of History, which renders men incapable in reading it.[56]

While the Romans continued free they adhered to this more generous and noble method, but when they came under the emperors who began to deteriorate and to love the shade rather than the sunshine, they also took to purchasing peace, now from the Parthians, now from the Germans, and at other times from other neighbouring nations. And this was the beginning of the decline of their great empire.[57]

Even more openly he denounces Christianity for having modified and humanized the rules of warfare, thus weakening Rome and preventing it from holding back the barbarians:

And though that empire was afterwards dismembered by those barbarians, yet the several parts into which it was cantoned never recovered their pristine vigour; for, in the first place, it is a very difficult matter and requires a long course of time to revive good order and discipline when it is once abolished; and in the next, the Christian religion has wrought such a change in the manners and customs of mankind, that they are now no longer under the necessity of defending themselves with such a degree of obstinacy and despair as they did in former times. For then, all such as were vanquished in battle were either put to death, or carried into perpetual slavery in the enemy's country, where they spent the remainder of their lives in labour and misery. If a town was taken, it was either demolished or the inhabitants were stripped of their goods, dispersed all over the world, and reduced to the last degree of poverty and wretchedness; so that the dread of these evils obliged them to keep up good discipline in their armies, and to honour all who excelled in the art of war. But at present those terrible apprehensions are, in a great measure, dissipated and extinguished; for after an army is defeated, those that fall into the hands of the conqueror are seldom or never put to death, and the terms of their ransom are made so easy that they do not long continue prisoners.[58]

Machiavelli transforms theology into human history. For instance, grace becomes virtue, the state takes the place of the church, and duty towards the country is substituted for obedience to God. The so-called Christian virtues, which softened life and brought about respect for the vanquished and humanized the relations between masters and slaves, are considered defects by Machiavelli.

14 The intellectuality of Machiavelli

Machiavelli is a scientific thinker who possesses the pride of the true scientist. For Machiavelli, knowledge is power. He subscribes to the concept of history usual in his time and, in a manner of speaking, canonical since the time of the Greeks and Romans and made popular by Cicero, that history is the teacher of life. He adheres to the facts and wants to offer prescriptions to help the heads of states restore the true life, that is the pagan one. Human life for Machiavelli is as changeless as that of the stars for Galileo. This immutability is the premise of his teaching. He blazes a new trail by recommending the reading of history not for pleasure but in order to imitate it. Machiavelli must have been very pleased with such a simple discovery. He advocates doing as physicians do who, having studied previous case histories of patients and cures, apply their findings to the present. Machiavelli is a convinced determinist. Russo, a critic who greatly admires him, has been justly amused at his mania for seeking motives behind every human event. Compared to histories by medieval writers, where everything stemmed from the mysterious will of God, Machiavelli may well seem extraordinary in his persistent attempt to reduce everything to human dimensions and passions. There is not a great difference between his history and the science of Leonardo. Men kill each other or become enemies, in the same way as some waters join or separate, bodies fall, and sands take form according to the direction of the wind. It is history, a physical event that repeats itself. It is history without mysteries. It can be taught *because* it repeats itself.

The principle of imitation was very popular then in art and literature. It deceived even the greatest and most original creators, who thought they had imitated the ancients when in reality they had created new worlds and new ways. For Machiavelli this principle became a law of politics. He himself makes the comparison at the end of his *The Art of War,* where he points to Italy "which seems born to bring back to life dead things, as is seen in poetry, in painting and in sculpture".[59] His personal ambition was to revive "dead things" even in politics. His political world is made up of models that are duplicated, of situations that are reproduced, of meetings of forces that recur persistently.

As exercise for the mind, the prince ought to read history and study the actions of eminent men, see how they acted in warfare, examine the causes of their victories and defeats in order to imitate the former and avoid the latter, and above all do as some men have done in the past, who have imitated some one who has been much praised and glorified, and have always kept his deeds and actions before them, as they say Alexander the Great imitated Achilles, Caesar Alexander, and Scipio Cyrus.[60]

If the same men should return to the world, as events return, a hundred years would not pass before those men would again be doing the same things.[61]

Four centuries later Nietzsche, looking out from the terrace of Sils Maria in Switzerland, suddenly realized that events would be eternally repeated. Going even further than Machiavelli, he thought that people would ultimately return to the world to lead the same lives all over again. This thought of inevitable repetition filled him with terror.

15 Religion at the service of the state

Only an intellectual would make religion a department of the state, and therefore of politics. For Machiavelli, religion is veneration of the supernatural which the people have acquired from wise and prudent men who may not believe in it. This veneration is to be maintained for the good of the state and therefore of the people themselves. It is a weapon of illusion, for the use of politics in the state's fight for survival.

In order to be believed, a religion must not use the language of politics and it should not become a separate entity—that is, it should not compete with the state:

> Princes and commonwealths that would save themselves from becoming corrupted, should before all things keep uncorrupted the rites and ceremonies of religion, and always hold them in reverence; since we can have no surer sign of the decay of a province than to see divine worship held therein in contempt. This is easily understood when it is seen on what foundation that religion rests in which a man has been born. For every religion has its root in certain fundamental ordinances peculiar to itself.[62]

It is clear that Machiavelli considers religions not revelations but social organizations. The accident of birth and the equality of religions could not be more accentuated than by the phrase "in which a man has been born", that is, not in terms of universal but by a geographical accident. It is still true today in the majority of cases that men are born to a given religion. They accept it and follow it if the heads of government favour and encourage it, even if they consider it false.

> The religion of the Gentiles had its beginning in the response of the oracles and in the prognostics of the augurs and soothsayers. All their other ceremonies and observances depended upon these; because men naturally believed that the God who could forecast their future weal or woe could also bring them to pass. Wherefore the temples, the prayers, the sacrifices, and all the other rites of their worship had their origin in this, that the oracles of Delos, of Dodona, and others celebrated in antiquity, held the world admiring and devout. But afterwards, when these oracles began to shape their answers to suit the interest of powerful men, and their impostures came to be seen through by the multitude, men grew incredulous and ready to overturn every sacred institution. For which reason, the rulers of kingdoms and commonwealths should maintain the foundations of the faith which they hold; since thus it will be easy for them to keep their country religious and, consequently, virtuous

and united. To which end they should countenance and further whatsoever is in favour of religion, even should they think it untrue; and the wiser they are, and the better they are acquainted with natural causes, the more ought they to do so. It is from this course having been followed by the wise, that the miracles celebrated even in false religions have come to be held in repute; for from whatever source they spring, discreet men will extol them and their authority give them currency everywhere.[63]

Therefore the advanced and scientific statesman must even allow the sect of haruspices (which Machiavelli puts on the same level as a sect of the Order of St. Francis) to urge people to believe in miracles, even if he knows them to be false. Miracles are an opinion, that is, a credulity, and they are a part of "false" as well as of so-called "true" religions. The authority of religion, no matter what its source, is of great importance to the state. All religions are good provided they serve to keep people virtuous and united.

After having cited many of the great miracles of ancient Rome, Machiavelli mentions a special one where the people believed that a statue nodded its head and seemed to advise a return to Rome.

But their faith and belief were wholly approved of and confirmed by Camillus and by the other chief men of the city. Had religion been maintained among the princes of Christendom on the footing on which it was established by its Founder, the Christian states and republics had been far more united and far more prosperous than they now are.[64]

It can be seen that the word religion is used interchangeably for pagan as well as for Christian belief, and that Christianity is defined as a republic, that is, it is considered a social organization. The beneficial results of religion are first political (Christian republics are more united than other republics) and second hedonistic (they are happier republics).

16   His criticism of the Church of Rome

Machiavelli, considering religions from a purely nationalistic point of view, was a critic not only of Christianity but of the Church of Rome. The reasons that impelled him to write "in opposition to the opinion that the welfare of the Italian cities stems from the Church" are two:

> The first is that, through the ill example of the Roman Court, the country has lost all religious feeling and devoutness, a loss which draws after it infinite mischief and disorder. . . . To the Church therefore and to the priests we Italians owe this first debt, that through them we have become wicked and irreligious.[65]
>
> [The second is] that by the Church our country is kept divided. . . . For though she holds here her seat, and exerts her temporal authority, she has never yet gained strength and courage to seize upon the entire country, or make herself supreme; yet never has been so weak that when in fear of losing her temporal dominion, she could not call in some foreign potentate to aid her against any Italian state by which she was overmatched.[66]

These two observations are consequences of two political premises—first, a people without religion cannot be led to combat because no oath would be respected from a person without a religion; and second, the unity and welfare of a country are dependent upon complete obedience to a republic or a prince. Machiavelli does not censure the Roman pontiffs for their corruption, or like Dante for moral and evangelical reasons, but for the political influence they exerted on Italians by making them unbelievers and therefore incapable of forming a state. He did not reprove the Popes for the formation of a temporal power, as Dante did, because this was contrary to the spirit of Christ, but because such power interfered with the establishment of a national state. For Machiavelli religion always has a political function. No one else has so exalted the power of religion in social life, but no one has placed religion in such a subordinate position to the state.

17 Modern states have adopted his ideas of religion

Modern states, democratic or not, have adopted the concept that it is advantageous to a state to have its citizens believe in a religion, no matter which one. While the state during Machiavelli's day recognized only one religion, today all of them more or less accept what is known as freedom of worship. No state objects if a citizen changes religion; nor does it force a citizen to believe in a stipulated religion. In certain states, like Spain, proselytizing of a religion that is not Catholic has been opposed. But states that believe in the so-called "separation of Church and State" are not indifferent to religion, and encourage their citizens to have a religion even though they themselves as states do not favour one religion over another. For instance, in the United States, where this separation has been affirmed and practised for a long time—although it does not appear in the Constitution, which only prohibits the establishment of a state religion—we see that the state allows its citizens freedom of worship, but only insofar as it does not conflict with its moral laws. The United States in 1882 and later did not hesitate to enforce with arms the abolition of polygamy, which was an article of the Mormon faith. Moreover, the United States does not accept any religion as valid until the state is assured that this religion will not be detrimental to the state itself. A minister, priest or rabbi, even of an accepted religion, cannot preach anything he wants from his pulpit. If he should order his flock to abstain from military service, or not to pay taxes, or to overthrow the government, he would either be arrested or harassed. Nor is this the only way the state affirms its superiority over any and all religions. It is the state that decides if a religion is acceptable, not a religion that decides if a state is valid. The state shows its interest in having its citizens believe in a religion by means of exempting authorized religious institutions from taxes. To grant exemption from taxes is nothing but a subsidy and it can be said that in the United States religions receive a subsidy from the state. The state does not subsidize one religion more than another, because like the wise and prudent princes of Machiavelli, even if it does not believe in those religions or in any religion, it is convinced that it is in the state's interest to favour them with a subsidy in the same way it concedes tax exemptions to cultural and medical institutions, because they are for the betterment of citizens. Even in Russia, provided it is not an obstacle to the state, the practice of religion is tolerated and was even favoured during World War II, when it was necessary to have the help of the Orthodox Church to spur the people to take arms against the German invader. And France, even though anticlerical after the separation of Church and State, continued to subsidize schools and Catholic religious Orders abroad, because they served as tools of power in international competition. To sum up, with the doctrine of the separation of Church and State, Machiavelli's concept that the state does not believe but wants its citizens and subjects to believe has triumphed throughout the modern world.

18   Machiavelli's religiosity

Since Walser began to react against the picture of Machiavelli drawn by Renaissance historians down to the present-day Russo who speaks of a religiosity in Machiavelli, attempts have been made to remove the stigma from Machiavelli of being irreligious.

Walser says: "Machiavelli, too, the inexorable sceptic, had his Paradise," and he quotes the famous letter Machiavelli wrote from San Casciano to his friend Vettori, filled with reverence for learning and admiration for men of antiquity, who had been concerned with political problems.

Russo does not hesitate to speak of a "profound internal religion" àpropos of Machiavelli's ironic remarks. And both these viewpoints are valid only if religion is given a different meaning from the usual one. It seems to me that religion means that which unites people in the specific performance of a rite. As a matter of fact, both Walser and Russo are forced to use a less strong term than religion. Walser calls it "the benediction of antiquity", and Russo says: "I don't hesitate to speak of a religiosity of Machiavelli, the religion of this technical virtue, of this economic virtue which has always governed a considerable portion of the things of this world, and whose inventor is not Machiavelli. . . . He is only the courageous revealer and confessor." But this is not religion, and it might be well to avoid the poetic abuse of the word "religiosity" because of the misunderstanding it can engender, like all words that lend themselves to vague interpretations.

19 The relativity of forms of government

Machiavelli stands deliberately against those philosophers, perhaps Plato more than any other, who dreamed of states that have never existed, that is, perfect republics. He has insisted, in fact, that no republic can last forever.[67] However, he does not always remain faithful to this scientific principle. Sometimes he shows a preference for certain forms of governments, like that of the Swiss who were a poor people with simple customs, believers, and disposed to fight strenuously for their independence.

[The Swiss], the only people who at this day, both as regards religion and military discipline, live like the ancients.[68]

Machiavelli believes implicitly that no single political system can claim superiority over another. The aim of a state is to survive, but the means vary according to the prevailing conditions of time, place, and people. Like a true scientist, Machiavelli uses the term *proportion* in order to describe the game of power politics:

It has been said by a wise man that if one is to hold a state by violent means, the force employed should be proportionate to the resistance offered. So long as this proportion obtains, it is to be expected that the violence will last; but should the violated be stronger than the violator, it is probable that the violence will some day cease.[69]

By means of this almost Euclidian formula, Machiavelli eliminates the idea of morality or of ideals from political conflict. This is indeed a prerequisite when writing about political science. The engineer who works with metals or cement never asks if the building for which these materials are to be used is to be a school or a house of ill-repute. The ability to withstand pressure and weight is the same in the one as in the other. Mathematicians have never spoken of a good or evil triangle and, if they had done so, science would never have made any progress.

Making use of the biological terms Machiavelli often indulged in, we could say that he studied the life principle of states. A doctor considers a liver good when it functions properly, whether it belongs to a rascal or to a saint.

20   The state as form imposed on the people

The Prince starts out with a famous definition: "All states and dominions which command or have commanded mankind were either republics or monarchies."

The use of the word *command* should be noted. The state commands mankind. Here is the focal point of Machiavelli's political thought—every state originates by means of violence, which is imposed on man just as form is imprinted on matter. It does not come from God, it does not spring forth of its own account, it is not an established agreement among men, nor a contract nor a conviction. Machiavelli makes use innumerable times of the words *form* and *matter* to describe the constitutions and the people, the law and the citizens. These words were part of the vocabulary of Aristotle, whose *Politics* Machiavelli had read; they were in common usage at the time. For Machiavelli a state has no life outside of the people, and its form does not exist if it has not given

47

shape to the people who, before assuming form, cannot even be called men, but beasts. (See the origin of the state, as treated in the second chapter of the First Book of *Discourses*.)

To give human form to beasts or to widely scattered savages is the basic function of the state. There are two important points to observe in this imposition of the form-constitutions on the matter-people. First, in order to assure the success of an imprint the form must not differ greatly from the matter (and therefore the success of the form should be conditioned by its possible agreement with matter and should be relative or proportionate to matter).

Different institutions and procedures should be prescribed for the governed according as they are good or bad, *since similar forms cannot subsist in matter which is disposed in a contrary matter.*[70]

Second, the imposition should always occur through the work of a single individual, a man who is stronger than the rest or, at a later time, by a wise and crafty individual.

At the origin of every state, whether monarchy or republic, there is according to Machiavelli the *virtù* of one man who has known how to grasp the opportunity provided him by fortune. Without opportunity there was no chance of applying *virtù*. His models of virtuous men range from those he takes from the mythical history of Greece, Rome and even from the Bible, to those of his own times, like Ferdinand the Catholic or Caesar Borgia. Their success is assured because they always dominate by organizing armed forces. (The matter-people is not only in need of force to be directed to the form-constitution, but the continuous use of force is essential in order to keep them in that condition.)

Although at times Machiavelli expresses himself in many ways, and sometimes in contradictory terms, no one can question the stress he places on armed forces in the life of a state. Moreover, he believes that it is of the utmost importance for the army of the state to be formed of its own people and not of mercenary troops. With his realistic sense, he understood that laws have no significance unless they are applied, that treaties are of no value if they are not respected.

The chief foundations of all states, whether new, old or mixed, are good laws and good arms. And as there cannot be good laws where there are not good arms, and where there are good arms, there must be good laws, I will not now discuss the laws, but will speak of the arms.[71]

Treaties between rulers are observed by means of arms and maintained only by them.[72]

Machiavelli knew that it was characteristic of men to make use of laws and of beasts to make use of force. For him politics is both law and force and the art of politics consists in combining law with force. "Study and books do not suffice to rule a State."[73] Even Moses, although considered the instrument chosen by God to carry out His orders, was forced to resort to means which did not differ from those used by pagan princes.

Laws are not good, or rather they are ineffectual without arms; and arms are not good, that is they do not function without laws. (Form without matter is invalid, and matter without form lacks reality.) For armed forces to function well, they should not be too different from the form of the state. Thus a national army is superior to mercenaries. Machiavelli does not draw this conclusion from pure reasoning, but as was his custom, from historical observation of past and present times.*

The idea of a citizen militia was taken up again by Machiavelli's successor and friend, Donato Giannotti, as Ridolfi reminds us in one of his historical works: "The militia was established in exactly the way it was suggested in a speech by Giannotti." And finally, armed forces are needed by the government to maintain internal peace. There can be no programme of improvement without military force. Those who succeed in persuading the people to

---

* The dream of a national militia is found in some of Machiavelli's contemporaries, but it is surprising to see it revived again in a work of one of Machiavelli's descendants, Piero Machiavelli: "*A Plan . . . to Rid Tuscany of French and Spaniards and to Establish a Tuscan Army*," 1560, published for the first time by Jarro, 1863, Florence.

accept a "new deal", but who do not consolidate their position with arms, fail as Savonarola did:

> Moses, Cyrus, Theseus and Romulus would not have been able to keep their constitutions observed for so long had they been disarmed, as happened in our own time with Fra Girolamo Savonarola.[74]

Machiavelli's belief in the necessity of arms was so strong that at times it caused him to exaggerate. However, to lie in order to make a point about history was accepted in his day as a way of instructing. In his *Florentine History* he uses as an example the bloodless battle of Anghiari carried on by mercenaries:

> And in so great a defeat and such a long battle, which lasted from 20 to 40 hours, only one man was killed—and he did not die of wounds or as a result of a brave feat, but was trampled on after having been thrown by his horse.[75]

However, among Leonardo da Vinci's papers, Solmi found notes in Machiavelli's own handwriting which provided the painter with detailed information of the battle. Leonardo is said to have used these notes to record the battle in a mural in the Signoria Palace. These notes record the great number of casualties in that battle. It is useless to insist on this point, but let us observe that Machiavelli's programme of a national militia became a reality in the nineteenth century, with the advent of the democratic movement. In opposition to the mercenary militia of kings, the French and the Americans adopted the idea of a national army and ultimately even of a national draft. It can be said that this turn of events is a direct result of the development of that Machiavellian and democratic thought that condemned mercenary arms.

It is Machiavelli's conviction that military training is the source of human virtue, inasmuch as it opposes indolence which breeds corruption, and forces the individual to make the greatest of sacrifices for society.

> Men attain greatness and show their virtue insofar as they are used by and led onwards by their leaders, their country or their king. . . .

He who considers a part of Europe, will find it to be full of republics and principalities which because of fear of each other were forced to keep alive military discipline and to honour those who excelled in it. It is therefore true that where there are more empires, there will be found more brave men; it follows of necessity that when these disappear, gradually virtue also disappears because of the lack of purpose which makes men virtuous.[76]

21   The state as an end in itself

For many philosophies and religions, the state is only a means whereby man can attain a superior end. Although Machiavelli does not explicitly say so, implicit in his thought is the belief that the state is the ultimate end and that there is nothing better in which man can participate. In *The Prince* he clearly states:

> And in the actions of men, and especially of princes, from which there is *no court of appeal,* the intention must be considered.[77]

Machiavelli says that since there is no court of appeal for states, one must consider the result. Clearly Machiavelli never thought of a universal state or a universal court of law and he excluded conscience or the church, or the judgment of God, which could settle differences between states. He never imagined a League of Nations or a United Nations, and hence he could not criticize them. If we follow his thought logically we would say that a court with an international police force could bring peace to mankind. But with peace, indolence would ensue, and corruption set in. From corruption there would spring forth a revolution, and we would then once again return to the cycle of violence.

For Machiavelli the state is the ultimate end for man in his striving for an ethical life. Machiavelli's clear and oft-repeated statement that private and public interests are sometimes incompatible shows that he conceived of the sacrifice of individual interests in favour of the state as *the only form of ethics.* It is simply untrue to say that Machiavelli places politics outside of morality;

he places it outside of Christian morality, but not outside of ethics.

He praises men and nations who possess the power to bend people to the will of the state. The citizens whom he most admires are those who subjugate their own ambitions and interests to those of the country. The two people whom he idealizes are the Romans of the past and the Swiss of his own time. They are both pictured without a flaw, as composed of individuals who put the interests of their country above their own personal ambitions. Today too this consideration carries great weight in public life, in lip service at least, when expressed by national leaders.

> For a citizen who is living under the laws of a republic, I think it is more praiseworthy and less dangerous to adopt the procedure of Manlius, since this way of behaving was entirely *in the public interest,* and was in no way affected by *private ambition,* for *it is impossible to gain partisans* if one is harsh in one's dealing with everybody and is *wholly devoted to the common good,* because by doing this *one does not acquire particular friends* or—as I have just called them—*partisans.* Wherefore, no procedure can be more advantageous or more desirable in a republic, since it neither fails to take account of the *interests of the public* nor does it suggest that *personal power* is in any *way being sought.*[78]

This common good is forever placed in opposition to the individual interest of the few or to personal ambition. Even in his letters he praises citizens who work and above all "love their country and the common good".[79] When you read Machiavelli you will find that in these frequent passages he has substituted the "common good" for the Christian love of God; both are opposed to self-love. What draws Machiavelli's ethical evaluations close to Christian ones is his passion for political action, and his belief that in no other way can an individual develop his own personality. Only within the state can man surpass human limitations and reach a self-identification with the common interests of the country. In his precepts and recommendations there is no less an asceticism than in Christianity, but it is an asceticism of the fatherland.

22 The end and the means

For Machiavelli the state or fatherland is the ultimate goal that an individual can reach if he wants to raise himself above the common herd of mankind and leave a record of himself for posterity, and thus attain glory. But is the accusation so often levelled at him valid, that he affirms the end justifies the means? It does not seem so to me.

It is my opinion that ends and means are indissolubly connected in our actions, and the end that we attain with certain means is never the same as the one we attain with other means. The same means seem different according to circumstances, as for instance there is a difference in reaching the peak of a mountain on foot by one's own effort, or in a cable car, or carried on someone's shoulders. Moreover, we might say that man never attains the end he seeks, nor does he ever succeed in using the means which he thought to be at his disposal because in action difficulties and unforeseen incidents arise. Only in a very limited way can we speak of having attained our goal, or of having used prescribed means.

Machiavelli gave no thought to these subtleties. He thought of means and ends as really distinct.

> The masses judge the end when it is reached, and not the means used. [80]

Let us consider what Machiavelli meant by the word "end" in this frequently quoted passage. It is clear that he insists above all on the fact that the majority of people, the masses, judge actions by their success. This is not to say that the end, that is the total view, justifies the means; what he wants to say is that *for the masses* the end (success) justifies the means. Many times in his public and private writings he dwells on this maxim and always insists that it is conditioned by the fact that it deals with the opinion of the masses; and with the use of the word "end", as meaning "the last moment of an action".

For men judge of actions *by the result*. Hence for all the ill that results from an enterprise the man who advised it is blamed, and, should the result be good, is commended; but the reward by no means weighs the same as the loss.[81]

And further on, in the same chapter:

Men in this respect *are blind* in judging good and bad actions *from the results*.

Also in his correspondence:

He said that in all things men considered more the *results* than the means.[82]

However, although not using the actual words *ends* and *means,* Machiavelli is prepared to "forgive" Romulus for killing his brother and companion, because "what he did he did for the common good",[83] and as we have already seen, everything is permitted for the well-being of the state "in whatever *way* it (the country) is defended". And in certain cases he approves of "extraordinary ways"—illegal means, rebellions, murder— according to the case. We can even say that one of Machiavelli's characteristics is to force the reader to face the fact that politics is too serious and important a matter to be sacrificed to scruples. It should be seen in its fullness of action, without considering the price demanded, including even perhaps losing one's soul, because the result will justify the sin.

[Borgia] was considered cruel, but his cruelty brought order to the Romagna, united it, and reduced it to peace and fealty. If this is considered well, it will be seen that he was really much more merciful than the Florentine people who, to avoid the name of cruelty, allowed Pistoia to be destroyed.[84]

Machiavelli is thoroughly convinced of the necessity of doing evil in order to act in the realm of politics. He sees action in its ineluctable form (of which evil is a necessary component) as sanctified by resulting in the common good. To avoid action because of moral scruples is worse than assuming the entire responsibility for the necessary moment of evil, even if it means breaking laws and spilling blood.

23 The "one man" or redeemer

In an almost mystical tone Machiavelli speaks of "the one man" whose duty it is to bring order to the many, in founding a state or saving it from ruin. It has been noted how Machiavelli makes use of examples of the aloneness and uniqueness of this "one man" from the dawn of society, when leaders were half-historical and half-mythical like Moses, Lycurgus, Solon, Theseus, Romulus (and although not mentioned by Machiavelli we might add Solomon, who killed his half-brother because of political ambition). This subject is dealt with in a chapter of the *Discourses* entitled "That it is necessary to be the *Sole Authority* if one would constitute a Commonwealth afresh or would reform it thoroughly regardless of its Ancient Institutions".[85]

And when the "one man" dies, the health-giving virtue dies with him:

> If in a state on the decline . . . a renaissance is ever to be brought about, it will be by virtue of some one person who is then living, not by the public as a whole, that good institutions are kept up and, as soon as such a person is dead, they will relapse into their former habits.[86]

Machiavelli admits that when people are not corrupt, a state can get along with laws alone,[87] but during the foundation of a state or its reconstruction, the force of one individual is a prerequisite. And we have seen that in these extraordinary periods everything is tolerated, even the murder of one's brother, as in the case of Romulus, in order to attain the required end.

It seems as though Machiavelli concentrated in this "one man", (superman, hero, etc. as he was to be called later) the ability to act, taking upon himself the responsibility of ethical violations

which that action necessitates. His "one man" will not be a sacri-
ficial "lamb of God", but assuredly he will take upon himself the
"sins of the world" or at least the "sins of the state". By spilling
blood if necessary, or cheating if necessary, he will bear for others
the weight of these sins. And in the case of the transformation of
Italy from a deeply corrupt to a well-ordered country, which he
hopes for and seeks, Machiavelli does not hesitate to call the "one"
a Redeemer. He will not be a soft-hearted man and he will not be
a saint (a term Machiavelli uses for Cato, naturally the early
Cato).[88] He will be an "evil" man from a Christian point of view,
but "good" politically speaking, capable of carrying out the good
for the many at the risk of losing his own soul.

The concept of "sin" in Machiavelli was quite different from
the idea of sin as breaking a Commandment. For Machiavelli
"sin" consists in not doing the things that are necessary for the
common good.

> *True, there are those who think that greed has been*
> *fatal to kingdoms, and that these may be*
> *destroyed by usury or carnal sin.*
>
> *They believe also that their greatness comes,*
> *and both their height and power thus derive*
> *from prayers and from fastings and from alms.*
>
> *But those who are more wise and prudent claim*
> *that all such things can neither ruin states*
> *nor keep on earth their power and their fame.*[89]
> (*Translated by Joseph Tusiani*)

And referring to the preaching of Savonarola, who interpreted
the invasion of Italy by Charles VIII as a chastisement of God for
the "sins" of Italians, he said:

> Those who said that it was owing to our *sins,* spoke the truth, but
> it was not the sins they meant, but those that I have related. And as
> it was the sins of princes, they too have suffered the punishment.[90]

Here Machiavelli is like a country doctor who assures the people that their sickness, whether diphtheria or typhus, is not a result of their having been irreligious or not having given alms to the poor but from not having observed the rules of hygiene—in Machiavelli's case, political hygiene.

The leaders of the people are "great men" who take upon themselves the "qualms of conscience" of others and do not "sin" against the technique of politics. For Machiavelli the great individual seems to shield and protect what he called matter and we now call the masses. The masses are well off when they obey laws, adhere to customs and pray to God. The great individual can on special occasions with impunity "lose patience and humility".

24 The return of the state to first principles

Characteristically applying physiological concepts to the state, Machiavelli contends that states are easily corrupted by the passage of time (we would say that they age). To save them from death, it is necessary to urge them to return to "their first principles" so that they can generate the same vitality and youthfulness they had at the start.

> Here I am concerned with composite bodies, such as states and religious institutions, and in their regard I affirm that those changes make for their conservation which lead them back to their *start*. Hence those are better constituted and have a longer life whose institutions make frequent renovations possible, or which can be brought to such a renovation by some event which has nothing to do with their constitution. For it is clearer than daylight that, without renovation, these bodies do not last.
>
> The way to renovate them, as has been said, is to reduce them to their *starting points*. For *at the start* religious institutions, republics and kingdoms have in all cases some good in them, to which their early reputation and progress is due. But since in process of time this goodness is corrupted, such a body must of necessity die unless something happens which brings it up to the mark.[91]

Machiavelli closely examines the regeneration of a state brought on by the pressure of a foreign power or by an internal impulse, the latter through laws or by means of an extraordinary man. However, it was almost an oversimplification on his part to specify the exact time, which he set as ten years, required for such a change. In referring to Christianity, he sees the return of the Franciscan and Dominican Orders to the Gospel as a good example of reverting to first principles. For Machiavelli, this principle is a natural fact. It is always a play of forces which reanimates organizations. At times it springs from an internal necessity, like war or foreign invasions, at other times from the influence of a strong personality, like St. Francis or St. Dominic.

Today we are seeing the resurgence of people towards an independent and free national life. They have accentuated this return to first principles by reinstating their old language and religion (like Israel, which has adopted the very difficult old-script Hebrew as the official language), as though by going back to origins the people could be renewed and reinvigorated. Other peoples have rejected the names that invaders or colonial dominations had given their countries and gone back to the original names, as in the case of Indonesia, Iran and Yugoslavia.

Machiavelli's principle is not to be taken too literally, but as a recommendation of a certain directive in national reforms: these are of more profit to the state if they spring from tradition rather than from foreign customs. The return to one's own beginnings cannot be carried out literally, because history never goes back; what is over is over. But Machiavelli's advice is valid in the sense that when an old and weak country wants to reawaken and transform the germs of its new life, it must revert to its own past and not adopt the ways of a foreign country.

This idea of Machiavelli became very popular. It is found again centuries later in the writings of no less a person than Pope Leo XIII, a man of exceptional intellectual qualifications and culture who could not fail to know its origin. In his encyclical "Rerum novarum" (1891), he said: "De societatibus enim dilabentibus illud rectissime praecipitur, revocari ad origines suas, cum restitui volunt, oportere." ("When societies that are deteriorating wish to restore their former greatness, they should be told to return to their origins.") If we were to use the language of certain of Machiavelli's adversaries or admirers, we would say the devil had placed a drop of ink in the pen of a pope.

25   Human nature and education

Compulsory military service—the draft—is the principal form of education for a people who want to live freely (independently) and a corrective for people corrupted by indolence (peace), Machiavelli says.

> *If you perchance are tempted to accuse*
> *Nature if Italy, so weary and wounded,*
> *does not produce so hard and bellicose*
>
> *a people, this, I say, is not sufficient*
> *to erase our cowardice, for education*
> *can supplement where nature is deficient.*
>
> *Stern education made Italy bloom*
> *in ancient days, and made her rise and conquer*
> *the entire world and for herself make room.*
>
> *But now she lives—if tears can be called life—*
> *beneath that ruin and unhappy fate*
> *that she has reaped from her long lack of strife.*[92]
>   (*Translated by Joseph Tusiani*)

With this we touch upon one of the inner and fundamental contradictions of Machiavelli's thought. On the one hand he seems convinced that man's nature is immutable and on the other firmly believes in the power of princes to modify people. Chabod has this to say: "Machiavelli ends up by contradicting himself; his theoretic pessimism suddenly becomes unlimited faith in the leader of government and also in the people who are awaiting the Redeemer, all ready to follow him. . . . Scepticism becomes transformed in the most moving cry of hope and faith, and the words of contempt for the wicked creature that is man become transformed into a religious invocation reminiscent of an exhortation of a Biblical prophet." But, Machiavelli is not aware of any contradiction:

> He who would foresee what has to be, should reflect on what has been, for everything that happens in the world at any time has a genuine resemblance to what happened in ancient times. This is due to the fact that the agents who bring such things about are men. Men have, and always have had, the same passions, whence it necessarily comes about that the same effects are produced. It is true that men's deeds are sometimes more virtuous in this country than in that . . . according to the type of education from which their inhabitants have derived their mode of life.[93]

Perpetuity and change go hand in hand. Machiavelli has great faith in laws, in the military draft, in the example given by leaders which can be followed and imitated,[94] and in religion. However, as we have already seen, he considers Christianity the cause of the weakening of old customs that strengthened the state; his criticism is aimed at the humanitarian and anti-belligerent content of Christianity.

> But though it looks as if the world were become effeminate and as if heaven were powerless, this undoubtedly is due to the pusillanimity of those who have interpreted our religion in terms of *laissez-faire* rather than in terms of valour.[94]

This passage has been interpreted by certain critics as an acceptance of primitive Christianity, but these critics have closed their eyes to the preceding passages which condemn Christian education for having exalted humility, contemplation, the acceptance of blows, and the endurance of hardships, instead of vengeance.

It is clear that by education Machiavelli often means things that make a man strong and hard, ferocious towards the enemy but obeying superiors. Clearly his ideal of education is that of the army

—his dream is a citizen army. When he thinks of educators, he does not imagine learned men but army leaders. The youth of a country should become accustomed to discomforts, hardship and work; they should practise long marches and foot races, get used to fighting, and not fear death.

Machiavelli is aware of the natural events that can influence the state and the people. He considers the best natural conditions to be those that force men to make an effort and to fight. And when these conditions do not exist, he advises the head of the state to create them. War is an excellent instrument of education:

> For discord in a republic is usually due to idleness and peace, and unity to fear and to war.[95]

The fertility of the soil is useful to the people for a limited time, but eventually it leads to corruption. Leaders must correct this threat to the well-being of the state:

> As to the idleness which such a situation may encourage, it must be counteracted by laws imposing that need to work which the situation does not require. It is advisable here to follow the example of those wise folk who have dwelt in more beautiful and fertile lands, i.e., in ... order to obviate the disasters which idleness induced by the amenities of the land might cause [such lands] have imposed the need for training on those who were to become soldiers.[96]

It cannot be said that Machiavelli would have been a friend of the "pursuit of happiness" listed in a modern constitution as man's inalienable right. And those who, like Villari, see Machiavelli as an exponent of Reanaissance civilization and its hedonism are completely wrong. If Machiavelli has an ideal, it is rather protestant and ascetic. He praises qualities developed by sports and hard physical exercise—in a word, warlike qualities.

> Hence it is said that hunger and poverty make men industrious, and laws make them good.[97]

26   Necessity and liberty

This leads us to an examination of another of the two-fold antitheses which often occur as a motif in his works—the antithesis of *necessity* with *election* (or freedom of choice). A law is an artificial necessity created by the superior man, as a substitute where necessity is lacking. Machiavelli believes that through the stimulus of necessity and the injunction of law, and therefore of doing things that are not pleasant but necessary, man works more satisfactorily—that is, he performs more virtuously.

> Men never do good unless necessity drives them to it; but when they are free to choose and can do just as they please, confusion and disorder become everywhere rampant. There is no need of legislation so long as things work well without it, but when such good customs break down, legislation forthwith becomes necessary.[98]

Passages like this show the preferences, inclinations and aspirations of Machiavelli. It should be noted that necessity is not only placed in opposition to choice or election, but also to reason.

> *Necessity* will lead you to do many things that reason does not recommend.[99]

Among the various pagan deities that Machiavelli introduces as substitutes for the biblical and Christian God, *Necessity* is the most sinister. The other deities that motivate his history are irrational: greediness, ambition, revenge, hunger, or simple boredom (men tire of good). On rare occasions there appear, to the great delight of Machiavelli, love of country or the liberation of the fatherland, but necessity leads them all. It is the ultimate god of mankind. It is superior to liberty, insofar as liberty alone causes one to consider one's own advantage. Necessity and law (artificial necessity) force man to actions of glory and of service to the common good, that is to the state. If you allow a brick freedom, it will fall because its nature is to be attracted to the centre of the earth; but place it by force with mortar in a wall, and necessity will make it into a useful support, a vital part of the building. The "virtue" which Machiavelli places above all others is born of necessity:

> Necessity engenders virtue, as we have so often remarked.[100]

27 Liberty

It seems to me the word "liberty" has been the cause of much misunderstanding in interpreting Machiavelli. The concept of individual liberty as used in our times did not exist at the time of Machiavelli. He had a very precise but to the present democratic point of view a very restricted idea of the limits of individual liberty:

> That nation is desirable in which wealth and friends can really be enjoyed, not the one where wealth can be easily taken away, and where friends in a time of necessity abandon you for fear of relatives.[101]

But the word liberty in Machiavelli becomes confused with law or order. This is what he means by *vivere civile* (civil life) and *vivere libero* (the free life of a city or state), terms which he frequently uses. He has given us a clear definition of this concept:

> It is true that when (and it seldom happens) for the good of a city or country a wise, good and strong man comes forth who makes laws that pacify the nobility and the plebeians, or is able to hold them in rein so that they cannot do evil, that city or country can be called *free* and can be judged stable and steady. Having been founded on good laws and on good order, it no longer has any need of the virtue of one man to keep it in good condition.[102]

Clearly, when Machiavelli refers to "liberty", it is not to that interpretation dear to the Anglo-Saxon tradition considered as the right of the individual to go against the state or, outside the state, to do what he wants provided it harms no one. Rather it is that law which imposes a "restriction" on various social classes, a limitation of one's own desires so that the common interest can triumph.

Limited to a republic, Machiavelli was aware of the advantages of what today we would call "freedom of the press", by indicating two aspects of it: the "proposal" of new laws and the "criticism" of citizens.

A tribune or any other citizen [in Republican Rome] could propose a law, in regard to which every citizen was entitled to speak either in favour of against, prior to a decision being reached. This institution was good so long as the citizens were good, because it is always a good thing that anyone anxious to serve the public should be able to propose his plan. It is also a good thing that everyone should be at liberty to express his opinion, so that when the people have heard what each has to say they may choose the best plan.[103]

No authority more useful and necessary can be granted to those appointed to look after the liberties of a state than that of being able to indict before the people or some magistrate or court such citizens as have committed any offence prejudicial to the freedom of the state.[104]

But in the majority of cases, and especially where Machiavelli gives vent to a romantic enthusiasm for liberty, the word only means freedom from tyrants and foreigners, for instance as he applied it to the Duke of Athens who was both one and the other:

Have you ever considered how important the name of liberty is in a city like this, and how strong it is? Force cannot subdue it [liberty], time does not consummate it, and it outweighs all other advantages [that tyranny can supply].[105]

Russo and Solari have clearly seen that the concept of liberty in Machiavelli takes on a hedonistic rather than an ethical colouring, that it is addressed to "the happiness of individuals and people, to their betterment, but not to human perfection" (Russo). This is because the task of leading men to perfection, according to Machiavelli, is a function of the state. Although less pessimistic than Guicciardini, Machiavelli still considers people, or the masses, only as passive matter.

Princes ought not to complain of any fault committed by the people whom they govern, because such faults are due either to their negligence or to their being themselves sullied by similar defects.[106]

Besides, Machiavelli makes a distinction between national groups. There are some that have been branded as servants and others that have enjoyed liberty and it is very difficult to change their basic nature:

It is just as difficult and dangerous to try to free a people that wants to remain servile as it is to enslave a people that wants to remain free.[107]

Liberty or servitude are like deep creases in a cloth—difficult and at times impossible to remove. When Machiavelli was questioned by the Medici, who had returned to power in Florence, he tried to convince them that an openly absolute government would have been appropriate for Milan, which had been accustomed to strong leaders, but not for Florence which had enjoyed freedom. From the scientific and Machiavellian naturalistic point of view, liberty and servitude are habits of the body politic. Each set of customs calls for a different constitution. Today this explains the caricature of systems of government imposed on people not accustomed or suited to them. It might be well to keep this in mind today when there is a desire to impose certain types of government on people completely unadapted to them. A case in point is the ludicrous imitation of democracy in South America and in some European countries.

28 Idleness and action

In the substitution of theological values that Machiavelli undertook, without even being aware of so doing, action is the new anti-Christian virtue which he sets in opposition to idleness. He always recommends the benefits of initiative and of courage:

Results are often obtained by impetuosity and daring which could never have been obtained by ordinary methods.[108]

He also combats the maxim,

'To enjoy the advantages of delay'—which now is on the lips of our wise men.[109]

Machiavelli encourages the heads of states to wage wars because "wars cannot be avoided, and a postponement is to the advantage of others".[110] He is also opposed to neutrality:

For if two neighbouring powers come to blows, they are either such that if one wins you will have to fear the victor, or else not. In either of these two cases, it will be better for you to declare yourself openly and make war.[111]

The neutral nation "is hated by the loser and not respected by the winner".[112] And even Fortune, which at times is called omnipotent by Machiavelli, favours the young and the brave:

Like a woman, she is always a friend to the young, because they are less cautious, fiercer, and master her with greater audacity.[113]

In this tendency of his to exalt men of action, he was ahead of his time. Intuitively, he realized the value of work, a concept which one day was to force monks and men of leisure to change their way of life in order to survive. "He who wants to form a Republic where there are many noble men, must first of all rid himself of them."[114] This is a passage of Machiavelli that the Russian revolutionists could have quoted, but it escaped Karl Marx—although it was used by Marxists like Gramsci.

Machiavelli attributes the direst of consequences to idleness, which he makes synonomous with peace, for to him it breeds corruption. The peace in the cloisters, and in the ivory towers of scholars, and that of medieval men of leisure who live on those who work, are all equally distasteful to him. A healthy life is attained by means of exercise, while corruption is the result of idleness. A republic that is inactive is not possible; it will end in extinction.

Machiavelli seems to say, Keep active at any price, even at the risk of doing evil. Anything is better than sitting with folded hands:

Because I believe, have believed, and will always believe that what Boccaccio says is true—it is better to act and repent than not to act and repent.[115]

Machiavelli had read Dante thoroughly and remembered the strange punishment meted out to those "who lived without sin and without praise". Dante had less respect for them than for sinners who dared to act. Machiavelli recalled the passage of Dante about Soderini's death. Although he had wanted to assume extraordinary powers, he did not do so because of constitutional scruples, and was thrown out of Florence by more daring rebels. In a famous epigram, Machiavelli places him in the limbo with children:

> The night Pier Soderini passed away,
> his soul was halted on the brink of hell;
> and Pluto yelled: "No hell for you—you fool!
> In children's limbo you can only stay."[116]
> (Translated by Joseph Tusiani)

In this case it is not success that Machiavelli sets as a standard of action, but action for its own sake. "Better to lose all with courage than a part with disgrace."[117]

29 Fortune

Machiavelli has trouble reconciling his predilection for action, and above all for prompt, direct and extraordinary acts, with his belief in Fortune. First of all we must remember that at times he used the word "fortune" just as he used the word God or "heavens", without attaching to it any special significance. Sometimes the word means not chance or whim but a social situation.

One thing, however, is certain. For Machiavelli Fortune never means what it did for Dante (except in the *Inferno*, VII, 7) that is the minister of God, guided by Him, the dispenser of earthly goods which men, because of blindness, do not see as a rational force. In other words Machiavelli's Fortune does not correspond to a divine and rational design. For him it is a power that is "varied", "unstable", "voluble", "fickle", "inconstant" and "changeable". It plays tricks on men, changes friends into enemies, an altogether irrational force beyond the control of men. In one case, at least, the spirit of man depends on it:

> Fortune, wanting to show the world that she and not prudence makes men great, demonstrated her strength on occasions where prudence could have no part *so that it is only possible to ascribe every-thing to her.*[118]

But much more often it is represented by Machiavelli as something which we would call the "condition" of human action. Its function is to provide the opportunity to virtuous or wise men so that they can demonstrate their greatness. Sometimes Fortune passively furnishes opportunities, sometimes it is pictured as the temptation and suffering of Christianity which serves as a trial for attaining sanctity. That is why believers consider fortune as grace from God. This indirect manner of acting is shown here:

> Fortune, especially when it wants to render a new prince great, who has more need of gaining a great reputation than a hereditary prince, raises up enemies and compels him to undertake wars against them, so that he may have cause to overcome them, and thus climb up higher by means of that ladder which his enemies have brought him.[119]

Confronted with Fortune, the people reveal their true nature. The Gauls, that is the French, for instance "are most humble in adversity—but insolent in good fortune".[120] In other cases Fortune doesn't act like this but in the opposite manner. Fortune, by means of its power, oppresses even those endowed with virtue, as was the case with Caesar Borgia according to Machiavelli:

> If his measures were not successful, it was through no fault of his own but only by the most extraordinary malignity of fortune.[121]

It seems to me that the contrast of fortune and virtue in Machiavelli is not only the exaltation of the power of man, but a sort of mechanism of life. There are conditions of fortune that destroy everyone, even the most courageous and virtuous.

At times Machiavelli seems to believe that even this irrational apparition is dependent upon the human mind:

> I believe that the fortune the Romans had, all rulers would have had if they had acted as the Romans and had had the same virtue.[122]

At times fortune is bound to an *inescapable* cycle and therefore is a consequence rather than an original force:

> Because that religion caused good behaviour, good behaviour resulted in good fortune and from good fortune came the happy successes of the undertaking.[123]

At times fortune is powerful, not because of itself but because of the paucity of virtues which are opposed to it: "Where men have little virtue, fortune greatly shows its power."[124] One need only learn from the ancients, and fortune can be dominated:

> Because fortune is fickle, so are the republics and the states—and they will always be thus until someone comes who is a great lover of antiquity, who can rule fortune in such a way that it has no chance to show, at every turn, how strong it is.[125]

On the other hand, Machiavelli often advised not opposing fortune but "adapting oneself to its fickleness".[126] Even to Soderini, fallen from power and abandoned by everyone, he addresses the following words:

> Lucky is the man in tune with his own time and unfortunate the man out of tune with his time and with the order of things.[127]

Although varied and inconstant, Fortune in Machiavelli has sufficient "constants"; for example it is not ever complete, but "accompanies good with evil and evil with good",[128] just as Nature does. Moreover, good fortune, if it comes quickly, quickly disappears. For Machiavelli it seems to manifest itself in change.

She does not like to favour the same man
forever, nor does she forever crush
beneath her wheel the one who's now in pain.[129]

(Translated by Joseph Tusiani)

The "permanence" of fortune is excluded by Machiavelli. To maintain it, *virtù* is essential. But we can ask, as we have already asked about the "grace" of Christianity, is it not already a "fortune" to be endowed with *virtù*? A useless question to put to Machiavelli because he never answered it. It might be said that for Machiavelli *virtù* and fortune are fundamentally the same things and that both are essential, as is seen in this passage where he speaks of Moses, Cyrus, Romulus, Theseus and others who became princes from the ranks by means of their own *virtù* and not because of fortune:

And in examining their life and deeds, it will be seen that they owed nothing to fortune but the opportunity which gave them matter to be shaped into what form they thought fit; and without that opportunity their powers would have been wasted, and without their powers the opportunity would have come in vain.[130]

In this passage Machiavelli seems to have settled the conflict between *virtù* and fortune, and to have succeeded in thinking of them as a single action in a synthesis that appears to surmount the attempts to determine their components. He thus achieves the formation of a new process.

What appears more characteristic in this synthesis of fortune and *virtù* is that the occasion is presented as greater in direct proportion to the difficulties and obstacles encountered. The more contrary is the occasion, the greater is the *virtù* of men who create a state. The similarity of Machiavellian *virtù* to "grace" could not be clearer than in his insistence that it was "necessary".

It was thus necessary that Moses should find the people of Israel slaves in Egypt and oppressed by the Egyptians. . . . [131]

It was necessary that Romulus should be unable to remain in Alba, and should have been exposed at his birth, in order that he might become King of Rome and founder of that Nation.[132]

It was necessary that Cyrus should find the Persians discontented with the empire of the Medes.[133]

These opportunities, therefore, gave these men their chance, and their own great qualities enabled them to profit by them, so as to ennoble their country and augment its fortunes.[134]

In his poetical composition, *Dell'Occasione,* he represents Fortune somewhat like a bald-headed woman, with a shock of hair falling over her face so as not to be recognized, moving along quickly with a foot on a wheel. Very few recognize her, so cannot grasp her, or else realize too late that she has passed by. She escapes, accompanied by Penitentia (assuredly a non-Christian remorse, since it springs from the sin of having allowed the opportunity to escape). It is true that this epigram was taken from Ausonius and is not Machiavelli's invention, but in any case he used it and it is certainly in agreement with his thought which exhorts men to act and to act quickly. It is the natural representation of those who believe in worldly success, and exalt intuition and the audacity of the gambler.

The necessity for seizing opportunity appears early in Machiavelli's thought. In his work *On the Method of Dealing with the Valdichiana Rebels* (1503), he speaks of men who "are aware of opportunity and know how to make good use of it".[135] In another passage, opportunity is offered to those same great men who knew how to become new leaders not through Fortune but through the stars or the heavens. This can be interpreted in two ways: either as divine Providence in which, it seems to me, Machiavelli did not believe; or the term stars or heaven was used as a physical cause of an influence on the destinies of men, in which we have proof that Machiavelli believed (astrology was then considered a science).

Really the heavens cannot give men (like Romulus) a greater *occasion* to attain glory, nor can men desire it more. And finally let us consider those to whom the heavens give such *opportunity*.[136]

Rather I would say that the uncertainties and contradictions of these passages, which refer to Fortune, express a conflict in

Machiavelli's mind between his naturalistic convictions and his heroic individualistic concept of political life. Although he never says so, it seems reasonable to assume that Machiavelli was acquainted with Democritus. However, he does not speak of atoms. Often he assigns to Chance an important function. Even his Rome, model of political acumen, was "guided" by chance[137] and thus to chance he ascribes the variations of government.[138] As liberal as were the governments of that time in respect to religious beliefs, and as relatively indifferent to heretical opinions as was the church then, it might well be that Machiavelli did not consider it wise to affirm publicly his Democritean concept of the universe. Among the few confessions that he has left us, he tells us that for a time he thought, as did Plutarch, that the grandeur of Rome was dominated by Fortune. I don't believe he ever resolved the contradiction between his faith and his emotions, just as no theologian has ever satisfactorily succeeded in settling the contradiction between the omniscience of God and the free will of the individual.

30 The national state

During the nineteenth century, especially among German and Italian commentators, Machiavelli enjoyed the reputation of having created the concept of the national state. He certainly deserves credit for having seen that a state founded on national unity has a greater chance to survive than the one that has differing languages, customs and laws.[139] In Machiavelli there is a notion of expediency, not expressed in the romantic and mystical form of "nationalism", that people have a "right" to form a separate state when they have a common language and similar cultural traditions. Machiavelli never speaks of rights and seldom of "nations". At times he means by the latter word the inhabitants of a certain city, for example the Florentines.[140] At other times he uses the word *province,* but only because he considers the country to which he refers as a part of the Roman Empire from which it was separated. It is not possible that Machiavelli had a "completely clear concept" of the nation (as Ercole says) because such a concept is not clear in anyone's mind. We have a clear concept of the state; but who can form a clear concept of a nation? We know where a state starts and ends geographically, and the extent of its powers. The nation is a sentiment, or an indistinct concept, and it is a cause of confusion. But what is important is the fact that Machiavelli, in his attempt to escape from medieval concepts, searches for the realistic basis of a healthy state, and finds it in uniformity of language, customs (religions), and order (laws and a militia).

His realism made him see that many states exist which are not national. He has indicated what norms a leader or a creator of a state must follow in order to provide for the missing bases of language and cultural unity. His remedies are the following: the prince or leader should live there or send colonizers, and in addition to destroying the aristocracy of the unformed country make friends with the people (as did the Romans). This proves he was not the apostle of the national state. He was the first to point out that a political organization is normally more vital in a national state than in one that is not. This rule is in general practice in all modern states which make a conscious effort to abolish the differences in languages either of an entire population (as republican and democratic France did with Provençal, Breton and Flemish), or of emigrated peoples (as the United States did by absorbing, principally by means of compulsory education up to 16 years of age, children of German, Italian, Spanish, Hebrew and Polish minorities). The development of compulsory elementary school attendance in the nineteenth century was not so much a democratic effort to distribute effort to distribute instruction to the underpriviliged as a nationalistic attempt to unite and absorb them. This was especially the case in Italy, where the populations were separated by dialects and where there was no common language by which they could understand each other. From the sixteenth century, first in France and later in other countries (for example in Piedmont, Italy), public officials were forced to put their records in the language of the country. These are the instruments that succeeded best in unifying different populations. As an exception there is the case of Switzerland, which without great difficulty has maintained statal unity despite the differences in languages, religions and cultures of the four federated peoples. In Austria the problem was so serious that it contributed to the dissolution of the Empire. In Russia the problem was studied by Stalin, who had lived in Austria, but it is too early to say with certainty if the freedom of languages and cultures of the people assembled under the aegis of the army and of the Russian police force has been wholly successful.

The diversity of religion in the two centuries following Machiavelli's death was a big obstacle to the functioning of modern states. During this period the Huguenots were expelled from France, in Germany the principle *cuius princeps eius religio* was affirmed, making compulsory the religion of the sovereign. From the maxims of Machiavelli we see that the uniformity of religion was one that worked best for the country. Today religions are seldom threats to the state, because states absorb all religions in a super-religion of their own. In the United States all religions function under the greater religion of the national flag, which is revered alike by ministers, priests and rabbis. The state declares itself superior to all religions and in a certain sense by practising the cult of the religion of the state has no need to bow to special religious cults. Only in the slightly anachronistic resurrection of the state of Israel (1949) have we had something similar to a theocratic state where a rabbinical language not used as a spoken language for centuries has become the state language.

The concept of "race" never appears in Machiavelli although he expresses something very close to "racism". He appears to believe firmly that people have a characteristic and immutable nature despite the changes in government, language, religion and customs. From the use he makes of the words Gauls and French, Etruscans and Tuscans, Romans and Italians, we might almost say he thought those people had remained the same for centuries.

Indeed when he wants to give an example of how wise men can foresee things that are to occur, on the basis of the past, he says:

> It is still easy to see a state maintain the same customs for a long time—being either *continually* greedy, or *continually* fraudulent, or having some such similar vice or virtue.[141]

As an example of this repetition, he does not hesitate to cite examples from ancient history and from his own time to show that the Germans could not tolerate the Tuscans (whom he calls Etruscans) and he adds:

> If Florence were not forced by necessity or conquered by passion and had read and understood the old customs of barbarians, it would not have been fooled by them, either this time or many other times, inasmuch as they have *always been the same* and have always and with everyone used the same means.[142]

In a consideration of linguistic cultural and religious "minorities", Machiavelli adheres to a uniquely political criterion. He saw that minorities became the natural allies of invaders, especially when they had been oppressed. He alludes to them as "strong minorities":

> The rule is that when a powerful foreigner enters a province, all the *less powerful inhabitants* become his adherents, moved by the envy they bear to those ruling over them; so much so that with regard to these *minor potentates* he has no trouble whatever in winning them over, for they willingly join forces with the state that he has acquired. He has merely to be careful that they do not assume too much power and authority.[143]

In the Second World War, the minorities which felt oppressed acted just as Machiavelli had foreseen. England encouraged separatism in Sicily, in the Ukraine the revolt against the Russians would have been stronger if the non-Machiavellian Hitler had exploited the situation. After the war, Russia abolished two of its republics and dispersed populations which had not been loyal to Russia. These were examples of ethnic minorities apparently not satisfied with the cultural liberties offered by Stalin.

31   Love of country above all else

Machiavelli places patriotism at the head of all his values. Every-thing is permitted for the good of one's country, which "is well defended, whether by ignominy or with glory".[144] This was echoed by Stephen Decatur and repeated by many Americans who would have been shocked to be termed Machiavellian: "Our country. In her intercourse with foreign nations may she always be right; but our country, right or wrong."

This love of country is "caused by nature" and is seen as a fundamental motivation of his heroes: "The love we bear our country, honoured sirs," say the conspirators of San Pier Scherag-gio.[145] It is the most noble motive that appears in his histories. It is supreme and transcends all religious and moral considerations. Therefore it seems right to him even to lose one's soul for one's country, as is seen in his celebrated exclamation in one of his letters to Guicciardini: "I love my country more than my soul."[146]

He probably took this expression from a popular saying that was found in the works of an old chronicler, Gino di Neri Capponi (1420). He used it more than once and applied it not only to his country but also to his friends. Of Cosimo di Rucellai he said:

> I don't know what was more his own (without even the exception of his soul) that he did not spend for his friends.[147]

Croce, commenting on the attempts to give to this expression a national heroic significance or a meaning not in opposition to Christianity, notes that it should not be taken too seriously since it reveals that

> Machiavelli's supreme interest was politics and the defence of politics of the country, and not the solicitude for his own moral perfection or the thought of the next world. This thought conditions all his works.[148]

32   The forms of government

At times Machiavelli gave a radical and decisive description of the forms of government in harmony with his incisive thought. At the beginning of *The Prince* he presents this axiomatic definition:

> All states and dominions which hold or have held sway over mankind are either republics or monarchies.[149]

This in other places is followed by other distinctions, always co-ordinated in the same precise and absolute way with the conjunctive *or* (a characteristic of his style) as though in his mind there could be no other alternative. He fixed some immutable structures or eternal models in the varied forms that are presented by history. However, he admits that there are states which have the appearance of one of these structures, but not their substance:

> Florence, as far as is known, without ever having been a state managed itself 200 years, for which reason it can really be called a republic.[150]

But along with this radical distinction, which is completely his own, he accepts another, derived from the Aristotelian tradition, without trying to reconcile or oppose it to his own. In this one, states are classified as Kingdoms, Aristocracies and Democracies, which are good in themselves but can become corrupted easily and give rise to three others which are evil. Kingdoms can degenerate into tyrannies; Aristocracies can become the government of a few who are not necessarily the best; Democracies can turn into anarchies.

It is my opinion that these distinctions have no importance in the work of Machiavelli, and in general not even in the history of political thought, because they are unrealistic. They have only served to provoke empty discussions on the merits of those forms. When a country is absorbed in these unrealistic questions, it only proves that it is politically immature. Rather we should note some of Machiavelli's cleverly affirmed similarities between systems of governments which seem different—like the government of Mohammed and the Papacy—both founded on a religious faith; and in both the head of the state is also the head of the religion:

> It is to be noted that this state of the Sultan is different from that of all other princes, being similar to the Christian pontificate, which cannot be called either a hereditary kingdom or a new one. . . . [151]

Attention should be given to his calling ancient theology "pagan mythology" and therefore to his tacit consideration of Christian theology as mythology. Unquestionably Machiavelli stands alone in the domain of history for concreteness, as in his observations on the change of names of countries, rivers and individuals, in which is manifest the transformation of ancient history into modern history. In generalities, he is one of many.

33 Machiavelli and the Renaissance

Machiavelli's attitude to his own epoch is one of dissatisfaction and of criticism. He was convinced he was living in a period of decadence following one of Roman grandeur. In this sense it can be said that Machiavelli was not in agreement with many of his contemporaries whom we call humanists. They believed they were living at a time in which the forces of the human spirit were giving evidence of a new life, comparable to the ancients, with respect to art, science, philosophy and techniques. During the century in which Machiavelli lived scholars were delighted at the ability of contemporary artists to emulate and even surpass the ancients. In the work of such men as Leon Battista Alberti and Marsilio Ficino there is felt an awareness of belonging to a new era of the world, and they openly say so. Even Machiavelli was in agreement with this general feeling about the fine arts and he explicitly says:

> This province [Italy] seems fated to resuscitate dead things, as has been seen in poetry, painting and sculpture.[152]

But for Machiavelli the most important things were not art and beauty, but political and military life. In this respect he is out of tune with his times. He wanted a renaissance but the artistic one did not suffice him. As a matter of fact, he looked upon the arts with suspicion as manifestations of inertia that corrupt human society. Here we see the new and unique attitude of Machiavelli. While in a certain sense he was also a humanist, in this respect he was not one at all. His esteem is for the ancients, especially the Romans whom he seldom criticizes. He quotes Livy in his *Discourses,* just as Christians quote the Bible, as a sacred text. He felt that his times had not been sufficiently freed from the decadence that took place at the end of the Roman Empire, with the victory of Christianity (in his words, the darkness that follows the sunlight). Leonardo's paintings and Ariosto's verses are not enough; he wants the valour of Alexander and of Caesar. In his criticism of Italian leaders he condemns all those qualities, real or legendary, that have made the Renaissance famous.

34   Breaking away from the Middle Ages

Some critics like Villari have made Machiavelli the exponent of the moral corruption of his times, but we have seen that this is not true. There are others who have made him the standard-bearer of a national church and therefore a reformer like Zwingli or Luther. This is not so. There are many, like Croce, who place him ahead of his time, in the nineteenth century which witnessed the affirmation of national states. But no one has been able to associate him with the Middle Ages.

Machiavelli is anti-medieval. He represents the complete rupture with the medieval world in a most extensive way—from the economic to the political, from the religious to the theatrical. He does not dream of universal monarchies or of eternity; nor is he concerned with the salvation of souls or the value of the contemplative life. Machiavelli was so completely emancipated from the Middle Ages that he was not even aware of the new middle ages which were springing up with the Reformation and the Counter-Reformation. Not only did he not understand them; he did not even see them. In this he was like some other great men of his time who saw Luther's rebellion only as a "monks' quarrel". Partial blindnesss of this type is not rare. This great historian Machiavelli understood the importance of the "national" formation of the big monarchies of France, Spain and England, yet he did not grasp the significance of Luther's revolt and its possible political and national consequences. He reduced to a common denominator of power the falling empire, the rising monarchies, the papacy reduced to a principality, the Italian communes and the Swiss, but he did not attach importance to the discovery of America. He saw that the modifications of military techniques and especially the appearance of an infantry influenced events, but he did not realize that artillery meant the end of the defence of medieval walled cities. He placed religion among the instruments of politics, but he thought it was possible to impose religious myths on people who did not believe in them and that religion could be useful even when it was merely superstitious.

35 Motives in history

Why do men act politically? An examination of the motives of human actions in the political field, as brought out by Machiavelli, is enlightening. Although in accord with his pessimistic principles, his analysis sheds a more noble ray of hope on human reason than is later to be found in Guicciardini.

The motive of political action that Machiavelli frequently repeats is *ambition,* followed by its natural consequence, *the fear of another's ambitions.* The second, a large category of motives, can be called *greed.* A third category falls under the heading, *boredom*— to escape from monotony, disgust, etc. But there is a fourth, the *patriotic* motive, such as a desire for one's country to be free, a desire to return to one's country, love of country, and even a *religious* motive, such as a pontiff's sincere interest in the welfare of people.

To Machiavelli, the one basic motive is the desire to tyrannize over others, to acquire other states, to conquer a city. *Envy* and *malice, timidity* and *fear* often arise. *Hatred* is a mainspring, sometimes inherited from forebears, sometimes from a social class, like the hatred of the poor for the wealthy. Other motives are the results of past injuries, foreign oppression, burdens (taxes), indignation, the desire to reclaim what once belonged to a person, the suspicion of being cheated. *Ignorance* and *vanity*—"in order not to seem less honourable"—are motives that of course are also listed. Since it is always a question of force, where there is more than one motive the strongest prevails, and in the event of a conflict the negative and positive forces even up (your weakness plus their ambition).

In examining facts from an historical viewpoint, Machiavelli is always a realist and a pessimist. Without human passions, there would be no history. But some human passions he approves in some men, or at some particular moment in their lives, if for no other reason than that they are directed at the common good of a society organized into a state. All these passions are *innate*. Even the love of country is praiseworthy because the land of our birth is not our deliberate choice, but an accident of nature. (We must remember that in Machiavelli's day acquiring another nationality was very uncommon.) Since Machiavelli's history is composed of human passions, the devil takes the place of God. History is the result of human transgressions and continues only insofar as man is impelled to sin, to want what does not belong to him, to surpass others, to assert himself, to satisfy his lust for possessions. Even in the least egoistic passion—the love of country—the question of possession enters into the picture.

The disenchanted eye of Machiavelli observes these manifestations with sadness. And even the highest motives, like the one of organizing a community, or of defending it from destruction, meet with ingratitude. This is the lot of those who work for others.

> *Go all over the world, from shore to shore,*
> *and you will find that few princes can be grateful,*
> *if you read well what history unbares;*
>
> *and you will see that those who free a state,*
> *or give their thrones away, are soon rewarded*
> *either with death or with the exile's fate.*

And at times this transforms virtuous people into savages:

> *But bold and evil slanders this obtain:*
> *they often make a mind, once meek and kind,*
> *tyrannical, and change a citizen;*
>
> *and, once a tyrant, often he forgets,*
> *and crushes every sign of civil life*
> *to save himself from Ingratitude's threats.*[153]
> (*Translated by Joseph Tusiani*)

36 Machiavelli's political formula

It is well known that many books of the Renaissance were written to instruct. At that time a number of books of conduct, rules, advice, and instruction were published. They expressed the conviction, not shared by the medieval world, that it was possible to mould the destiny of mankind. Characteristic of the new era, these books were also a clear sign of the belief that benefits were to be derived from human intelligence and everything does not stem from God. Man can fend for himself, or at least he is empowered by God to know how to do things by himself. Alberti's *The Book of the Family* is, on first reading, a book of domestic economy: how to manage your own home. His *Treatise on Painting*, on which Leonardo worked for many years without giving it final form, was intended as a manual on how to paint a landscape, a storm, etc. Cellini's treatise on the art of the goldsmith, though more technical, also belongs to this category. *The*

Courtier of Castiglione shows how men and women can become perfect courtiers. We might even say that the *Spiritual Exercises* of Ignatius was a book of this type, inasmuch as it shows how faith can be strengthened. At this time there also appeared the first grammars of the Italian language and the first dictionaries. The educated people of that period were becoming conscious of their manner of expression, and of the helpful books at their disposal.

All of these attempts to instruct impinge on the general concept of art. These human activities were taught like the arts, which copy or repeat nature externally. Machiavelli's art is the imitation of history; and just as in the imitation of the other arts models were chosen, so Machiavelli chooses as his models the nations and the great individuals who originated a political system that met with success.

His principal works (*The Prince, Discourses, The Art of War*) are technical treatises on politics, the first two on politics in general, the third on that part of politics which is warfare. They are conceived as a study of events that can occur, and of how to act or what remedies to adopt:

> Either you talk of a republic that wants to create an empire like Rome, or of one that just wants to maintain itself as it is. In the first case it is necessary to do everything as Rome did; in the second case it can imitate Venice or Sparta.[154]

Or what should be avoided:

> It was necessary for Roman legislation to do one of two things if they wanted Rome to be peaceful like the two above-mentioned republics—either not use the plebeians in wars, like the Venetians, or not to open the way to foreigners, like the Spartans.[155]

These are rules of an art, that is to copy history by studying the best examples. This holds true even in war:

> When one wins, one must with great haste follow up the victory; in this case imitate Caesar and not Hannibal who, for not having moved after defeating the Romans at Cannae, lost the Roman Empire.[156]

83

Hence, in reading Machiavelli's works, one is struck by the fact that they are filled with counsels, prescriptions, formulas, commands, warnings and remedies. And it was inevitable that collections of maxims should have been made from them.

Machiavelli describes situations common to various periods of humanity which in his estimation are principally two: the ancient or pagan, and the modern or Christian. He is like a doctor who diagnoses a sickness of his patient, then prescribes a remedy, telling what was done with success in the past and indicating what can bring about immunity in the future.

Many of Machiavelli's "counsels" deal with the actual "theory" or "technique" of politics and statecraft. For example, he considers whether it is worthwhile to build fortresses, whether colonizers should be sent to conquered countries, or whether the infantry or cavalry is to be preferred in a certain situation. But some also deal with the conflict between morals and politics, an aspect that Machiavelli so courageously exposes. His morality and politics, taken out of their context, caused much antipathy to Machiavelli, and have always provided critics the means of attacking him.

37 His dialectics

It does not seem as though Machiavelli in his concept of the march of historical events ever gets away from criteria of an almost mechanical causality. Human passions are direct causes of actions; they come in the forms of leaders who are ambitious or states that want to conquer or avenge offences; or in the form of states that want to expand; or of exceptional men who want to accomplish immortal deeds. These are some of the motives of history.

At times it seems as though Machiavelli feels that what happens in the course of history is not so simple nor so direct. He has a curious insistence on a certain kind of miracle: the reaction of a people who have reached the lowest point of their existence and *just because of this* are likely to rise again and accomplish great deeds. Machiavelli often said that Italy was in this situation. He depicted it as the most desperate plight imaginable—disunited, unarmed, disorderly;[157] more corrupt than any other country;[158] without religion because of the Church of Rome;[159] more enslaved than the Jews; without a leader, beaten, torn apart, and often occupied.[160] However, *just because of this* Italy is in a position to be saved by a great leader, just as the Jews were saved by Moses.[161]

Or consider the advice he gives the Florentines who have sent for a preacher: choose one who would teach them "how to go home by way of the devil," because "I believe this would be the way to go to Paradise; to learn the way to Hell in order to avoid it."[162] This too is a causality, made up of antithesis.

He is aware of the fact that the same actions do not always produce the same results:

> Seeing that various governments attained the same thing, just as a certain place is reached by various roads, one attains the same ends by acting in different ways. . . .[163]

Despite all this, we cannot say that Machiavelli had any inkling of what has been called the dialectics of history, one of the more elegant ways of connecting historical events and a favourite intellectual pastime of our century. This method more than any other lends an organic cohesion to accidental events and is a sort of poetic justice for reality as it appears to us in the world.

II

MACHIAVELLI'S
PRECURSORS

It was only by the end of the eighteenth century that it became clear that several of Machiavelli's ideas were to be found in the writings of some of the most respected thinkers of antiquity. With the great interest in historical studies that developed in the nineteenth century, Machiavelli's "sources" rapidly multiplied and attempts were even made to show similarities and influences where none existed.

It should be remembered that first, while it is easy enough to find certain ideas of Machiavelli in the writings of other thinkers, there is a tone and special quality to Machiavelli's thought that is completely his own and that is not to be found in other authors. If this were not so, why did the ideas of a thinker as famous as Plato create such a furor when they reappeared in Machiavelli? I do not mean to say that Machiavelli had his own system, but he does have a way of considering life which is extraneous to earlier authors. Secondly, some of these resemblances are only coincidences; it is perfectly possible for scholars, centuries apart, to reach identical conclusions when studying the conditions of human society. As a matter of fact, in many cases it would be more profitable to discover why some writers do not mention facts or ideas that struck others long before them; "silences" should be noted as well as "repetitions". (I hope that some day a study will be made of "literary and philosophical silences"—that is, why certain events and ideas were subconsciously ignored or not touched upon by great writers.)

When Aristotle counsels the tyrant to leave the women among his subjects alone, and Machiavelli repeats this, does this similarity prove that Machiavelli had read Aristotle, as Ranke suggests, or is this merely a reasonable thought that happened to occur to both

writers? This reminds me of the wonderful sentence with which
Ranke opens his work on Machiavelli and Aristotle: "Lofty souls,
however different they are, emerge from the masses and meet and
shake hands over the centuries." No one has commented on the
relationship of Machiavelli with other thinkers with so sure a
touch as Ranke, who was himself a lofty soul when looking at
these two great men.

1 Plato

Plato was certainly the chief theorist among those who wrote of
states as they *should* be, instead of as they really are. Compared to
Plato and the other Utopians, Machiavelli seems like an iconoclast.
Plato wanted wise men at the helm of the state (these men would
be called egg-heads today). Plato imagined a republic constructed
rationally and founded on the division of labour, where the
abolition of property and the common sharing of women would
remove conflicts. Plato's theory of the state springs from a belief
that man's work is complete only if it is undertaken with other
men. These positions are antithetical to those of Machiavelli.
However, it is strange that Plato, more than other philosophers of
antiquity, justified lying and encouraged the use of what Machiavelli would consider "extraordinary measures", for the sake of the
state. In Plato, the common good even justifies violence and fraud.
Like Machiavelli when he compared the politician to the doctor,
Plato says:

> We respect doctors whether they cure us by love or by force,
> whether they cut us, burn us, or inflict other painful remedies.[164]
>
> It seems to me magistrates will often be forced to resort to lies and
> fraud in the interest of their subjects.[165]
>
> A lawmaker would gladly create a new constitution and laws
> without tyrannical force and with the mildest of purgatives but the
> more severe punishments like death and exile are those that attain
> results.[166]

Such phrases and ideas caused some University of Chicago professors in the nineteen-forties to declare that Plato was a Fascist.

The concept that the welfare of the state takes precedence over any moral aspiration is found in Plato. It is also found in Machiavelli, but Plato's thought has nothing in common with the realism of Machiavelli.

2 The Sophists

As they were described by Plato, especially in the *Gorgias* and in the character of Callicles, the Sophists seemed to be the prototypes of Machiavellism. "This is the real Machiavelli", exclaims Menzel in his study on Callicles. But the imputation does not hold true. However, there is a suggestion of Machiavelli's ideas in the discourses of Callicles where he makes mention of the "insatiable desires of man".[167]

In Machiavelli the thought goes like this:

Nature has so constituted men that, though all things are objects of desire, not all things are attainable; and inasmuch as the desire is always greater than the power of acquisition, there is dissatisfaction with what one possesses. The variety of men's fortunes—some desiring more, others fearing to lose what they have—results in enmity and wars.[168]

It would have been another one of Machiavelli's strokes of genius if he had connected his ideas to those of the Sophists, thereby anticipating by centuries Hegel and Grote whom we credit with having re-evaluated this line of thought. I do not believe Machiavelli ever considered this at all, and I would even venture to say he had never read the *Gorgias*.

Moreover, Callicles speaks differently from Machiavelli. For him, too, force is the law of politics, but from this concept he justifies the dominion of masters over slaves and of the few over the masses—in the interests of the few and of the masters. Callicles who does not think of a Redeemer, is a precursor of Nietzsche, not of Machiavelli.

3 Euripides

Machiavelli did not know Greek, but in his time many Greek classics were translated. We do not have a complete list of translated works and even with such a list we would not know much more than we already know, because manuscripts of translations were lost. Machiavelli knew some passages from Greek authors through quotations in the Latin classics, with which he was well acquainted. For example, let us take the case of an idea in Euripides that could pass as one of Machiavelli's. Machiavelli probably read this in the translation of Cicero, who apologizes for rendering the verses of Euripides so crudely:

> *Num si violandum est ius, regnandi gratia, violandum est; aliis rebus pietatem colas.* (If wrong must be done, it is best to do it in the pursuit of power: let us attend to virtue in other things.)[169]

In Euripides' play, *The Phoenician Women,* this is an accidental proposition that serves to depict the character of Eteocles, but not to set forth a political theory.

4 Thucydides

Germs of Machiavelli's thought can be found in the political discussions of Thucydides. Meinecke quotes such a passage, where the Athenians are discussing the fall of Meli:

> But you and I should say what we really think, that is, that we are only searching for what is possible because we both know that in discussing human affairs, the question of justice only enters into the

picture when the pressure of necessity is equal, the powerful exact what they can obtain, and the weak concede what they are forced to forsake.[170]

5 Aristotle

Machiavelli belongs more in the Aristotelian than in the Platonic tradition. In certain respects he is thoroughly Aristotelian. He knew Aristotle's *Politics*.[171] From Aristotelian terminology, common in his time, he derived those concepts of *form* and *matter* he frequently uses, not always in a very Aristotelian manner. Though Aristotle, like Plato, constructs an ideal state, it is within the limits of possibility (*Politics,* IV, 4); and his lessons contain a description of the means by which various constitutions function. But he is in search of the *best* state, the one capable of supplying the means of living in accordance with virtue (IV, 1). Aristotle is a finalist and Machiavelli, even though he may have studied him, does not agree with him in this respect. Machiavelli is a scientist in the Galilean rather than Aristotelian manner.

On the other hand, Machiavelli lifted from Aristotle the division of governments into three forms. This is found in his work without logical coherence and in contrast with the repeated affirmation of his incisive nature that there are really only two forms of government: monarchy and republic. Perhaps he did not take this directly from Aristotle but from Polybius, or more simply from the contemporary culture of his day. But this classification, which opposes to the good forms the three evil forms of government (monarchy that degenerates into tyranny, etc.), is an external importation. I would say it remains like a cyst on the organism of Machiavelli's thought, whose originality consists in seeking not so much the good or bad forms of government, but the conditions of the existence of states of whatever form (even if he prefers a certain type which might generically be called republican).

For Aristotle, man is by nature a social being, and the state takes precedence over the individual. For Machiavelli, the state has an origin which might be called natural and which comes from the act of will of a strong individual. Aristotle is a philosopher and he believes in the innate idea of justice. He contends that for men to be worthy of the name there must "first be a state". Machiavelli is not a philosopher and he does not even take Aristotelian thought into consideration. He is a naturalist who accounts for the development of a state from the bestial to the human by means of an act of will (mechanical). This development gives birth to justice.

Ranke, Lutoslawski and Meinecke were able to show several similarities in the thought of Aristotle and Machiavelli that are striking, but some of their comparisons are not convincing. For example, Aristotle in his *Politics* (III, 4) considers "whether the virtue of a good citizen and of a good man are identical". This might almost make us suspect that Aristotle admits a different morality for the statesman and the private individual. But this is not so. The virtue of the leader differs from that of a private individual because "the citizen is like one who makes the flute but does not play it, while the leader is the one who plays it", says Aristotle. Here he applies the principle of the division of labour which is unknown to Machiavelli.

Another more impressive example at first sight is the passage in Aristotle where the Greek philosopher seems to advise the prince, as does Machiavelli, to encourage observances: "It is always necessary to *seem* to give thought to religious matters above anything else," (*Politics* V, 2), but when the context is closely examined it is seen that Aristotle speaks of the "tyrant" who, according to him, is the corrupter of the monarchic form of government, while Machiavelli applies the principle to all states, kingdoms and republics.

The ethical concept of human life is not the only thing that separates the two thinkers. The naturalistic observations that Aristotle makes on politics (for Aristotle the state is nature), when he deals with "examples" taken from history, or "norms and rules" which the philosopher gives for the various forms of government, become a part of a vaster vision of the world. Aristotle's horizon is infinitely more extensive than Machiavelli's.

The passages in Aristotle which seem to commentators to have been borrowed by Machiavelli in *The Prince* are almost all contained in the second chapter of the fifth book of the *Politics*. Here the Greek philosopher examines two ways tyrants remain in power—one a real tyrant, that is, an evil one; the other resembling as much as possible a good king. Aristotle describes the tyrant as a man who likes to wage wars—this is in agreement with the advice Machiavelli gives to princes—but Aristotle's reasons are very different. The tyrant will provoke wars "so that his subjects will have something to do. . . . They always feel the need of a leader." Aristotle also says that "the tyrant will do his best to impoverish his subjects", but he does not attribute to poverty the value that Machiavelli gives it, and he makes use of historical examples that Machiavelli never mentioned, like the building of the pyramids whereby Egyptian tyrants kept the people busy and impoverished. Aristotle evidently did not believe in the benefits of poverty.

Campanella oversimplified the matter when he stated that Aristotle had generated Machiavelli: *"Ex Aristotelismo postea ortus est Machiavelismus."*

6 Polybius (204?–123 B.C.)

With this historian, we approach the solid domain of affinities. Machiavelli's thought goes hand in hand with the scientific spirit of Polybius. When we find ideas that are so similar, we can with justification speak of derivations.

Machiavelli resembles Polybius more than any other writer of antiquity in a number of ways. Polybius stands out as a fine example of an impartial thinker. A Greek, conquered by the Romans, he tried to explain objectively by means of natural causes, why the Romans had succeeded in conquering the Greeks.

Like Machiavelli, he was an independent thinker and did not believe in the religion of his time. As an historian, in certain respects he was more modern than Machiavelli inasmuch as he sought for documents and proofs. The two men were similar in their dispassionate observations of the motives of political actions, although Polybius was not as cynical as Machiavelli, and in the stress each placed on the importance of military organizations. In a certain sense Polybius is the Machiavelli of antiquity, just as Machiavelli is the Polybius of his time.*

Both Polybius and Machiavelli believed that inasmuch as events repeat themselves, one can learn from history (*Histories,* VI, 5); and that there are no "accidents in history, but causes" (II, 38). The two men held the following beliefs: The primitive life of man was wild and untamed and at first the strongest person was the leader (VI, 6). Revolutions, constitutions and other political movements follow a cycle of events (VI, 9). Rome's constitution was not formulated theoretically, but through struggles and conflicts (VI, 10). It is not worth while to discuss the Platonic constitution, because it would be like comparing a statue with a living person (VI, 47). Kings (Machiavelli would say princes, heads of states, even of republican states) consider everything from the viewpoint of expediency (II, 46). Rome conquered because it did not use mercenary troops, whereas Carthage lost because it made use of them (VI, 52). Religion is a deception, invented to keep faith among men (VI, 56). Men would not face danger with courage, without hope of divine aid (X, 2). Man's nature is fickle and gratitude is rare (X, 36).

These and other ideas inspired by the same historical positivism are frequent in Polybius and they give evidence of one of the clearest and more illuminated minds of antiquity. Polybius could not fail to have delighted Machiavelli.

---

* I believe the first person to note Machiavelli's imitation of Polybius was the erudite scholar Fabricius (1668–1736, *Bibliotheca Graeca,* Vol. II, 756–7, note, not mentioned by Norsa). He called attention to a passage from the sixth book of Polybius' *Histories,* and compared it with Book I, 2 of Machiavelli's *Discourses.*

7 Plutarch

From Plutarch, Machiavelli acquired a great deal of biographical information. Some of Machiavelli's passages dealing with Greek personalities seem to come from *The Lives* of Plutarch. And he also made use of what he had read in the *Moralia* and in the *Praecepta*.

The most important passage that Machiavelli mentions is the one which treats of the relative importance of fortune and *virtù* in accounting for the greatness of the Romans:

> Many people, Plutarch among them, were of the opinion that the Romans in acquiring their Empire were more favoured by fortune than by *virtù* And among other reasons he adduces the fact that they ascribed all their victories to fortune inasmuch as they erected more temples to fortune than to any other deity. It seems that Livy is in agreement with this opinion because seldom does he have a Roman speak of *virtù* that he doesn't also mention fortune.[172]

But this is not Machiavelli's opinion. He adds: "I cannot accept this in any way—nor do I think it can be upheld."

In contrast to Plutarch's thesis, an attempt to minimize Rome's accomplishment in having subjugated Greece—inasmuch as he was not satisfied, as was Polybius, in attributing purely human reasons, natural and political, to the event—Machiavelli places the force of the Roman will and intelligence (*virtù* and prudence).

In the same treatise (*Moralia,* vol. II, Teubner) where Plutarch treats of the fortune of the Romans is found a passage illustrating the course of this divinity who bestows her gifts on the people of this earth:

> Fortune, having abandoned the Persians and Assyrians, flew in haste to the Macedonians and removed Alexander the Great, and after having passed over Egypt and Syria and having helped the Carthaginians, finally flew over the Tiber on the Palatine Hill, and there deposited the wingéd sandals of Mercury and his deceptive globe.

Machiavelli reverses this process by applying the same theory of favours distributed by a divinity, but his divinity is not fortune but *virtù*.

The world remains the same. There was only this difference that whereas Virtue first bestowed its favours on Assyria, it then gave them to Media and Persia, and finally to Rome in Italy.[173]

There has been an attempt to find in Plutarch's life of Lysander, the origin of the lion-like or fox-like comparison when referring to politics, but the passage deals only with war: "He laughed at those who believed that the descendants of Hercules should not use deceit *in war;* because where the skin of the lion is of no use, it must be replaced by that of the fox."

Another passage of that same life is often quoted because it disavows the obligations of princes to keep their word: "[Lysander] recommended deceiving children with dice, and men with oaths." But Plutarch takes Lysander to task for this attitude as not being very honourable for a leader, fit only for a tyrant and encouraging indifference to the god on whom the oath was made.

8 Carneades

The Greek philosopher Carneades (born 214 or 213 B.C.) is presented by Cherel as a source of the negation of the justice of states. But the passage of the Christian writer Lattanzio that refers to it does not mention states; it is only a negation of *human* justice, in an attempt to exalt the only real justice, that of God:

Men established laws for the purpose of their own use, naturally changeable according to the prevailing customs; and also changeable according to the times. A natural right does not exist; all things, men and animated objects, are created by their nature according to the law of expediency; and consequently there cannot be justice or, if it ever should exist, it would be very stupid because it would harm itself in order to serve someone else's interest.[174]

These arguments of Carneades were presented by him as his ambassadorial report before the Roman Senate, where the Greek philosopher one day sustained justice and the next day refuted it. Cicero referred to them in his *De Republica III*. These remarks were taken up by Lattanzio and Augustine. Among those ironic arguments there is one of timely interest: Carneades dared tell the Romans, who boasted of being just, that if they really wanted to be just they should give back all that they had conquered and return to their huts around the Tiber. But the law of life does not allow such a turning back of history.

Carneades enjoyed indulging in witticisms: "If you are just you are stupid. and if you are wise you are wicked; there is no alternative."

9 The Romans: Cicero

As we have already stated, Machiavelli did not know Greek and read many Greek authors in translation. He read a great many Latin authors, but like the Humanists of his time he doesn't seem to maintain a clear distinction between Greek and Roman writers. The end of antiquity seemed to him the ruin of a world *greater* than his, more noble, courageous and intelligent. With contempt he was the first to note the linguistic variations from the Latin to the Romance languages in the Middle Ages. Instead of being called Caesar and Pompey, men bore the names of Peter, John and Matthew.[175]

Ellinger, Krapp and Burd have diligently collected a number of quotations from authors whose names Machiavelli does not always mention. Among the Latin ones there are Cicero, Sallust, Seneca, Valerium, Maximus and more often than any other, of course, Titus Livy whom he commented upon at length in his *Discourses*. Each one of these authors merits investigation, but one name stands out as demanding special attention: Cicero.

If there is a person who can be considered the antithesis of

Machiavelli, it is Cicero, the lawyer—I almost wrote His Honour Cicero. Cicero examines the case of the murder of Remus by Romulus but only as an example of the strength of individual force against honesty—while Machiavelli speaks of it as though the event were responsible for the grandeur of the Roman Empire. Machiavelli's thought is more realistic and radical than Cicero. Cicero is aware of the problem but he skirts around it. In Cicero is found the famous definition of politics made up of reason and force, that is human and bestial:

> Nam, cum sint duo genera decertandi, unum per disceptationem, alterum per vim; cunque illius proprium sit hominis, hoc bellarum, confugiendum est ad posterius, si uti no licet superiore.[176]

It would seem that Machiavelli did nothing more than appropriate Cicero's words and translate them:

> Therefore you must know the two ways of fighting—one with law, the other with force. The first is characteristic of men, the second of beasts. But inasmuch as at times the first does not suffice, one must have recourse to the second.

To the words of Cicero, he adds the legend of Achilles' education by a Centaur, half-beast and half-man: "This means only that a prince must not use either one or the other nature alone. One without the other is of no value."[177]

For Cicero reason is preferable, force being but a deplorable substitute; while for Machiavelli in politics the two natures are indissolubly bound. The Centaur is for him the symbol not of what man and beast are separately, but of one who contains both natures.

10 St. Augustine (354–430)

So far as I know, only Meinecke compared the thought of Machiavelli with that of St. Augustine. "Remota itaque justitia, quid sunt regna, nisi magna latrocinia?"[178]

This Christian problem has been interpreted in various ways. Is it, as some believe, a condemnation of *all* states, or is it only a condemnation of non-Christian states? Truly I would like to ask, where has there ever existed, in Augustine's time or after, a Christian state—one that is morally just?

"*Vera autem justitia non est nisi in ea republica, cujus conditor rectorque Christus est.*"[179] For Augustine the only real justice is found in the City of God, where Christ reigns; human justice will always be lacking, in the mind of such a Christian. And therefore the passage should not be translated dubitatively (*if* justice is lacking) but affirmatively and causally (*inasmuch as* states do not provide justice). What are states if not large enterprises of brigands?

The impression one gets in reading *The City of God* is that the author tried to show that Rome was the result of the greatest effort made by humanity, with all the means at its disposal, to provide decent order to the world. Yet, he adds, what were these greatest men of the world, these Romans, but thieves, pigs, etc.?

In addition to Rome, Augustine openly condemns all states—or rather politics—because they originate from Cain. Romulus too, let us remember, was a *fratricide*. Machiavelli dwells on this aspect of the origin of a state. The object of the condemnation of Augustine and of Roman moralists becomes for Machiavelli the benefactor of humanity, while the opposition of the two societies, earthly and divine, is always at the root of Augustine's thought.

Inasmuch as we cannot be moral without religion, at least in a Christian sense, it is clear that the opposition between politics (love of self to the point of contempt for God) and religion (love of God to the point of contempt for oneself) is the same opposition as that between politics and Christian morality. This idea is at the core of Machiavellian thought.

It has been said that Augustine affirmed the "diabolical character of the state". However, I do not think it is possible to say that he had an influence on Machiavelli.

11   Dante (1265–1321)

It would be impossible to imagine two worlds more remote than those of Dante and Machiavelli—one medieval and the other modern; one which believes in the Roman Empire of his time, and the other only in the reality of national states; one Christian, the other upholding only regulations that can be successfully put into practice; one inspired by the ideal of justice, the other acknowledging only the moment of force.

Professor Francesco Ercole (1884–1945) while acknowledging the difference between Dante and Machiavelli tried to establish a bond between them and found it by using perspicacity rather than doctrine; first of all in the love each bore his country (even though this was for Dante only the Garden of the Empire) and in the importance both writers attach to will power—in doing evil as well as good. Dante keeps the hesitant, the irresolute and the trimmer even out of the Inferno and refers to them with contempt; and Machiavelli, as we have seen, believes in action at all costs, as did Boccaccio who felt that it was better to act and sin rather than repent for not having acted.

For Ercole there is a *continuity* in the world of Dante and of Machiavelli, notwithstanding the abyss that exists between their doctrines:

> If Dante closes the Middle Ages, he inaugurates Humanism, and if Machiavelli inaugurates the modern age, he closes Humanism. . . . In other words, Dante is the first link in a chain of which Machiavelli is the last. . . . If humanism already exists in embryo in the medieval thought of Dante (a period which Machiavelli closes), that abyss must in some way be bridged because the history of thought, like all histories, continues uninterruptedly. Humanism is the bridge across which Machiavelli's thought joins the thought of Dante.[180]

Two centuries ago no one would have dreamed of linking Dante with Machiavelli. The connection exists only in Ercole's mind. But this is the real life of ideas and of men who generate them. It does not proceed along ways opened by scholars, but follows the route excavated by political and religious passions and interests, by imagination and by men's desire to invent, repair, concede, neglect. Men are not satisfied with words and precise facts and are ready, like Ercole, to "bridge the gap". When the pressure of the historical moment is over, the abyss remains.

12 The Humanists

Following largely the model of the *Cyropaedia* of Xenophon, a pedagogic and political "novel", many Humanists wrote treatises, aphorisms, counsels and rules which refer to the ideal education of a model prince. Many of these literary compositions deal with the same subjects touched upon by Machiavelli in his *Prince*. A diligent reader of these, Professor Allan H. Gilbert, made an interesting study of the subject which leads him to maintain:

> Few of the ideas expressed in *The Prince* are completely new; the greater part of them is found in medieval and Renaissance works which belong to the category of books giving advice to sovereigns. Perhaps a study and a thorough reading of treatises of this type would leave Machiavelli *without anything substantially new.*[181]

The conclusion of this scholarly work is erroneous. None of these authors considers princes of the "new" light shed on them by Machiavelli's fundamental concepts which are, first of all, seeing them as living examples of natural forces; and secondly, considering them subject to the law of the necessity of evil. Except for these essential differences, the verbal points of contact are many. It could be said that Machiavelli used the old treatises as an antique frame to adorn a new picture. Professor Gilbert even seems to agree on this point later on in his book when he says: "The real originality of Machiavelli consists in his philosophy of politics."

In addition to the many treatises examined by Gilbert, the work of the humanist Aurelius Brandolini called "Lippo" (who died in 1497) can be added to the list without making him a precursor of Machiavelli, as E. Mayer did in the year-book of the Hungarian Academy of Rome (Vol. II, 1937). In Brandolini's *De comparatione republicae et regni,* dedicated to Lorenzo dei Medici, he is in search of the "best prince" and therefore he is not a pre-Machiavellian. However, Machiavelli's ideas were well enough known inasmuch as Brandolini writes in opposition to the idea held by a "few" (that is, Machiavelli) which attributes to Christianity the blame for the decadence of modern times in comparison with ancient times and especially the end of the Roman Empire. Like Machiavelli, Brandolini praises the military vigour of the Greeks and Romans and favours their very severe military training, deploring the use of mercenary troops, whose only interest is to prolong wars. And again like Machiavelli, he is even against the use of the cavalry because it is so heavily encumbered that the soldiers cannot attack the enemy even though they protect themselves from the enemy.

Among the many humanists mentioned by Gilbert there are two that can be rightly termed precursors or companions of Machiavelli, at least in spirit. They are Leon Battista Alberti (1404–72) and Lorenzo dei Medici (1449–92), one with a theoretical knowledge, and the other with a practical experience of political life. Leon Battista Alberti, as does Machiavelli, seems to be aware of belonging to and representing a new epoch and of breaking away from the medieval world. The subjects treated by Alberti resemble those dealt with by Machiavelli. First of all both men exalt the will power of the individual:

> It is said that man can do what he wants, when he uses all his power in doing what he wants.[182]

The similarity is also seen in the activist theory they both subscribe to:

> Let us realize that man is not born in order to become saddened by leisure—but to undertake great and magnificent things by means of which he can first of all please and honour God and also have the satisfaction of perfect virtue—which leads to happiness.[183]

Alberti, more than any other writer before Machiavelli, prefers *virtù* to fortune:

> Fortune can dominate you only if you allow it. So we may affirm that fortune is completely incapable of depriving us of the least of our virtues. We must realize that *virtù* is capable of conquering and taking posession of every sublime and lofty thing, like the most powerful state, the greatest praise, eternal fame and immortal glory.[184]

And moreover in his "intellectualism"—the power of thought to dominate the world—he says:

> If the solicitude of a professional instructor can teach a beast to perform human actions, if this can be done to a beast by discipline, why should it be less efficacious on a human intellect—which is certainly capable of learning the most difficult things imaginable? The intellectual power of man is capable of accomplishing anything.[185]

And also in the determining power of *nature* which gives form to men, he says: "If you observe from his first days the desires of a child, immediately you will know the inclinations given him by nature."[186]

We might add that Alberti is a Christian to such a small degree that he never mentions Christ in his book on the family; and he considers religion only as a pedagogic means, or a habit to observe for "honour and fame of a family tradition". Nor does he ever stress the Christian virtues, such as charity and compassion but, like Machiavelli, the "common good". Even in his respect for and faith in the Florentine language as opposed to Latin, he approaches Machiavelli. Like Machiavelli, the activist theory he subscribes to shows an awareness of the importance of economic well being, so that "earnings" are considered by Alberti as logical results of action (in opposition to the theory held by the Church in the Middle Ages), and poverty (in an almost American manner) is the result of negligence, laziness and backwardness. Machiavelli was in agreement with Alberti in maintaining that Rome dominated the world while it was *united, strong and in harmony.*

In the Medici dynasty there must have been an hereditary strain of irony characteristic of men with political power, who were in a position to see the frailties, the stupidities and the cowardice of men. None more than great leaders with intellectual acumen can better measure the depths to which the majority of people can sink in an effort to feed their vanity and appease their desires. In addition to political judgment, Lorenzo and Cosimo were possessed of this ironic vision of life, shared also by Machiavelli.

Truly Machiavellian is the phrase that Machiavelli reports of Cosimo dei Medici who more than any other Humanist epitomizes the incompatibility of Christian morals with politics: "States were not governed by us with rosaries in our hands."[187] Machiavelli realized that such a saying provided the means "of spreading slander about the man who made it, as of one who loves this world more than the next".

Of all the writings of Lorenzo, Machiavelli chose to quote a drama which has no special poetic merit but which is filled with political humour. It deals with Emperor Constantine who, in order to please General Gallicano, promises him his daughter's hand in marriage. This marriage becomes an affair of state.

> Shall I give my beautiful daughter who is so dear to me to a commoner? If I don't give her to him, my state is in great danger. And who will then repair the damage?

The advice of the daughter, Constantina, is slanted towards "realistic" politics. Take your time, she says to her father, lead him on and make him think I will marry him:

> Whenever a choice is difficult from all angles and the issue is not clear and success not certain, I have heard said that the wise man temporizes, talks a lot and bides his time. Although I am a woman of little sense, Father, I would suggest you promise me to him, make him think he will have me, then send him on an urgent mission.

In this same play, the evils of division of power are described by Constantine:

Whoever wants to succeed in dominating the people must make sure to keep the power in his own hands; if it is divided, the ruler will eventually lose control.

Julian seems to believe that the Roman Empire declined because paganism had been abandoned. This is an idea dear to Machiavelli:

At the time when the Roman eagle was unfurled, the world trembled like a leaf in the wind; now we have so little power that any small town wants to assert itself. Since the sacrifices to Jove, Mars, Phoebus, Minerva and Juno were abolished and the statue of Victory removed from the Senate, the Empire has lost its glory.

In certain rules for those who are called to command are seen ideas similar to those held by Machiavelli—the "common good" and good example (inasmuch as all people look up to the leader): "He must not think of personal gain or of pleasure, but of the common good of everyone." If Machiavelli had not quoted this work of Lorenzo, it might be a matter of coincidence that the two men were in agreement. And it is not much more. Such ideas and expressions were indeed common at that time, but it was a coincidence of which Machiavelli was aware.

III

HIS WORK

All of Machiavelli's principal works were written at about the same time, one single manner of thinking animates them all, and none of his important works has been lost. Modern criticism has not discovered any essential change in any of his texts. *The Prince*, the *Discourses, The Art of War* and the *Florentine Histories* form a single unit with differences stemming only from non-essentials or methods of exposition.

Machiavelli differs from many authors in that it is not possible to speak of a development or transformation of his thought caused by events or by a maturing of his ideas. Even before 1516, and at the time of his significant works, his mind was already formed; it was an adult mind from the beginning. The young or adolescent Machiavelli does not exist for us. His style always bears the same serious, severe and mature imprint—a rare quality in Italian literature. There are no uncertainties in his thought. The fundamental concepts of political life are already clearly presented in his early works; at times they are expressed by means of the same formulas in which years later they reappear on other occasions.

Machiavelli died relatively young. He only wrote when an adult and while in exile, when he felt impelled to write because of inactivity. It is almost as though he considered the period of his political activity as being too important to waste time in writing about it. For his principal works we are indebted to his political misfortune, which deprived him of employment. (This is also true of Castiglione, who wrote *The Courtier* while unemployed.) Not only were Machiavelli's works written almost contemporaneously—indeed two were written almost simultaneously and in the three principal ones he refers to the others—but in almost all of them, in his minor works as well as in the humorous ones, his thought is always consistent.

In making this statement I differ from those who have tried to establish an essential difference between *The Prince* and the *Discourses,* seeing the former as a work that idealizes the monarchic or tyrannical form of government and the latter as exalting the republican form. There are differences between the works, but they are not essential, and united they complement each other to form a complete body of political doctrine. It isn't even true to say that in *The Prince* Machiavelli was concerned only with monarchies and that in the *Discourses* only with republics. *The Prince* was written between the first and second book of the *Discourses,* and it was composed almost accidentally, for a special event. In a certain sense we might say that the *Discourses* are the most systematic exposition of Machiavelli's thought, that *The Prince* is a sort of intermezzo, written for a special occasion, and that *The Art of War* and the *Histories* are, above all, the application of his theories.

1   Report on the Florentine Republic's efforts to suppress the Pistoia Factions

When I read these three pages of Machiavelli, I am reminded of the reports of an F.B.I. agent. This composition could serve as a model for a good report. There is nothing extraneous in it. Machiavelli immediately attacks the question, reports the events, and stops when there is nothing more to say. The account is like a hydraulic problem where the balance is determined by pressure and force. Pistoia remains orderly when the Florentine forces are present, reverts to tumult when they are withdrawn, resumes order again when they return. "To use force", "that land remained without force", "forces so well ordered" are frequent phrases. To him force is the opposite of disorder, tumult, thievery, arson and murder. It is similar to the contents of one of the letters from the Legations (I.1355), explaining how to bring order to a city of that time. The commander must "prohibit, quell and annul the factions". The Report was written in 1500.

2 Description of the Method used by Duke Valentine in Slaughtering Vitelli and Others

This famous pamphlet of 1502 is noteworthy for the scientific detachment with which a political operation is described—much like a surgical operation (and for the one responsible for carrying it out it was just that). Suppressing adversaries was typical of the time in which Machiavelli lived. It was resorted to before and after Machiavelli and it is more effective than certain historians are ready to admit. Political assassination is reprehensible but no one can say that it is not effective, even today. Machiavelli attended this atrocious event much as he would a game of football. The pamphlet should be compared to his description immediately after the deed, in which Machiavelli says he is reporting every detail because of the "quality of the thing which is indeed rare and memorable".[188] He attributes its success to chance and fortune in addition to the ability (*virtù*) of the Duke. He educes a general rule: in a world in which men are not good, whoever does good and not evil will soon be finished off.

3 Words to Be Said on Providing Money

This short speech dates from March 1503 and was probably written to be pronounced in the Grand Council but perhaps remained on Machiavelli's desk like a repressed desire. This essay, wherein are contained the germs of his political thought ready to blossom forth into life, is typical of Machiavelli and is expressed in his characteristic deductive manner. The theory that gold does not replace iron is dramatized by Machiavelli by means of an historic anecdote. In these pages is found one of Machiavelli's most revealing principles, that private morality cannot be applied in public affairs: "Among private individuals it is by faith that laws, writings and pacts are observed; but among heads of states only arms succeed in making them observed."

This work, which contains his belief that cowards and idlers are not favoured by fortune, his appeal to force, swift decisions and to independence which he believes is every man's inalienable right, might well be considered a little résumé of Machiavelli's thought.

4 Of the Methods of Dealing with the Rebels of Valdichiana

This book, written in 1503, is Machiavelli's first little work of importance. It deals with a "counsel" given to the Florentine Republic. All of Machiavelli's thought is already clear in this work, ten years before he wrote *The Prince*: his straightforward tone, his consideration of the substance of the question, his clear-cut resolution, his habit of contrasting either-ors; his tendency to radical solutions, his detachment in suggesting atrocious but necessary measures; his realism in the face of solutions that might seem crude at first sight and in the end are the best; his love of rapid decisions ("when deliberation is necessary, it must be carried out quickly"), and his frankness to the leader he is counselling. The motif of this counsel given to the Florentines, which is repeated by Machiavelli in parts of his other works, has become famous.[189] It is that rebellious people who have been vanquished must either be "benefited or killed" by the conqueror.

Here too are found the basic principles of his writings. "History is the master of our actions", "the world has always been inhabited by men with the same passions", and therefore "it is not a bad idea to follow the example of those who have been masters of the world (the Romans)." There is the inevitable quotation from Livy which serves as a springboard for the reflections that follow, the final eulogy of Caesar Borgia and of Pope Alexander VI, and the acknowledgment that "even great men at times must trust to fortune".

This is Machiavelli in a nutshell—tasty, dry, nodulated, a little bitter and as hard to digest as a nut.

5   I Decennali (Annals of Italy)

These are two poems in *terza rima*. The first deals with the history of Italy from 1492 to 1503; the second, which is unfinished, covers the period from 1504 to 1509. The first, composed and published in 1508, he called "the chore of 15 days". The date of the second is not known, but from a reference in it to his own misfortunes, would seem to be at least 1512.

The importance of these two compositions lies in the fact that they came from Machiavelli's pen before he started writing seriously. However, they give evidence of a rapidity and a simplicity in his ideas on politics and on the men of his times. He made use of symbols that are easy to interpret and transposed names or used hieroglyphs that are decipherable. They were well received, the first one especially, by his contemporaries who noted the primary quality of his style, his gift of "marvellous brevity" (letter of Vespuccio, Feb. 1596).

Machiavelli was not a great craftsman in writing verses and he is not always successful with the requirements of rhyme and rhythm; however, here and there are found passages of energy and colour. One couplet has become famous, where he makes use of puns in speaking of the Capponi who did not succumb to Charles VIII:

> *The din of arms and of horses could not drown out*
> *the voice of a capon among a hundred roosters.*[190]
> (*Translated by Joseph Tusiani*)

6　The Prince

This, Machiavelli's best known work, is the one that has made his name so controversial. It was written in 1513, as shown by Machiavelli's letter to Vettori on December 10 of that year:

> And because Dante says it does not produce knowledge when we hear but do not remember, I have noted everything in their conversation which has profited me, and have composed a little work on Princedoms, where I go as deeply as I can into consideration of this subject, debating what a princedom is, of what kinds they are, how they are gained, how they are kept, why they are lost. And if ever you can find any of my fantasies pleasing, this one should not displease you; and by a Prince, and especially by a new Prince, it ought to be welcomed. Hence I am dedicating it to His Magnificence Giuliano. Filippo Casavecchia has seen it; he can give you some account in part of the thing in itself and of the discussions I have had with him, though I am still enlarging and revising it.[191]

These words have given rise to various questions. Clearly this was a work of improvisation, written for a practical purpose, to call himself to the attention of the Medici who at that moment seemed to have the greatest chance of political success. Inasmuch as Giuliano had died, Machiavelli dedicated it to Lorenzo. Like many works of improvisation written for special occasions, it is sincere and has assumed great importance (like Lincoln's Gettysburg address). In describing his topics Machiavelli does not include those discussed after Chapter XV. This and the mention of padding, or additions, lead Meinecke and his disciple, Weichert, to think that The Prince was composed at two separate times. But two passages of Chapters III and XII and others of a similar nature seem to bear out Chabod's contention that this was not the case. They maintained that The Prince, in the version we possess, was written at one period and is all of one piece. Until the twentieth century no one questioned this.

The form of Machiavelli's compositions is always disorderly. Even in his Discourses he doesn't seem to proceed according to a set plan, despite the fact that at times he mentions things he intends to say later. A study of his work method leads one to think he wrote by fits and starts rather than methodically. This was caused by his desire to get at the core of ideas at the centre of a given problem. And the connections which lend a natural manner to ideas so unified and unhesitating as those of Machiavelli were probably added later.

Even critics who agree on dividing *The Prince* into various parts differ as to the divisions. For example Ranke (who, I believe, was the first to have tried to make this separation) says: "The first eleven chapters deal with the enlargement and maintenance of principalities, the three following with the art of war, and the remaining with separate maxims." But Tommasini, although accepting the division in three parts, does not agree with this, and finds first of all that it deals with the kind of principalities Lorenzo could use; secondly with the description of the nature and quality a prince should possess; and third with military institutions which, as he says, "crown the final sublime exaltation" of the last chapter.

From the point of view of style, it seems clear that *The Prince* gives evidence of three models: an official humanistic one, for the dedication; in the body of the text up to the last chapter, the real style of Machiavelli, dry, clear-cut and precise, eager to convey what is on his mind and to make distinctions; and, in the final chapter, a sort of prophetic rhetoric that is very different from his usual expression.

From a literary point of view, *The Prince* is *not a unified work.* And while it is clear that the dedication was written after the book was finished, as is the habit of many authors, the final part is rather a surprise and does not seem actually related to the rest. I realize that what I say will seem almost a sacrilege, but I am of the opinion that from a literary point of view the final chapter of *The Prince* is an addendum. The style of the core of *The Prince* is that of a scientific work, possessing an air of seriousness and a competence which technical matters give even to literary works. The end does not fit in with the rest.

I reached this conclusion by dividing *The Prince* rationally into sections. The first nine chapters follow a thread which might be called a description of the formative and continuing process of principalities, of which the first chapter contains the general plan. After this it is not possible to find a logical sequence. Chapter XXIV, for example, "Why Italian Princes Lost Power", should follow chapter XXVI, "Exhortation to Free Italy from Foreigners", of which in a certain sense it is the preface, but in between there is the chapter on Fortune which separates rather than unites them, dealing with a universal and not a specifically Italian problem. Chapters XV to XXXII form another group "How to Perfect the Basic Qualities of a Condottiere". Chapters XII to XIV are treated separately from the rest—"The Problem of a National or Mercenary Militia". Chapter XI, "Ecclesiastical Principalities", is a solo, partly ironic and partly flattering, and Machiavelli seems to be holding himself in check. However, he ends up by saying unpleasant things about popes, but he realizes that Lorenzo and Julian are related to the reigning Pope and that their fortune is dependent upon his power. This accounts for the final statement:

> His Holiness, Pope Leo X, therefore, has found the pontificate in a very powerful condition, from which it is hoped that, as those Popes made it great by force of arms, so he through his goodness and other infinite virtues will make it both great and venerated.[192]

As a matter of fact, between this part of *The Prince* and the *Discourses* there is no difference in construction, or rather lack of construction. Gilbert is right when he calls *The Prince* "loose".

In *The Prince,* as in the *Discourses,* Machiavelli makes use of the system of two-fold expressions, one from ancient and the other from modern history, but I get the impression that in *The Prince* the modern example illuminates the classical one, whereas the opposite is true in the *Discourses,* where the classical example clarifies the modern. Machiavelli sees the "new" Prince so vividly as a real model that it was inevitable for him to view ancient history in the light of the present. But in the comments of Livy, the present is judged from the highest peaks of the great past. The

Romans appear like mountains that cast their shadows over the surrounding hills.

There are many interpretations of *The Prince*. Some think it was written seriously and others find hidden motives in it. For many *The Prince* was a satire on tyrants, or a revelation of the arts of tyrants to teach people how to prevent them from seizing power. For others it consisted in a series of written counsels so false that the Medici, by following them, would be ruined. For still others it was seen as a series of counsels written with the connivance of Lorenzo d'Urbino so that the road would be paved for him to seize the throne of Italy. This, as a minor hypothesis, would make it the work of a flatterer, a courtier of the Medici. Some interpret it only as a joke composed to give vent to the author's feelings; or a book with a special and personal aim, with no pretence at being a serious work. For some it mirrors the moral and political conditions of the times, but of that epoch only and not of all times. For some it does not express the real ideas of Machiavelli, who expounded them instead in the *Discourses,* where he seems to favour a republican form of government; for others it is the revelation of what sovereigns of all times have done. This final interpretation is the first that grasps something real in Machiavelli's thought and opens the way to the modern belief that Machiavelli is the philosopher of the *pratica,* in Croce's meaning of the word. And finally some have even said that *The Prince,* according to a Freudian interpretation, is the work of a frustrated person and should be considered only as a compensation for his personal disappointments. This seems to me to be the least serious interpretation of them all.

7 Discourses

These were written between 1512 and 1516. The first book was written before *The Prince,* and the last two books afterwards, as is shown in various passages.[193]

In the first book Machiavelli had planned to treat of "the deliberations of the Romans about the internal affairs of a city"; in the second book of things "that the Roman people did for the aggrandizement of their Empire"; and in the third he planned to "narrate and talk" of special individuals who had made Rome great and "brought about such great results in that city". In this plan the first book deals with internal affairs, the second with foreign affairs, and the third with eminent citizens (not including the kings of Rome). But we cannot say that Machiavelli kept to this plan. On reading the *Discourses,* we get the impression that they are disconnected reflections on politics in general. They have even been compared with two masterpieces in the field of essays— those of Montaigne and Francis Bacon. At times there is no mention of Rome, as in chapter 26 of the first book, where he deals with David and Philip of Macedon, and this might well be a chapter from *The Prince.* The same might be said of chapter 27, "Most Seldom Do Men Know How to Be Wholly Evil or Good". Nor does chapter 13 of Book II have anything to do with the foreign affairs of Rome—"Great Fortune is Attained More by Fraud than by Force". We see that Machiavelli followed the course of his thought rather than his "plan". From what Giunta, one of his first publishers, tells us, the *Discourses* were not finished and the proofs were never corrected. We might add that as Machiavelli proceeds he stays less closely to the text of Livy. The book is actually a series of lectures that Machiavelli delivered to a group of friends who met in the Orti Oricellari of Rucellai's home in Florence. It is dedicated to two of the closest and more faithful of the group, Zanobi Buondelmonti and Cosimo Rucellai. The dedication is in the same rhetorical form as that in *The Prince,* but with different expressions of humility. In both is felt Machiavelli's resentment at being left out of the active life of the state. But whereas the dedication in *The Prince* is purposely and artificially humble, that in the *Discourses* is violently critical of those who occupy the position of the Prince without possessing the necessary qualifications of a suitable mind. Both dedications stem from Machiavelli's conscious awareness of having been trained for political action by his participation in contemporary politics and by his meditation on the past.

> That knowledge of the deeds of great men which I have acquired through a long experience of modern events and a constant study of the past. (*The Prince*)
>
> What I know and what I have learned through long experience and continuous study of the things of this world. (*Discourses*)

8 The Comedies

Machiavelli has left three comedies: *L'Andria,* a translation from the Latin of Terence; *Clizia,* an adaptation from the Latin of Plautus; and *Mandragola,* which his nephew Giuliano de'Ricci called "a new invention". There is no general agreement about the dates of these comedies. A. H. Gilbert believes that *Clizia* could not have been written before 1509; for *Mandragola,* he is inclined to accept the date 1512, given by Calimore, although Russo places it near April 1520. By literary reasoning they may have been written in the following order: *Andria* (copy), *Clizia* (imitation), *Mandragola* (invention), but who knows? Another play, *The Masks,* a satire on the people of his time, was unfortunately lost; perhaps it was the best of them all. Of the three we possess the *Mandragola* is the only one of importance, one of the most brilliant and original comedies of the Renaissance. Italian drama, which influenced playwrights of all countries in the western world has been surpassed in force of expression and in characterizations, with one exception—*Mandragola.* It possesses almost nothing of the Roman comic dramas and took very little from Italian short stories to which most comedy writers of Europe, including Shakespeare, owe many of their plots. The *Mandragola* is new in subject matter and in spirit; it is realistic, witty, amusing. I would also say symbolic. In short it is a master-piece which, like all masterpieces, forever lends itself to new interpretations. One returns to it again and again and continues to discover something new. The interpretative currents are two which I will give in the words of two eminent critics:

At times there had been an attempt to discover a more profound meaning in Machiavelli's comedy than he probably put in it. To his contemporaries it seemed a pleasant joke—nor do we have any indication that Machiavelli wanted to do anything more than amuse. If the prologue is a lamentation of the decadence of old virtues . . . this is a commonplace which is found also in Pietro Aretino and in Doni and the word "virtue" should not be interpreted as it is used today, but as courage and intelligence.[194]

The intention of the author was to lay bare social corruption, a family undermined by the family friend and by the priest. The slow inevitable decadence, various incitements, the lack of honest people, credulity, fickleness, and malice are the real drives of the comedy. It is all a deception, not a jest. The author looked closely at universal revelry but he was not happy at what he saw (compare instead Bibbiena). Here there are no filthy or low creatures—as in Bruno and Aretino—but people from the middle classes. It is a picture of general corruption.[195]

The *Mandragola* has always met with great success, starting with Machiavelli's contemporaries who performed it perhaps in 1520 before Pope Leo X. It was given twice in Venice in 1523 at the same time as Plautus' *Menaechmi* which the audience found "a dead thing compared to *Mandragola*", up to our own day. Karl Marx even liked it. Voltaire, who admired it, found it more beautiful than Ariosto (I quote this judgment as a matter of curiosity). In our own time it has caused a great deal of comment. A philosopher found a similarity between the heroine Lucretia and Michelangelo's Eve. De Sanctis was critical of the play and found that it lacked artistry, was "rough material", and was applicable only to the society which was represented in it almost with disgust, and that it died with that society. Croce re-established it by discovering in it an unusual poetic tone in Machiavelli's "painful feeling", proving that Machiavelli was not a pure scientist and observer.

I do not feel that the dominant note of the comedy is that "resigned perspicacity" of which Croce speaks, but rather the violent joy of a person of great intelligence who is superior to the ordinary man and who ridicules imbeciles and their superstitions. It is the revenge of effectual truth and natural law over mediocre minds, the precepts of religion, and social laws. It can be likened to a modern ballet, accentuated by outbursts of laughter, ridiculing the fictional world of the credulous, the hypocrites and the lawmakers.

However, in this comedy love does not ring true. Callimaco's falling in love through hearsay is a romantic and medieval concept of which his character seems to be a complete negation, and the sudden change of Lucretia from a faithful wife to an adultress is not plausible. On the other hand Ligurio's intrigue, which reveals the force of human intelligence without moral scruples, concentrating only on success in a given situation, is convincing and well expressed by Machiavelli. The husband's gullibility, the mother's cowardice, the monk's corruption are all well realized. Politics, which meant more to Machiavelli than anything else, was never far from his mind. The characters in the play are painted in such a way that they also symbolize problems of the time in the Italian family and in the church. "Zo criticize" was Machiavelli's favourite pastime, as he himself said. Throughout *Mandragola* there is a sort of cruel joy in striking at and destroying stupid people, hypocrites, and those who, like Nicia, have a position (in this case the husband of Lucretia) that they are incapable of filling. Isn't *Mandragola* perhaps Machiavelli's revenge against those who occupied the position that was rightly his, if only life were as it should be? And aimed at those whom he had to serve?

I am sorry I cannot agree with Russo when he says that it was "the bitter taste of contemplation", although I go along with him when he states that the comedy was inspired by events of the period. Machiavelli does not have an "aristocratic scorn for corruption"; he delights in it, because it is further proof of his convictions and confirms his pessimistic beliefs, and also because he has a personal dislike for the many stupid people with whom he had to deal, and with the clergy who belonged to a state in competition with Italy. And I don't know how this comedy, filled with jeers, taunts, double meanings, caricatures and vulgar obscenities can seem to be "aristocratic". If I am not mistaken, one of the clearest impressions derived from *Mandragola* is that the author is enjoying himself, while at the same time he is aware that "the subject matter is not dignified and serious". We can almost see him on the stage, gloating over Nicia's stupidity.

9   The Art of War

Among Machiavelli's principal works, this is his third book in order of time; among the theoretical ones it is also the third in order of value. It is inferior to *The Prince* for courageous conclusions, and to the *Discourses* for vastness of panorama. Because it seemed a technical work, it was, together with the *Florentine Histories,* better known than the two former and was published in the period in which *The Prince* and the *Discourses* were being denounced. No one then saw in *The Art of War* the same ideas that are in the other two books. It was also the first of his books to appear in translation in countries like Russia and the United States, where the public accepted the idea that Machiavelli could teach them the art of waging war, but not the art of politics. It was written in 1520 and published in 1521 and was one of his few works that he was able to correct in proof. It is not known exactly when it was started, but of very few works is it possible to say when they started to be "written" in the mind of an author. In this book there is a personal element that is well worth noting— Machiavelli's work in support of the Florentine militia and of the draft that personally cost him seven years of feverish activity, riding great distances on horseback, preparing memoranda and reports. All this effort culminated in the disaster at Prato (1512), when the "national" army prepared by Machiavelli with such great care and diligence shamefully fled before mercenaries who were, among other things, veterans. This book is the result of a delusion, and might be called an apology for an illusion.

The animating spirit of the book is the same found in all of Machiavelli's works, but here it seems burdened with technical and contemporary historical problems and of humanistic reminiscences that make it seem archaic. The structure, in form of a dialogue, is fictitious. It is not important to know from whom he acquired this didactic inspiration, in common use in the Renaissance. (Castiglione at that time also wrote in dialogue form a book in complete opposition to Machiavelli's, but not intentionally since the two men did not even know of each other.) Some of the characters in the dialogue of *The Art of War* are friends of Machiavelli: Cosimo Rucellai, Zanobi Buondelmonti, Battista della Palla, and Luigi Alamanni. The one with an historical name, the great General Fabrizio Colonna, is really Machiavelli himself idealized.

The general inspiration comes from the concept of "country". Citizens must defend their country at all costs, and war in that case is to be glorified. If it is waged instead by private individuals, like the "condottieri", it is thievery and a "dishonest" way of life.

War is an art which men at all times cannot practise honestly. Only a republic or a kingdom can make use of this art and both of these, when well ordered, never allow any citizens or subjects to use it as an art; nor has a good man ever used it as his own art.[196]

The militia, however, represents the individual's sacrifice for the state and therein lies the value of military discipline, showing the capacity of a people to be free of foreign occupation.

Along with this fundamental inspiration are found the problems which correspond to the military crisis that Italy underwent between 1492 and 1539, its period of decadence and the end of the country's independence. For Machiavelli the problem was to create an Italian infantry capable of conquering the Swiss and Spanish infantries that were triumphant on European battlefronts, as opposed to the cavalry, the favourite arm of the superannuated medieval aristocracy. This was an organic and technical problem.

One part of the book consists of a criticism of mercenaries and of Italian princes who recruited them; this can therefore be called a formative and political problem. On the other hand—this is the technical problem—he proposes to restore the Roman Legions! This humanistic and antiquarian proposal reduces the value of the modern aspects of Machiavelli's book. Yet he clearly saw, ahead of his time, the development of modern national and democratic armies that have culminated in total warfare. The national democracies of the nineteenth century justly claimed Machiavelli as their patron; it was they who introduced compulsory draft and transformed the small wars of princes into wars of nations.

From the point of view of today's reader, the most important theoretical part of the book is the dedication to Lorenzo di Filippo Strozzi in which Machiavelli affirms the unity of a country's civil and military life. Today this concept is not accepted by those who believe that only in civil life is a country's civilization to be found. Machiavelli very clearly states that the civil and military life of a nation are indivisible and that war is therefore a necessary and vital moment in the life of a nation. In our own words, the armed forces of a country are the expression of the general capacity of a nation. In them the moral, technical and intellectual forces of a people are fused and put to the test of survival.

Unlike those who think that wars, whether lost or won, cause no change and have little importance on the life of a nation, Machiavelli saw grave consequences in military defeat and maintained that after them a country is never the same again: "Any mistakes I may make in writing can be corrected to no one's hurt, but these errors made by soldiers are only corrected by the ruin of empires." There is no doubt that a bad poem, poor novel or inferior painting have little importance in the life and future of a nation; but a stupid general, dishonest industrialist, opinionated statesman and treacherous scientist can create havoc in a country.

The technical classical sources of this work have been revealed by Burd and seem less changed than in the political writings, especially Vegezio's *De re militari;* Polybius' *Histories;* Livy's

History of Rome; Frontino's *Stratagems;* Josephus' *Hebrew Wars,* Plutarch's *Lives,* Caesar's *Gallic War* and perhaps Aulus Gellius' *Attic Nights.*

Technically nothing new appears in *The Art of War* that is not found in *The Prince* or in the *Discourses,* including Machiavelli's distrust of fortresses, the false hope they inspire, and the time lost in constructing them; and his opinion on artillery, in which he did not see the great technical novelty that was transforming the wars of the time.

As the secretary of the Ten of Liberty and of Balia, who were in charge of war expenditures, Machiavelli went into the field with troops recruited by the Florentines for the war against Pisa and could see the consequences of having to deal with soldiers who would not fight until they were paid. To understand *The Art of War,* one must read his letters of that time. Machiavelli's bitterness comes from his experiences during the war with Pisa. The scorn and hatred for mercenary troops was felt in Italy for centuries, but the idea of a citizen militia was even less popular. Nor did Machiavelli think of a national militia in the modern sense of the term. The one he proposed was accepted and he himself was put in charge of it. He recruited only from a certain section of Florence, where one would expect to find faithful soldiers.

The Art of War should be considered together with Machiavelli's other works, such as his *Discourse on Calling the State of Florence to Arms* (1506), his *Discourse on the Law of Forming a Florentine Militia* (1596), and his *Provisions for the Florentine Republic* (1506-12). In these we see Machiavelli as a precise and detailed "organizer", but never losing sight of the general principles that govern his thought.

10   The Life of Castruccio Castracani

In 1520 Machiavelli was sent on an official mission to Lucca

(Legations and Commissions, IV, 267-76) to settle some small business matters, intrigues of merchants and political questions of a group of students. Nothing of real importance. But during this visit he composed a report entitled "Summary of City Matters of Lucca", and *The Life of Castruccio Castracani*.

The first is an interesting report of comparative legislation, in which the system of selecting magistrates in Lucca is compared by Machiavelli with those used in Rome, Venice and Florence. At times he gives the advantage to Lucca and at others allows the people of Florence to judge for themselves where his sympathies lie.

The second is a little work that today would be called fictionalized biography, or an imaginary portrait. Machiavelli pictures Castruccio Castracani as a "new Prince" of the time. He possesses some qualities of the Borgia. But Machiavelli does not judge him with the same criteria with which he judges Borgia. He ascribes his own misfortunes to the evil deeds of Castracani, and the objective manner in which the treason and execution of rivals are narrated would give a psychoanalyst food for thought. It makes one wonder if, as in the narrative of the slaughter of Rimini, this is not a sort of reprisal on Machiavelli's part against the enemies who had humiliated him.

But those who investigate sources solve the problem in an easier way by declaring that it is fictional, or an imitation. Machiavelli's model is found in the life of Agatocle, the Greek tyrant who became prince *"per via nefaria"*, by evil means.[197] But how could such a Prince, considered evil by Machiavelli, be the model of an ideal prince? There is something about this little work that does not ring true. Perhaps this accounts for the strange hypothesis it gave rise to, like that of Paolo Giovo who sees Machiavelli only as a nationalistic historian who prefers Florence to Lucca, and compares his portrait of Castracani with that of the historian Tegrini, one of the principal sources. In 1700 it was the general opinion that the book was "poetic" and "exemplary". Leibnitz, who called it a "fable", was perhaps the first to see that it contained Machiavelli's desire for Italy to rid itself of foreigners. And a very little known French translator of Machiavelli in 1700 stated that the book was written like a great poem by a poet who, after having propounded "all the principles and rules of an epic poem, proceeds to compose one on that model".[198]

The Life of Castruccio Castracani was finished on July 29, 1520, and immediately sent to Florence. Probably the author touched it up several times.

The final part, which seems like an appendix, is composed of a series of sayings attributed to Castruccio, but almost all of which are taken from the *Lives* of Diogene Laerzio that Machiavelli had read in the Latin translation of 1475. His friends, who were the first to read it, immediately noted these aphorisms in the book. They were so striking that they were also noted by the humanists, until Luiso found that not one of them was of popular origin and had come, almost in the same order, from Laerzio's *Lives*. Particular importance is given to the following saying, which perhaps gave rise to the legend of Machiavelli's famous dream (see page 186):

> Asked if in order to save his soul he ever thought of becoming a monk, he answered in the negative because, he said, it seemed strange to him that Fra Lazzero should go to Paradise and Uguccione della Faggiuola to Hell.

But even this saying is derived from Laerzio, although Machiavelli translated it freely and adapted it to shock Christian believers. He believed Paradise should be reserved for great statesmen and not for friars who practise humility and lead an inactive life.

11 The Florentine Histories

Ever since the works of Gervinus and Ranke in the first decade of the nineteenth century, this work of Machiavelli has served as a study of the history of Italy along with that of Guicciardini, who covered the period up to 1534, where Machiavelli left off, and perhaps even that of Botta who carried the reader up to the French Revolution. Today Machiavelli's history has outdistanced the two historians, just as a racer outdistances his less swift competitors. Now, however, it is generally read to understand Machiavelli's ideas and to flavour his style. Machiavelli was a born writer, even when he didn't try to be, and even though he arranged the facts to fit his convictions. Machiavelli had no intention of presenting facts with documents, nor of following them in their development; rather he sought to find in them another proof of his own political philosophy and his aspirations for Italy. We know that Machiavelli wrote the *Histories* on behalf of the Officers of Study of Florence (November, 1520), presided over by Cardinal Giulio de' Medici, who became Pope Clement VII while Machiavelli was writing the histories. In other words, Machiavelli wrote them for the Medicis and was paid for them by the Medicis. In 1525 he went to Rome to present the eight books to the pontiff, but they were not published until 1532.

Book I is a sort of preface on general events of the history of Italy from the fall of the Western Empire up to the beginning of the fifteenth century. Then come three books on the history of Florence from the origins of 1434, in which Machiavelli stresses above all the development of internal affairs, inasmuch as Bruni and Bracciolini had already dealt with foreign affairs. In the four final books Machiavelli considers the entire history of Florence against the background of Italy. He ends with the death of Lorenzo the Magnificent, which adumbrates the change in the destiny of Italy. Bruni and Bracciolini maintained that he stopped there in order not to become involved with contemporary politics.

Fueter rated highly the advance made by Machiavelli's history over the Chroniclers. Machiavelli is the first, he says, who sees the connection between foreign and internal affairs, between armed forces and the constitution, and the first to realize that the history of Florence cannot be written apart from the history of Italy—the political destiny of that city being inseparable from the fate of the peninsula. Fueter further observes that the talk Machiavelli puts in the mouths of his heroes does not result from the situation in which they find themselves and is often unconvincing. The heroes do not speak as they really spoke, or even according to the rules of rhetoric, but they speak as Machiavelli does—such is Fueter's comment. However, this was the first history after Aristotle and Polybius that sprang from a naturalistic consideration of human life. Fueter is right in saying that the selection of facts taken from sources (Biondo, Bracciolini, Simonetta) is "accidental". One feels that Machiavelli is writing from a sense of duty but every so often, when he is interested in a person or an episode, he is enthusiastic and his tone becomes elevated.

Those who read the *Florentine Histories* today can distinguish between the connective tissues and the vital organs. The passages that stand out from the background are those on heroes or heroic deeds. It is not a history of the people, nor of classes, nor of institutions, nor of masses. It is a history of individuals and of feats, each one of which serves as an example and teaches a lesson.

Men are described in the history as they appeared to Machiavelli—evil, selfish, traitorous, and above all mediocre, petty, servile, except for the few who emerge because of great deeds, good or evil. Such a history might have been written by a great Catholic, very pessimistic about human nature. *Virtù* is always in opposition to circumstances—with this little difference, that God is not seen in the general design nor in any special intervention. Machiavelli judges facts like a Catholic, according to good and evil, but *his* good and his evil are not those of a Catholic. Thus popes here are blamed for the lack of Italian unification, and his good and evil are based on his political philosophy, making him consider the formation of a national Italian state as the highest good for Italians.

This is a human history, made up of human motivations but presented against a background of chance. In general scholars pay tribute to Machiavelli for the connection that he established between events. Gervinus rightly said: "Machiavelli's way of writing in the first book is of great value to any one who can differentiate between the annals of chroniclers, the rhetoric of

Latin writers, the pragmatism of diplomats and memoir writers, and the scientific philosophy of Machiavelli."[199]

Machiavelli always tries to find a law in events. But the general essence of his history is, in my view, that of uncertainty in men's lives, always threatened by forces that come from far off and create unforeseen dangers and unexpected upheavals.

Forced by necessity to narrate events, which he does not always succeed in presenting in a logical sequence, Machiavelli in his *Florentine Histories* ascribes a larger measure to chance or fortune than he does in his other works. Proof of this is the number of times he uses the word *accidente* or chance. It is no longer human passions that motivate actions; actions seem to spring from nothing and are bent on destroying the plans of men, even of the most politically astute, like Borgia. He states that because of the coincidence of Borgia's illness, the Principality of Central Italy, which he created with so much ability, is destroyed. The fever that robbed Borgia of life is in this case an ironic accident that demolishes valour and destroys the most elaborate designs of man, forcing him to acknowledge the irrational foundation of life: "Thus the plans of degli Oddi could not be carried out by reason of such a weak *accidente*."[200]

For Machiavelli there are weak accidents[201] and others that are strong and difficult.[202] At times he attributes to little accidents[203] serious consequences such as "those that make one lose popular favour"; or else "give birth to results"[204] as serious as a revolution.

At times he equates accidents with "necessity".[205] At others he calls them "strange", "unhoped for", "sudden", and "unforeseen", thus doubling by the use of the adjective the meaning of the word. Sometimes he makes use of an astrological concept, the "heavens" that "wanted things that way". The accidents are always presented as a force against which "there is no remedy". It seems to me that their quality is that of "being extrinsic" to the logic of political facts, or else stemming from powers that have no relation to politics, while at the same time however, influencing it to the point of altering destiny. To them Machiavelli opposes "intrinsic prudence", the "event", "order", or the "nature" with which an authoritative man is born.

Into the category of "accidents" also enter nothing less than the plebeian revolt of Michele di Lando of 1378 and the tyranny and the expulsion of the Duke of Athens,[206] events of first importance and of great significance in the history of Florence.

This concept of accident is also indicated by Machiavelli with circumlocutions and verbs such as "to be born", "to follow", "to need", "to rise", or else with such temporal phrases as "in the middle", "when", etc. At times the verb "to be born", which is most frequently used, redoubles its value by being close to the noun "accident":

> And while the war in the Kingdom was being waged, there *was born* an accident which robbed Giovanni d'Angiò completely of his reputation and his chance of winning that enterprise.[207]

Even in theory, in his general discussions of historical principles, Machiavelli attributes to "chance" the variations of governments[208] and the statute of Rome in opposition to that of Sparta made "on purpose" by Lycurgus.[209] In final analysis, the spectacle of human facts seemed to him more dependent upon fortune than has been admitted by theoreticians of Italian idealism.

If the facts do not concern some of his heroes, Machiavelli narrates them from a sense of duty and almost wearily, bringing them up every so often with a telling sentence, with a condemnation or exemplary reproach, with irony or jest. All this springs from his sense of intellectual superiority over human ignorance and stupidity and he bitterly shows the contradictions and changes of the spirit of the people:

> When the Count entered Rome, he was received with great and marvellous acclaim by those who, not long before, had maligned him with such hatred.[210]

12 Discourse on Reforming the State of Florence at the Instigation of Pope Leo

This was supposedly written in 1520. In style and ideas it gives evidence of a more cautious, more staid, more circumspect and even more Machiavellian spirit than his other works. Many years had passed in which Machiavelli had met with great adversity and disillusion. The bold spirit, the interjections, ironies, interrogations and self-answers of the "counsels" given to the Republic were no longer appropriate; nor do they now flow easily from Machiavelli's pen—or perhaps he suppresses them. However, there is no lack of general ideas and above all of the very intelligent concept of the relation between the historical temperament of people and the constitutional forms they adopt.

This your Holiness should keep in mind—that in all cities where citizens have equal rights, a princedom can only be established with the greatest difficulty; in cities where citizens do not have equal rights, a republic cannot be established. In order to establish a republic in Milan, where citizens do not have equal rights, one must get rid of all the nobility and reduce it to equality with the other citizens. And on the contrary, to establish a princedom in Florence, where there is great equality among citizens, it would be necessary first to make inequalities and create many nobles in castles and villas who, together with the prince by means of armed force, would keep the city and the whole province under control.

13 The Golden Ass

This is an unfinished poem in *terza rima* which should have continued beyond the eight chapters we have. Perhaps more than in his other works the pessimism of Machiavelli is shown, not only for human wickedness but also for the misery of mankind. He recounts the myth of Circe, the sorceress who transformed men who fell in love with her into beasts, but unlike Homer, these beasts have no desire at all to return to their former condition: it is easier to live as a beast than as a man. As for cruelty, man is worse than a beast. More often than in his other verses, intentional or not, here there is a sort of parody of Dante. This work illustrates his philosophy of the movement of human events that are forever changing; the uselessness of religion, when it is not accompanied by a will to act; and an apology of nature. In a certain sense this might be called the anti-comedy of Machiavelli, filled with irony and parody. Machiavelli condemns avarice no less than Dante, but his irony is seen in choosing the pig as an orator who talks like Cato.

14 The Capitoli

These are four treatises in verse, dedicated to friends, in which he gives vent to melancholy sentiments. The themes are ingratitude, fortune, ambition, and opportunity—forces of history that we have already met with in his prose writings. Here they are presented under a more painful and pessimistic aspect than in the *Discourses* or his *Histories*. It is noteworthy that he omits *virtù*. Machiavelli's verses are not in general very good, but in this book they possess a certain vitality. The general tone of the book is one of lament and sadness: the world seems to be at the mercy of fortune, people and princes are equally ungrateful; it is best therefore to adapt oneself to conditions furnished by opportunity.

15 Dialogue on Language

The books in which artists discuss their techniques and work tools are always attractive and at times can even be moving. Italian literature is particularly rich in these works, giving evidence of a people not only artistically creative but enamoured of art as a phenomenon worthy of reflection and discussion. From Dante to our own day the question of language has fascinated Italians. It would almost seem that they did not know what language they were actually using, so frequent and ferocious are the disputes over what language could or should be used.

In this century-old dispute Machiavelli has left a famous document, his *Dialogue* (with Dante) *on Language*. It was first published anonymously as late as 1730, but since then due to Rajna's important research, philological critics accept it as Machiavelli's. Here we see Machiavelli's enthusiasm in defending the language in which he as well as Dante wrote, but against Dante's theory of language. Machiavelli had a more modern and broader concept of the life of a language than did Dante, although his scientific knowledge of language and of Italian dialects was inferior to Dante's.

It is particularly notable how Machiavelli interprets the way a national language absorbs the words of other languages that penetrate it by reasons of commerce or human contact. I am in agreement with a young and reputable contemporary philologist who says: "The most brilliant idea in the Discourse or Dialogue written by Machiavelli on the question of language, is the one where he speaks of the capacity of assimilation possessed by a powerfully constructed language in the face of neologisms and elements from abroad, and also in its own capacity of neologistic production."[211] But I would add that these modern reflections should be considered together with the contents of the first book of the *Florentine Histories,* where Machiavelli is seen as understanding, before all philologists, the importance of the change that took place in the western world by the transformation of Latin into the neo-Latin language:

> Among these ruins and these new people, there sprang forth new languages, as seen by the way the French, the Spanish and the Italians now speak. This new speech, a combination of the language of these new people with the old Roman, results in a new way of talking. Moreover, the people have changed not only the names of

the provinces, but of lakes, rivers, seas, and proper names of people. It shows that France, Spain and Italy are full of new names and feel estranged from the old ones. For example, the names Po, Garda, Archipelago are very different from the old ones, and even men's names have been changed from Caesar and Pompey to Peter, John and Matthew.[212]

In this passage we can admire not only his knowledge of philology (where he mentions the mixture of languages preceding the Roman) but also his insistence on the word *new*, and finally his contempt for the decadence that followed paganism. Was it intentional on his part to compare the names of antiquity—warriors like Caesar and Pompey—with names from the Scriptures—Peter, John and Matthew? It is not without importance for an understanding of Machiavelli's thought to see that he noted the changed names of lakes, rivers and seas, as well as of men. All these are natural objects and would especially strike Machiavelli.

16 The Letters

Machiavelli's letters are of two kinds: the official ones, when he was secretary of the Committee of Ten of the Florentine Republic, written either from Florence or from various other places where he was sent, that are called "Legations"; and those that he wrote on his own account, called "Familiar" letters. He kept copies of these which have fortunately been handed down to us by his nephew, Giuliano de' Ricci. They are business, political or personal letters, sometimes gay, sometimes serious, to family and friends, and they are the most reliable documents we possess for an understanding of his personality, creating an image of another Machiavelli, different from the Machiavelli of political philosophy.

The "Legations" are models of clear and precise correspondence, revealing an honest public servant who knew more than his superiors, but who never ceased to treat them with due respect, making use of all necessary formalities, but at the same time not holding back the truth from them. They are real documents of contemporary history. Inherent in them is a contrast between the poor, intelligent and talented underling whose fate is to serve others, and the often mediocre superiors who order him about and often make use of a diplomat of wealth when it comes to the formal signing of an important document.

The "Familiar" letters are frank, sincere, honest—qualities that are rare in Italian correspondence which moreover is not a popular form of Italian literature. They vividly portray social environments, customs, situations and people of all types. Through them we are introduced into Machiavelli's inner circle of close friends. They were people of wit who said what they pleased, possessing no religious faith, or respect for authority. They formed a nucleus that was free of prejudices and formalities, the kind of rare group found at few moments of history—Athens in the fifth century, Paris in the eighteenth century. This group, free from prejudice, was made up of cultured people from the middle classes, fundamentally honest, who appreciated good food, reading matter that was not pedantic, drinking without drunkenness, and love without worrying about official ties. They had such a ready tongue that no matter what they found to talk about—a pile of logs to be divided among friends, or jokes about homosexuals—it became a real conversation piece and was related in such an animated manner that it seemed as important as a political event (although it was understood to be not so important). We can visualize them seated on the stone benches of the Piazza del Duomo, on the little benches of the Capponi, or on the steps of the Portico dell'Annunziata, arguing with vigorous gestures about business, love, intrigues, poverty and wine, or gossiping about politics, rumours current in the city, sermons, or the great dignitaries and ambassadors—all viewed as humans, without servility and envy. These were real people!

The "Familiar" letters begin in 1497 and continue through 1527, that is, throughout Machiavelli's lifetime except for his youth, which remains clouded in mystery. Some of his correspondents were important men, like Francesco Vettori, Ambassador of the Medicean Republic to the Pope, and Guicciardini, a man almost as famous as Machiavelli. But among the most vital letters are those to his personal friends in that spirited company, beginning with his faithful office companion, Biagio Buonaccorsi, who makes up for the mediocrity of his historical thought with his unswerving loyalty to and admiration for Machiavelli, Filippo Casavecchia, Agostino Vespucci, Francesco del Nero. Contemporary politics occupy a large portion of the letters to Vettori and Guicciardini. They reveal a man who is not always a good prophet (he feared the Swiss would take over Italy). We see these men, burdened with greater responsibilities than those of Machiavelli, capable of enjoying themselves and amusing others. Vettori, who was Ambassador of the Medicean government to the Pope of the Medici, amuses himself when he has free time with a widow and her daughter. Guicciardini in the midst of the affairs of state, of which he was a loyal executive, finds time to be concerned with the production of Machiavelli's *Mandragola* and plans how to deceive some provincial monks in order to get the play produced. The fundamental note of this correspondence is found in the famous passage of Machiavelli in which he speaks of the double nature of man:

> Anybody who saw our letters, honoured friend, and saw their diversity, would wonder greatly, because he would suppose now that we were grave men, wholly concerned with important matters, and that into our breasts no thought could fall that did not have in itself honour and greatness. But turning the page he would judge that we, the very same persons, were lightminded, inconstant, lascivious, concerned with empty things. And this way of proceeding, if to some it may appear censurable, to me seems praiseworthy, because we are imitating Nature, who is variable; and he who imitates her cannot be blamed. And though we have been accustomed to this variety over many letters, I wish to practise it this time in one, as you will see, if you will read the other page. Now spit.[213]

Through his letters we not only see Machiavelli's family life—

his affectionate relations with his wife, his advice to and his concern for his children; but also his partiality for bohemian and clever women who offered solace to this great man and took his mind off his miseries—such as the actress Riccia, the widow of San Casciano ("gentle creature", he calls her). What is particularly moving is his concern for his small mule; when war was approaching Machiavelli suggested the mule be freed in the fields.

The letters show us a wiser Machiavelli than in his books, one who does not pretend to command Lady Luck but instead is content to adapt himself to her.

I believe that as Nature has given men different faces, so she has given them different dispositions and different imaginations. From this it results that each man conducts himself according to his disposition and his imagination. And on the other hand, because times vary and affairs are of varied types, one man's desires come out as he had prayed they would; and that man is fortunate who harmonizes his procedure with his time, but on the contrary he is not fortunate who in his actions is out of harmony with his time and with the type of its affairs. . . .

And certainly anybody wise enough to understand the times and the types of affairs and adapt himself to them would always have good fortune, or he would protect himself always from bad, and it would come to be true that the wise man would rule the stars and the Fates. But because there never are such wise men, since men in the first place are short-sighted, and in the second cannot command their natures, it follows that Fortune varies and commands men, and holds them under her yoke.[214]

IV

HIS LIFE

Machiavelli's life can fairly easily be divided into three periods. The first, of which we know almost nothing, extends from his birth on May 3, 1469 to the time he became clerk of the second chancery of the Republic of Florence, on July 14, 1498. The second, when we can follow him almost day by day, extends to the downfall of Piero Soderini, gonfalonier of the Republic of Florence, and to the dismissal of Machiavelli by the new Medicean régime on November 7, 1512. The third, to which we are indebted for his principal works and the greater part of his private correspondence, extends from 1512 to his death on June 22, 1527. His education is unknown, his career is well known, and his thought has been a matter of discussion and re-interpretation from his death to the present day. When he started writing, his mind was already formed; all he did was to express himself quickly, without research, hesitation or regret. It is well to keep in mind that his life is a work of art, greatly to be admired, and set in the same key as his writings.

Machiavelli was poor and honest, endowed with the qualities of an average person except that he possessed a profound intelligence and a need to question the appearance of things in order to discover their permanent quality. He was courageous and independent in facing the truth without fear of consequences, and desirous of working for what he considered the good of the country beyond the political form of government. He was tormented, like all men of thought. He was badly treated by his social superiors, but found compensation in the love of women of easy virtue and in the affection of some friends who were friends more in words than in deeds. He had no admiration or compassion for the common herd, and a deep respect for exceptional men. He was simple, sincere when he did not force himself to be hypo-critical, measured in the tributes that a man of good sense pays those who command, disliked by stupid people, and imitated by crafty ones. No one then realized that this little clerical worker was an exceptional person. To have made such a niche in history, to have lived his interior life by himself, apart from others, is assuredly a source of wonder. Machiavelli's life is itself one of his masterpieces.

Ordinarily critical temperaments are not suited to a life of action. In his poem *The Golden Ass* he revealed that nature had made him critical and that his mind, bent on "biting this and that",[215] was stimulated by his love for independent thinking. He had little respect for the so-called "wise men" of his country.[216] One of his acquaintances, Luigi Guicciardini, describes him as one who "questioned everything—the things he was expected to believe, as well as those he could laugh about".[217] But above all he wanted to be active in politics, even in his subordinate position, which was fatiguing and full of risks, "urged on by that natural desire which was always a part of me, to participate, irrespective of what the work entailed, in those things that I believe are of common benefit to all".[218]

He was filled with distress by the humble position he held until 1516 and by the enforced inaction that followed his political misfortune. Distress is a note which is continually re-echoed in his writings. In *The Art of War* he laments that nature, which made him an expert on state matters, did not provide him with the opportunity of putting his ideas into action.[219] When in exile, in the country, he feels he is "useless" and he deplores the "quality of his sordid and inglorious life".[220] He says he is wasting away among lice (Letter from San Casciano) and in the prologue to his play, *Mandragola,* he mentions his grief at not being able "to show his valour by means of other enterprises". In sum, he is aware of his own value and of the fact that he is not appreciated and even held in contempt.

He was unhappy, like all men who have not become easily deceived or blinded by an exalting religion or philosophy, but in

his misery he had consolations, above all that of his own intelligence which raised him above mediocrity (when describing the
Romans he uses the same word he uses for himself, *undaunted*).
It is important to note that the other consolations came to him
almost always from simple people, like those obscure women
who loved him—the gentle widow of the Impruneta; Sandra di
Piero, who comforted him after his Medicean torture; Riccia;
Mariscotta; the actress Barbara, who granted him her favours and
gave the benefit of her acting talent to the production of *Mandragola;* and his wife, who was tranquil, patient and affectionate.
Then there are his intimate friends who today are practically
unknown, like Filippo Casavecchia, a gourmet who talks always
of "trout and wine", and that whole group of impertinent,
slanderous, irreverent, middle-class Florentines with whom he
spent his evenings, sometimes brawling, none of whom would
have come down in history except for their connection with
Machiavelli. But during his lifetime, which is what counted while
he was alive, these affections and consolations meant more to him
than any posthumous admiration and fame. He found greater
comfort in them than in the little his employer, Piero Soderini,
and Cardinal Giulio dei Medici, later Pope Clement VII, did for
him, or in the small encouragement that miserable wretch,
Lorenzo d'Urbino, gave him. The latter is said to have accepted
the gift of *The Prince* with less enthusiasm than "two hunting-
dogs" given to him at the same time.

1   First period:
    Early years, 1469–98

He was born in Florence, son of Bernardo di Niccolò, attorney,
and of Bartolomea Nelli, who tradition has it was a religious poet.
His family was poor but prided itself on a noble ancestry in whose
coat of arms appear those nails or *clavelli* which are part of his
name. It was one of those families like others of the time in

Tuscany, still to be found in the south of Italy, which are always in the process of suing for lost feudal rights and turning to authorities for help in winning their case.

Machiavelli tells us himself in his *Florentine Histories* (Book VIII) about the events and people he knew in these years of preparation and how he judged them. The most important men of that period were Lorenzo il Magnifico, Savonarola, Ludovico il Moro, Charles VIII of France, and Pope Alexander VI. The chief events were the Pazzi conspiracy, and the arrival and then the departure of the French. At the end of this period Machiavelli wrote a famous letter, his first interesting one, in which he describes to Riccardo Bechi a sermon of Savonarola in an ironic, disdainful and irreverent vein, accusing him of being a politician who "changed his cloak" as soon as he felt protected by the Signoria (the government of Florence) and kept on "working with the times and making his lies less plausible".[221]

2 Second period:
To his dismissal by the Medici, 1498–1512

When Machiavelli first occupied his modest position, in 1498, Florence was at war with Pisa. During this time, two events must have struck his imagination: the betrayal of Paolo Vitelli, soldier of fortune, corrupted by the Venetians (he was arrested on September 28, 1498 and met his doom on October 1, 1499); and the revolt of the Swiss mercenaries who, when they were not paid, kidnapped Luca degli Albizi, the Commissioner of Florence (July 9, 1500, Leg. I, 56). If Machiavelli had not already inwardly condemned the outside mercenary troops, these events would have convinced him. As it was they added fuel to his convictions.

His first assignment of foreign affairs was small indeed—he was sent to Pontedera on March 24, 1499, to settle a dispute with Jacopo d'Appiano, Condottiere of Florence.

The second assignment was a little more important and has left its mark in history. He was sent to Forlì on July 12, to speak to Catherine Sforza about hiring her son, Ottavio Riario, as a Condottiere for Florence.[222]

The third assignment was the most important, but he was only second in command, under Francesco della Casa. By reason of his humble origin and modest position, Machiavelli was never given a post of importance in the Florentine Republic. Even when his mission was successful, the official credit went to others. He was away from Italy from July 1500 to January 14, 1501. This assignment was in France, to get more help from the King for the war against Pisa. Here he was never paid on time, nor enough, and he had to contend with other Italian agents who were jealous of him or who were enemies of Florence. But he gained a thorough knowledge of that foreign country.[223]

The mission to Pistoia, to quell the local factions, brought Machiavelli to that city three times in 1501. See his work, *Report of things done by the Florentine Republic to put an end to the factions of Pistoia*.[224]

In August 1501 he was sent to Pandolfo Petrucci, *Signore* of Siena to discover the plans of Duke Valentino (Caesar Borgia), who was roaming around the confines of the Republic of Florence, carrying on intrigues. In May 1502, he went on a mission to a *Signore* of Bologna, Giovanni Bentivoglio. That year he went three times to Arezzo which had revolted at the instigation of Vitelozzo Vitelli. See Machiavelli's writing *Of the Method of Dealing with the Rebels of Valdichiana,* where he suggests remedies which possessed a quality of grandeur but were not accepted by the small minds of his contemporaries. On June 22, he was sent on a mission to visit Caesar Borgia in order to find out what he was plotting, perhaps against Florence. This visit from a dramatic point of view was to be of the greatest importance to the development of Machiavelli's thought. He saw Borgia twice, once with Francesco Soderini when Borgia was at Urbino, and the second time alone, for a longer and more important period, when he followed him in his adventures across central Italy. This ended with the ambush, capture (by means of a betrayal) and death of

Borgia's enemies. This was the period from October 1502 to January 1503.

Machiavelli's political imagination responded to this adventurous personality and made him consider Borgia for a time as the ideal Prince. He thought of him as one who in that historical moment could have created an important dominion in the centre of Italy, and perhaps could have put an end to the false pretensions of the Patrimony of St. Peter, by transforming the papal states into a hereditary kingdom—if Borgia could have been elected Pope. It must be said that Borgia seemed to have the necessary qualifications. He was a "basilisk", a determined man without scruples, who kept his plans to himself, and then put them into immediate action with assurance and rapidity.

From the first mission to the Court of Borgia, Machiavelli observes:

> This gentleman is very splendid and magnificent, and so brave in warfare there is no great thing that doesn't seem small to him, and to attain glory and to conquer countries he never rests, nor does he know weariness or dangers. He reaches a place before anyone knows he is on his way there; he is well liked by his soldiers; he has gathered together the best men of Italy—all of these elements make him victorious and to be feared—and added to this is his perpetual good fortune.[225]

In this letter, written "before daybreak", one senses a love-at-first-sight situation. It was to last a long time, even after Borgia was defeated by an "evil" fortune, imprinting on Machiavelli the intellectual conviction that made him always consider Borgia's actions as models to be copied. (Prince, VII, 15, 1513; letter of Jan. 31, 1514, p.896; A. VII 359 and this is in 1521). He not only admires him as a conqueror (foreign affairs), but also as a pacifier of the Romagna region (internal affairs.) He understands immediately that Borgia would seek revenge on those who had betrayed him even though in appearance he seemed to be full of affection for them; he realizes that "even children would laugh at the pacts Borgia makes with them". Machiavelli observed that he acted with the pure joy of an artist carrying out his designs. Borgia was the enemy of Machiavelli's republic, but this did not prevent him from admiring him and from praising him to his superiors. He understood the inferiority of the leaders of the Florentine Republic and of their policies in comparison with those of Borgia. Machiavelli also delighted in personalities like Ferdinand the Catholic (1452–1516), and later was charmed by that captain of fortune, Giovanni dalle Bande Nere (1498–1526). He was also to idealize mythical figures like Moses, Cyrus, Romulus and Theseus whom he chose from pre-history before the dawn of established social forms. But Machiavelli's "first love" was for Valentino, as Borgia was called, and his exploits always remained embedded in Machiavelli's imagination. This is the first time he knew a man who put into action those principles that Machiavelli had already fashioned in his mind. Knowing Borgia served to clarify these principles and to fill out the details of the picture.

In 1502 Machiavelli married Marietta di Ludovico Corsini. The marriage did not change the course of his life. There is no indication in his correspondence nor of that of his friends that she was a jealous woman or a source of trouble to him. She was probably a beneficent influence on Machiavelli's life, which was so lacking in other gratifications. They had six children—Bernardo, born in 1503; an unnamed daughter, who probably died soon after birth; Baccia, Ludovico, Piero, born in 1514, who more than the others remembered the doctrines of his father; and Guido. To Giuliano, son of Baccia, who married Giovanni Ricci, goes the credit for preserving a large number of letters and most of the secondary writings of Machiavelli.

In 1502 an important change in the constitution of Florence was made. Troubled by the fluctuations of political events and influenced by the example of Venice, the democratic group in Florence sought for greater stability by instituting the lifetime position of gonfalonier (August 26). Piero di Tommaso Soderini, who admired and liked Machiavelli, was chosen to fill this post.

In 1503, towards the end of his mission at the court of Borgia, Machiavelli wrote his *Description of the method used by the Duke*

Valentino in assassinating Vitellozzo Vitelli, da Fermo, Pagolo and the Duke Orsini.

In April 1503 Machiavelli was sent to Siena to see Pandolfo Petrucci. Pope Alexander VI, father of Caesar Borgia, died at Rome on August 18 of that year from an illness contracted also by his son. This prevented Caesar Borgia from becoming Pope, "either by good or evil means" as he had hoped. The pope who was elected, Pius III, died soon afterwards in October. His successor, Julian della Rovere, who became Pope Julius II, was a strong personality and an enemy of Borgia.

The first *Legation* or diplomatic report of Machiavelli from the Court of Rome was made when the Florentine Republic sent him there to attend and report on the election of the new pope. He arrived in Rome on October 27, 1503 (Leg. II, 297–467). Machiavelli realized immediately what destiny would await Borgia in this new election. He made a serious study of the election and of the various interests of the factions, with great detachment and free of any element that was not motivated by human desires. According to him, the choice of the pope was not the result of the intervention of the Holy Ghost as much as the promise made by Julius II to all the cardinals "except for four" that he would comply with all that had been requested of him. Machiavelli knew that the Pope hated Borgia, and he could not help smiling at Borgia's self-assurance. He wondered why Borgia believed "the promises of others more than his own" and he awaited "the judgment of time", which he considered "the father of truth". Time soon proved Machiavelli right about the end of Borgia's power. All that Borgia could do was to return to Spain, where he died in obscurity as a soldier of fortune on March 12, 1507. Machiavelli's mission was completed at the end of September 1503 and was greatly appreciated by the new Gonfalonier Soderini and praised by Cardinal Soderini in Rome.

In March Machiavelli wrote a speech, to be delivered by some one else, about the financial crisis that had overtaken the Florentine Republic in March 1503: *Words to be said on providing money, with an Introduction and an Apology.*

In 1504 Machiavelli went for a second time to France to the court of Louis XII to seek help, leaving on January 18 and returning at the end of February. There he worked in a secondary position to the regular ambassador, Nicolò Valori. This same year he composed his first *Decennial* on Italy and on his disappointments since 1494, and perhaps a comedy, the *Masks,* that has been lost.

On April 9, 1505, he was sent to Giovan Paolo Baglioni of Perugia, one of the Signori that the Florentine Republic paid to defend Florence. He found him at Castiglion del Lago and was convinced that he would not defend Florence and was in fact planning to join forces with the enemy. To assure himself of what Baglioni intended doing, Machiavelli did not hesitate to make all sorts of inquiries that made him fear "that from one day to another I will be taken for a spy".[226]

Immediately afterwards he was sent to the Marquis of Mantua (May 4), but he returned from there without having accomplished anything. On July 16, he was sent to Petrucci at Siena for the third time, and was ordered to find out what His Magnificence (Petrucci) intended doing about his neighbour, Bartolomeo d'Alviano, who was troublesome to Florence. Machiavelli was told, "The better to find out the truth, turn him every which way,"[227] and he was also expected to make use of his great proverbial tact. Though they paid him poorly, they expected a great deal from him. The mission ended on July 24, and his report is interesting to read in that it shows the game of dissimulation played by both sides in their conversations.

Bartolomeo d'Alviano, who threatened Florence, was defeated by Antonio Giacomini. The latter was the true ideal citizen of Machiavelli, a merchant soldier-of-fortune and a kind of George Washington ahead of his time who, after victory, retired from command of the army and returned to the selling of cloth, meeting with ingratitude from the Florentines who were not at all like eighteenth-century Americans. Machiavelli was next ordered to go to the siege of Pisa, when Giacomini was sent against that city (Aug. 21–25). This undertaking ended badly for the Florentines and for Giacomini.

In 1506 another period of Machiavelli's life started. He succeeded in obtaining from Soderini political support for his great idea of a national militia. Like a man of faith, he was ready to pay for it with his life and went personally to the countryside of Florence to take charge of the recruiting. The people were not used to this new idea of a national militia. However, by dint of physical labour and pleading, he formed the militia within one year under the auspices of a commission called "The Nine of the Ordinance and Florentine Militia".

In the middle of 1506 Pope Julius II initiated his programme to reconquer the church's lands from Perugia to Bologna and sought the help of Florence, which he obtained. Machiavelli was assigned the task of bringing the Republic's answer to the pope. This was his second mission to the Court of Rome. He met the pope at Nepi on August 27 and joined him on the expedition.

At Perugia he witnessed an event which made a lasting impression on him. Giampaolo Baglioni, who was already tarnished by a great many crimes, did not take advantage of a situation wherein he could have kidnapped the pope and all the cardinals with him, and killed them all to prevent them from succeeding in their mission. Instead Baglioni timidly allowed them to enter Perugia unarmed.[228] Machiavelli remained with the Pope until October 27. Perhaps as a reward for having formed a national militia, the Signoria gave Machiavelli a title of nobility (May 1507), but no rise in pay; titles and words have always come easy in Italian governments.

In August Machiavelli was sent to Siena to surprise Bernardo Carvajal, the cardinal of Santa Croce, when he was sent on a mission by Pope Julius II to the Emperor of Germany who was authorized by his Diet to proceed to Rome to be crowned King. It was a question of knowing what the Pope wanted of the Emperor, but Machiavelli only heard rumours. Maximilian's descent on Italy put Florence in a difficult position because of her association with the King of France. An ambassador, Francesco Vettori, was sent and at Soderini's request Machiavelli went with him. He left Florence on December 17 and passing through

Switzerland reached Bolzano. He remained in the cities near Trento and Innsbruck from January 11 to June 8.

This was Machiavelli's first contact with the German people. From their way of living he formed an idea which is not exact in detail but true in substance. As he did in the case of Borgia, upon hearing from people who lived there (he did not know German) about the simplicity of the life of the Swiss mountain folk, the independence of the Hanseatic cities, and their serious and religious life, Machiavelli found a concretion of his ideals. He concluded the treaty with Maximilian and offered him fifty thousand florins from Florence in order to keep away from that Republic. There is an account of this trip called *Portrait of Things of Germany* (perhaps written in 1512 or 1513, as Burd maintains).

The troops of the Republic recruited by Machiavelli were used for the first time in the renewed war against Pisa, where Machiavelli was sent on August 16, 1508. He returned there again February 1, 1509, for a longer time. The enterprise was brought to a head by hastening the siege, paying the King of France for permission to "get back their own things" (as Guicciardini ironically said later), and repelling the attempted help of the Genovese. Finally the Pisans surrendered and on June 8, 1509, the Florentines entered the long-desired city at an hour Machiavelli had chosen as the most propitious after consulting an astrologer. This successful enterprise greatly elated the Florentines, increased the fortunes of the popular government of Soderini and brought a measure of fame to Machiavelli.[229]

As a result of the wars of the Confederate States instigated by Pope Julius II against the Venetians, the restless Emperor Maximilian returned to Italy to ask the Italians and the Florentines for money. Machiavelli was sent to Mantua to deal with him (second mission to the Emperor)[230] on November 10, 1509, and he was engaged on this mission until January 2, 1510. All he seems to have gotten out of it was a knowledge of Verona, which he visited on this occasion and described twice. There are interesting variations between the descriptions to be found in his official letters and in his *Florentine Histories*.

While on this trip Machiavelli barely escaped a danger that had arisen in Florence, showing that he did not lack for enemies who were jealous of the little fame he had attained. The affair is a bit mysterious and not well documented. Apparently there was an anonymous denunciation of Machiavelli, claiming that because of his father he should not have held his office. The delation had some legal basis, at least in the interpretation of those who were ill-disposed towards Machiavelli—and it seems there were many. In a letter of Buonaccorsi to Machiavelli of December 27, 1509, we read: "Please believe me when I tell you I have not slept since I heard this, because there are so few who want to help you and I can't find out where this rumour originated." Perhaps Machiavelli's father was illegitimate, or had served a prison sentence. Nothing definite is known and there seems no way to determine the truth. But it made an impression in Florence. Buonaccorsi is quoted as saying: "The case has become public, and it is bandied about even in brothels." But apparently nothing came of this denunciation.

This same year, Machiavelli wrote the second *Decennial* and perhaps the *Capitolo* called "On Ingratitude". The first part of 1510 was spent in still organizing his beloved militia. In Italy civil wars continued which gave aid and comfort to foreigners and wars between foreigners caused Italians to fight against Italians. The Pope tried to keep Italy from becoming powerful by making trouble among the Italians themselves, then between Italians and foreigners, by pitting Milan against Venice, and setting the Swiss against the French. Because these conflicts kept changing aspect, with new alliances every few months, Florence in 1510 was forced to choose between two powers that heretofore were traditionally her friends: France and the Pope. Soderini, placed with his back against the wall by France, sent Machiavelli there (third mission to France).

He left Italy on June 24, 1510, and was forced to concern himself with things that did not seem feasible to him, like the threat of Louis XII to replace the Pope with a Council of Cardinals, an idea distasteful to Florence. Machiavelli passed through Lyon and found the king at Blois.[231] He was soon replaced by an accredited ambassador and returned to Florence in October. It is thought that Machiavelli's writings on France and on her political constitution and the character of her people date from this third visit. They include his *Portrait of Things in France* and *De Natura Gallorum,* which is written in Italian despite its Latin title.

In the first part of 1511 Machiavelli continued his work of recruiting the militia, this time for the cavalry, in various parts of Tuscany. On May 1 he went to Siena to renew for another twenty-five years the Treaty of Friendship, with a pact restoring Montepulciano to Florence. On May 11 he was sent to Luciano Grimaldi, Prince of Monaco, to conclude another Treaty of Friendship, returning to Florence on June 5.

Very soon afterwards he had to face the problem of a meeting of the Council of Cardinals against Pope Julius II that the King of France, without much tact, had summoned at Pisa, in the territory of the Republic of Florence. After trying to postpone it, Florence with heavy heart had to consent to the designs of the King of France. Machiavelli was entrusted with this difficult mission, and went to Pisa on September 10 to receive the four Cardinals who alone had accepted the invitation. Finally pressure from the Republic of Florence was successful in transferring the Council to Milan, after only three meetings in Pisa proved it to be a failure.

From Pisa Machiavelli was sent to France (fourth mission) where he remained until November 2, after having obtained the postponement of the Council.[232] He then returned to Pisa to persuade the four Cardinals to leave. At the end of the year, Machiavelli was again busy looking for "new men to be cavalry officers" (Dec. 5, 1511), and he continued in this work for all of January 1512. Except for a trip to Siena, when Pandolfo Petrucci died, he was busy with reports and visits in connection with his favourite brain-child, the militia, and in obtaining the leaders that were needed.[233] He went to the Pisan countryside, to Val di Chiana, to Montepulciano, to Scarperia, to Firenzuola, trying to settle local troubles such as partisan murders and delinquent payments, and to bring comfort to the local authorities.

1512 is the year of Machiavelli's misfortunes and disillusionment. Everything seemed to crumble about him: his militia, his own commune, even his meagre salary, earned with such effort and always paid late. His patron Soderini was sent away into exile. Machiavelli was poor when he started working for the Republic of Florence, and poor when he was discharged. His ideals and his practical life were shipwrecked at the same time. Like a derelict abandoned on the beach, he was forced to retreat to his small country house to write, not being able as he said to do "anything better". However, his loss was our gain.

Because of the dissension with Pope Julius II that Soderini did not succeed in preventing, a reorganization of Italian states was planned in which Florence was to return to the rule of the Medici. An army under the command of Raymondo di Cardona, made up of veteran mercenaries, attacked Prato. Its defence was entrusted to the militia of the commune of Florence, organized by Machiavelli. It was on this militia that he and Soderini relied. But these men, with a cowardice that even shocked Italian historians of the period, allowed the enemy to enter and to sack the city (August 29, 1512) in such an atrocious manner that only the Sack of Rome fifteen years later surpassed it.

After this victory, the group in Florence favourable to the return of the Medici made itself known and asked Soderini to resign. He consented and chose Machiavelli and Francesco Vettori to settle the terms of the surrender. Machiavelli wanted Soderini to resist and frankly said so. Later he wrote comparing Soderini to Savonarola, placing him in the category of the "virtuous and weak".[234] The Medicean revolt took place without the violent reprisals which were and are usual in Italian cities during such upheavals, and this without doubt is due to the lamblike conduct of Soderini. One of Machiavelli's epigrams about Soderini being debarred from hell and consigned to limbo is quoted on page 67.

The events that lead to the Sack of Prato and to the expulsion of Soderini were recounted with great impartiality in a draft of a letter from Machiavelli to Alfonsina Orsini de' Medici.[235]

3 Third period:
To his death, 1512–27

On November 5, 1512 Machiavelli was dismissed, and three days later was interned in the Florentine countryside. When for personal reasons he asked permission to visit the city hall in Florence, he was only allowed one day. (On December 4 this was extended, but this was only in the period during which the Commission of Ten were still in charge.) These events marked the destruction of his life.

In February something even worse happened. A conspiracy against the Medici, led by Pietro Paolo Boscoli and Agostino Capponi was uncovered. Luca Della Robbia gives a beautiful description of this (*Archivio Storice Italiana*, I, 274–312). The conspirators were arrested on February 18 and met their doom four days later. In a list of people whom the conspirators *might* have asked to participate, the name of Machiavelli was found. He was arrested and put to the torture (tightening of the rope six times), which he endured without confessing. His friends did not come to his aid and were probably afraid of becoming involved. In verses Machiavelli besought help of Giuliano dei Medici; perhaps being a poet was of greater assistance to him in being freed than any effort of his friends:

> I wear, Giuliano, chains instead of shoes,
> and round my shoulders goes a rope six times;
> and I won't tell you all my other woes
> since thus are treated those who deal in rhymes.
>
> Upon these walls I see such squat lice climb,
> they look like butterflies, so fat they grow.
> Neither at Roncesvalles nor in the slime
> of the Sardinian woods was ever so
>
> sordid a stench as in my dainty place. . . .
> > (Translated by Joseph Tusiani)

His brother, Totto, sent a courier to Francesco Vettori, who said he "could not help him at all". It seems that Giuliano dei Medici and Paolo Vettori were instrumental in getting him out of prison on March 13.

Machiavelli's spirit remained undaunted. What a vignette he paints for us, on celebrating his release from prison:

> And every day we go to some girl's house in order to regain our strength, and even yesterday we saw the procession pass by from Sandra di Piero's house; and thus we kill time in this universal merriment, enjoying the remainder of our life. I feel I am dreaming.

Deprived of participating in the active life of politics, Machiavelli began to meditate upon what he had learned from ancient historians and from modern politics. His little house in San Casciano, where he then lived, has become famous from his descriptions of it in his writings. This is the culminating moment of his genius. He writes, almost simultaneously, the *Discourses* and *The Prince*. He also carries on a correspondence with Francesco Vettori, ambassador in name only at the Holy See, where now there was another pope, Leo X.

Never was Machiavelli's genius so brilliantly penetrating and humorous as in this period when he shut himself in his study, grieving over his great loss, but stimulated by a ray of hope of taking up his former work again by some means or other. Though Francesco Vettori was a strong man, he was not powerful enough to be of use, but he might become so. Both of them often change tones in the same letters, going from the intimacy of companions in merrymaking to profound and keen interpretations of contemporary events (the period from March 1512 to about January 31, 1514).[236] Clearly Machiavelli was trying to curry favour with an influential person, but his motives were honest and sincere and, as often happens with men of genius, the results of an attempt go far beyond the attempt itself. As in *The Prince,* when his reflections on politics rise to a much higher level and open a vaster horizon than his modest personal request to be once again employed in service to the state, so in the correspondence with Vettori one feels that his ideas take over. He seems to derive a certain bitter pleasure from the painful truth, just as at the end of *The Prince* he has this definition of Italians that could well serve as an epigraph to many ancient and recent periods of Italian history: "We are cowards, poor and vain."[237]

The most famous of these private letters is the one to Vettori dated December 10, 1513. Among other things, it gives us the date of the composition of *The Prince*. It is famous for many reasons, but above all for a portrait of Machiavelli himself:

> On the coming of evening, I return to my house and enter my study; and at the door I take off the day's clothing, covered with mud and dust, and put on garments regal and courtly; and reclothed appropriately, I enter the ancient courts of ancient men where, received by them with affection, I feed on that food which only is mine and which I was born for, where I am not ashamed to speak with them and ask them the reasons for their actions; and they in their kindness answer me; and for four hours of time I do not feel boredom, I forget every trouble, I do not dread poverty, I am not so frightened by death; I give myself entirely over to them.

In other words, Machiavelli of the spirit rises above Machiavelli of the everyday body and becomes one of the great ancients, conversing with them as their peer, sitting at the right of Caesar and Alexander and at the left of Aristotle and Polybius. This is his compensation for having been forsaken, and for the misery and poverty of his position. It is a beautiful transfiguration (I have no hesitation in using a religious and Christian term). But one feels it is an escape from reality and a form of vengeance against adverse fortune, rather than an ecstasy of the moment that makes one unhappy in returning to everyday life. At the end of this letter, without transition, he writes of practical matters and of his greatest desire—being recalled to work:

> In addition, there is my wish that our present Medici lords will make use of me, even if they begin by making me roll a stone; because then, if I could not gain their favour, I should complain of myself; and through this thing, if it were read [*The Prince*] they

would see that for the fifteen years I have been studying the art of the state I have not slept or been playing; and well may anybody be glad to get the services of one who at the expense of others has become full of experience. And of my honesty there should be no doubt, because having always preserved my honesty I shall hardly now learn to break it; and he who has been honest and good for forty-three years, as I have, cannot change his nature; and as a witness to my honesty and goodness I have my poverty.

It has been suggested he wrote the *Capitolo,* "Of Ingratitude", in 1515, but any date after 1512 would be appropriate. But is the date of the composition of a work important? His life during those years explains it, if something can be explained in intellectual creation. This work is full of bitterness, completely understandable after the disappointments of 1512.

In 1515 he was working on *The Golden Ass,* which he never completed. At this time he wrote letters to his relative, Giovanni Vernacci, full of affection for the family, and showing a sense of duty and stoicism:

As for me I have become of no use to myself, to my family and to my friends, because my sad fate so decreed. I have nothing else to say; the only good left to me is the sanity of myself and of my family. I am biding my time, waiting to seize any good opportunity that may come my way, and if it should not come, I will have patience.[238]

In 1518 Machiavelli, spurred by necessity, accepted the commission of a group of Florentine merchants to go to Genoa (March and April). His confinement at San Casciano having been mitigated, he could go to Florence to the meetings at the Orti Oricellari among his friends Jacopo Nardi, Filippo de'Nerli, Zanobi Buondelmonti, and Luigi di Piero Alamanni. Jacopo Nardi, who profited greatly from Machiavelli for his historical style, has this to say: "Nicolò was greatly loved by them, and they delighted immensely in his conversation, valuing highly his writings."

In 1519, at the death of Lorenzo d'Urbino, when Cardinal de

Medici took over the reins of government in Florence, with a more liberal programme, Machiavelli was questioned along with other Florentine citizens about what constitution to give Florence. He then wrote his *Speech on the Reform of the State of Florence,* published with a dedication to Pope Leo X. And according to some scholars, he also wrote the *Mandragola* at this time, before 1520. In what relates to his life, only the prologue of this play is important. The theme of his grief at being kept inactive is recurrent:

> *And if you find this matter much too light*
> *and not worthy at all*
> *of one who wants to seem both grave and wise,*
> *forgive him! Doing this, he only tries*
> *to make his own unhappy time less sad,*
> *for nowhere else can he*
> *turn his afflicted eyes:*
> *with other deeds he's not allowed to show*
> *a nobler virtue, for*
> *there's no reward for what he did so far.*
> (*Translated by Joseph Tusiani*)

During these years Machiavelli had time to write *The Art of War,* which he refers to as *De re militari* in letters to his friends. In 1520, July-September, he goes to Lucca on behalf of the merchants. The source of a writer's inspiration is unknown; but after this trip he published the *Life of Castruccio Castracani,* an historical fantasy, and also the *Summary of Matters of Lucca,* which deals with the constitution of that Republic.

His friends turned to the pope and to the Medici at Florence to try to procure him a position. The efforts of his friends and (today this seems incredible) his historical fantasy *Life of Castruccio Castracani* helped him obtain in November 1520 the commission to write the *Florentine Histories.* He finished this work in 1525.

When Soderini, his old patron, who was at that time in Rome, under the protection of his brother the Cardinal, heard of this commission he offered Machiavelli the post of Secretary to Prospero Colonna. Even earlier, when at Ragusa, Soderini had tried to get Machiavelli to come there. Machiavelli however refused both offers. It would be going openly into the camp of the enemies of the Medici.

On May 11, 1521, Machiavelli received a small offer from the Guild of the Arte della Lana (Art of Wool) to choose a Lenten preacher! It meant he had to go to Carpi where the Franciscan monks were congregated. In addition the Commune of Florence entrusted him with a commission to these same monks to try to persuade them to form a "Province" in Florence separate from their Order.

This double errand gave rise to one of the most fascinating correspondences of the time with Francesco Guicciardini, who was serving the pope as Governor of Romagna and the Bolognese section. The ironic tone is set by the first letter of Guicciardini of May 17:

> The honourable officers of the Art of the Wool Guild have certainly shown good judgment in having commissioned you to select a preacher—it is the same as if someone had asked Pacchierotto, if he were still alive, or Ser Sano [two almost legendary characters who had become real caricatures of the low life of Florence of the period] to choose an attractive and beautiful wife for a friend. I am sure you will serve them according to their expectations and to your honour—which would become tarnished if at your age you became a bigot, and inasmuch as you have always lived in another fashion, they would attribute to you senility rather than virtue. Let me urge you to hasten your departure (from the monks) as soon as you can, because by remaining there you are exposing yourself to two dangers: the first, you might contract hypocrisy from those holy monks; and second, the air of Carpi might make you into a liar, for that is its nature, not only at the present time, but for many past centuries.[239]

The two friends enjoyed poking fun at Machiavelli's mission, at the monks and at the Bishop of Carpi, and they took delight in a mockery in a Boccaccian vein, with the solemn Guicciardini helping the rascal Machiavelli to assume an air of importance with the monks from whom he wanted "hearty meals" and "glorious beds", which he would not have obtained had he been a person of small account. They both had contempt for the intelligence and honesty of the monks, and they were happy to sow discord among them. The correspondence (Lett. CLXXVIII–CLXXXIII) of May 1521 reads like a comedy which might be entitled *The Republic of the Wooden Shoes,* in reference to the shoes of the monks.

In 1521 another anti-Medicean conspiracy was uncovered at Florence, this time involving close friends of Machiavelli—those that used to meet at Orti Oricellari: Zanobi Buondelmonti, Jacopo da Diacceto, Luigi di Tommaso Alamanni and Luigi di Piero Alamanni, who had supported the Medici when they first came into power. Machiavelli was not implicated. Jacopo da Diacceto and Luigi di Tommaso Alamanni were captured and beheaded for having plotted to kill Cardinal dei Medici; Zanobi Buondelmonti and Luigi di Piero Alamanni succeeded in fleeing. Later the historian Jacopo Nardi, who tried to blacken Machiavelli's reputation, unjustly wrote: "Nicolò was not without blame in connection with the plans and actions of these young men," despite the fact that acts of violence and the use of the stiletto as punishment for tyrants proposed by Machiavelli were offset by his universal condemnation of all conspiracies. In the writings of Luigi Alamanni there is no indication that he heeded the teachings of Machiavelli.

In the fall of that year, when Raffaello Girolami was sent as Ambassador to Spain by Charles V, Machiavelli wrote for him a series of shrewd, practical and memorable counsels—*Instruction for an Ambassador.*

In 1523, a fragment of a letter to Guicciardini informs us that Machiavelli was still in his country house, "waiting to write the history". But he had misgivings which he communicated to Guicciardini in a letter dated August 30 1524:

> I would pay ten *soldi*—but no more—to have you by my side so that I could show you where I am, because, having come to certain particulars, I need to learn from you if I give too much offence either by raising or by lowering these things. But I shall keep on

taking counsel with myself and shall try to act in such a way that, since I tell the truth, nobody will be able to complain.[240]

In February 1525 his friend de Nerli tells him that his comedy (*Mandragola*), produced in Florence, has become famous even in Lombardy. And from Rome Francesco Vettori writes that the Pope is awaiting the *Florentine Histories* and tells him to bring them to Rome. In a letter to Vettori, the Pope said: "He should come, and I feel sure his books will be well liked and read with interest."[241]

The reconciliation with the Medicis was now almost complete. In the following year Machiavelli went to Rome to present his *Florentine Histories* to Clement VII who received him cordially. Machiavelli took advantage of the occasion to try to convince the Pope to organize his own national militia! The pope sent him to Guicciardini at Faenza, where he arrived on June 19. But Guicciardini was not in favour of giving arms to the Romagnoli, knowing that in true Italian fashion they would use them to fight among themselves and not to drive foreigners from the land.

Nothing more was said of Machiavelli's idea of a papal militia. Guicciardini's commonsense prevailed over the dreams of Nicolò. Machiavelli returned to Florence at the end of July, then on August 19 he was sent to Venice for matters referring to certain merchants. It seems, but it is not certain, that at Venice he gambled at lottery and won two or three thousand ducats, but this did not appreciably improve his financial situation. On September 15, he returned to Florence where he was finally declared eligible for public office.

The complicated and ever deteriorating political situation in Italy prompted the Medici to refortify Florence. Machiavelli in 1526 was at first consulted and then appointed secretary of a new Commission called "Five Engineers of the Walls". As a result of an inspection made by Machiavelli, he wrote a report in terms of military engineering on fortifying Florence.[242]

During these years the correspondence with Guicciardini continued. It is of great significance and almost timely now. On behalf of Florence, Machiavelli went to see Guicciardini and then at the suggestion of Guicciardini, he visited various sections of Italy. In August he was in Lombardy with Guicciardini, in September at the allied headquarters at Cremona, on November 30 again with Guicciardini, and in December he returned to Florence. The two friends considered the political situation of Italy with great pessimism. Nevertheless both of them in their own circles of action—Guicciardini's very vast, Machiavelli's very limited—carried on their work and their duties. But the gravity of events, the lack of foresight of the leaders, and the complication of the vested interests did not dampen their practical and farcical Tuscan spirit. Machiavelli's last hope for Italy was expressed at this time. It would seem that a man in love, even a genius of great perspicacity, is easily blinded. In a letter to Guicciardini dated March 15, 1526, Machiavelli says:

> You know, and everybody knows it who can think about this world, that the people are uncertain and foolish; nevertheless, even though they are, often they say that something is being done that should be done. A few days ago it was said throughout Florence that the Lord Giovanni de'Medici [known as Giovanni of the Black Bands] was raising the flag of a soldier of fortune, to make war where he had the best opportunity. This rumour stirred up my spirit to imagine that the people knew what ought to be done. I believe anyone who believes that among the Italians there is no leader the soldiers would more gladly follow, and whom the Spanish more fear and more respect; everybody also thinks that Lord Giovanni is bold, prompt, has great ideas, is a maker of great plans. We could then, secretly making him strong, have him raise this flag, putting under him as many cavalry and as many infantry as we can.[243]

A little later, Giovanni of the Black Bands (1498–1526) was to die of a serious wound, and Machiavelli was also to leave this world of uncertainties that is made of beliefs not of knowledge, where almost everyone, even wise men, end by trusting the guiding light of men who are "fickle and mad".

In February 1526, Machiavelli was sent to Guicciardini to ask him to provide for the defence of Florence. He went with him to Bologna, Imola, Forli, Brisighella. Perhaps he returned to

Florence. In May, on behalf of Guicciardini, he went to confer with Andrea Doria at Genoa. By the time he returned to Florence, the great catastrophe of the Sack of Rome had taken place (May 6). In Florence the Republican faction took advantage of the situation to rebel against the Medicis, and among them the extremists got the upper hand. Machiavelli now hoped to return to his old office at the Magistrate of the Ten which, together with others of the popular government, had been restored. But on June 22, 1527 he died suddenly of an acute abdominal sickness, before learning that the restored Republic had appointed someone else to fill his old position.

V

HIS FRIENDS
AND CONTEMPORARIES

1 Buonaccorsi (1472–1522)

During his years of service as one of the clerks of the Florentine Republic, Machiavelli's closest and most faithful friend was Biagio Buonaccorsi, who is also the person to whom are addressed most of the letters in the earlier portion of Machiavelli's personal correspondence. He was always affectionate and loyal, devotion personified. Although his judgment is founded only on generalities, it is to his credit that he felt for Machiavelli that rare devotion and admiration, free of envy or a sense of rivalry, that restores one's faith in the world. But what did he understand of Machiavelli? I would venture to say nothing, if we are to judge by the chronicles he wrote. From an historical point of view, we know that he presented one of the first copies of *The Prince* to a mutual friend, Pandolfo Bellacci, in 1514.[244]

2 Savonarola (1452–98)

In the first letter in Italian we possess of Machiavelli, to an unknown correspondent, we read his account of a sermon of Savonarola's that Machiavelli had heard and that he comments upon with evident sarcasm. From this episode, many people attribute an open conflict between the spirit of Machiavelli and that of Savonarola. But when we read Savonarola we reach a different conclusion.

I have not only preached here in Florence, but throughout Italy. I have remained in Florence because, as God willed, it is the heart of Italy and from here the voice is carried forth and all Italy hears it, just as the vital spirit originates in the heart and goes throughout the body.[245]

In his analysis of the ills of Italy, he too deplored wealth, corruption of the Roman Church, the factions, the disunity of the country:

> The barbers [a play on the word *barbarians*] will come and shave Italy to the bone . . . Italy is completely disunited and her portals are wide open.[246]

But besides these commonplaces of the period, we find some maxims of Savonarola that are striking for their Machiavellian tone, as when he states that it is not enough for a statesman merely to be virtuous:

> If there are two men to choose from, one wise and one virtuous, elect the first, that is the wise man.[247]
> Beware not to elect a man who is the most virtuous when he is also naive; if you have a choice between a virtuous Christian and a good citizen who loves his country, elect the latter. Of course it would be desirable if he also possessed Christian virtues.[248]

"If he also possessed Christian virtues"—even in Savonarola there is that same plaintive note that is heard in Machiavelli for an ideal man possessing the qualities of a capable man and an angel, a politician and a righteous man—a combination that scarcely ever exists in reality.

In addition to the Savonarola who talks like Machiavelli, there is the Machiavelli who preaches like Savonarola, but in all fairness it must be said that in this respect Savonarola is more successful. An example of Machiavelli preaching like Savonarola is found in the final chapter of *The Prince*. Is it possible that he wrote those phrases in all seriousness? He must have known perfectly well that they were literary devices, or imitations of the Bible or of Savonarola. Or did he think they would make a good impression on the petty mind of Lorenzo? Was it over-enthusiasm? Was it rhetoric? Was it, as in some second-rate musical comedies, a show of bravura by means of which Machiavelli wanted to express his hopes in a language he had heretofore never used? As if his own did not suffice, why did he also add the rhetoric of Petrarch?

3 Francesco Vettori

All who have read Machiavelli's correspondence know what an amusing person was his friend Francesco Vettori and what an interesting philosophy of life he arrived at as a result of his life in Rome where he received the salary of an Ambassador *sine cura*, without working for it. He was the Ambassador of a Medici to a Pope who was also a Medici. He divided his time between reading the classics, walking around the city, seeing an occasional girl and writing to Machiavelli. Among Machiavelli's correspondents, Vettori is the most authoritative witness of the fact that Machiavelli's ideas were not shocking—indeed they seemed completely acceptable and were re-echoed according to the degree of articulate ability of those who listened to him. In his *Summary of the History of Italy*, Vettori says:

> In speaking of things of this world frankly and truthfully, I maintain if we were to have a Republic such as imagined by Plato or as the English writer Thomas More described in his Utopia, perhaps it might be considered not tyrannical—but all republics and principalities of which I know through history or that I have seen, are to a certain degree tyrannical. And to come to cases, and to speak honestly, all governments are tyrannical. I should like to be shown the difference between a king and a tyrant. If we were to examine well the origin of kingdoms we would find they had all been founded either by force or by ruse.[249]

The difference between Machiavelli and Vettori is one of degree. They both read the same histories and had participated in the same political misfortunes and they both believed the world had always been the same.[250] Machiavelli has a more acute sense of the meaning of events and a broader outlook on life, and he became more emotionally involved in politics than Vettori. When Vettori goes to Germany as Ambassador, he is accompanied by Machiavelli, but it is amazing to read reports of the same trip by the two men. From his knowledge of the German people, Machiavelli depicts a Germany in the vein of Tacitus. While at the same time seeming to report faithfully on the constitution of the free German cities, and of their relation with the authority of the Emperor, he actually presents the picture of a Utopian state— poor and religious, an ideal dear to his imagination, and contrasts it with the over-refinement, waste and wantonness of Italian princes. Vettori on the other hand takes occasion to recount tales, in the vein of Boccaccio, of innkeepers and girls, interspersed only here and there with some political observations and reflections.

4 Alamanni (1495–1556)

Luigi Alamanni was a third friend of Machiavelli of a later period, the years 1516–1520, when he and his friends met at Orti Oricellari. Reading the poetic works of Alamanni, who fled to France when the anti-Medici plot was discovered which resulted in the beheading of Diacceto, one is tempted to ask if he (Alamanni) even knew Machiavelli. There is only one reference to Machiavelli's words but only to uphold the opposite viewpoint. Where Machiavelli feels that a leader must possess the qualities of a lion (force) and act like a fox (astuteness), Alamanni is of the opinion that only arms are necessary, as is shown by these verses of his:

> The cruel brave lion, not the clever fox,
> conquers by force, never deception.

When Machiavelli died, Alamanni laments him by means of a purely literary sonnet which ends as follows:

> Now that our Secretary's soul
> is in heaven, and his bones in the earth,
> Death, I no longer fear you.

For him [Machiavelli] it was good to be alive,
for him only I feared Death's bitter battle;
now that he's gone, you cannot wound me.

It can truly be said that Machiavelli did not leave a strong impression of his political ideas on his closest friends. By means of great effort we can find some traces of his conversation, but not of his spirit.

5 Leonardo da Vinci (1452–1519)

Leonardo and Machiavelli met perhaps for the first time in 1502 at Urbino, after Caesar Borgia had suddenly occupied that city. But they assuredly had personal relations later in connection with the enterprise conceived by Leonardo, and strongly supported by Machiavelli, of changing the course of the Arno River in order to block the supplies that were reaching Pisa, a city that had been besieged in vain for years by the Florentines. Besides it has been proved from a page of the Atlantic Code of Leonardo that some notes for the history of the battle of Anghiari, which Leonardo had been commissioned to paint for the city hall of Florence, were handwritten by Machiavelli.

It would be more interesting to picture them discussing politics together as novelists and even historians have done, but there is no documentation to prove this. Ideally they are two representatives of the scientific spirit of the time. In certain respects they are alike. They both scorn authority and respect experience, and they both have a tendency to define things, but Machiavelli's definitions are more mechanistic than those of Leonardo, who is inspired by animism.

6 Fregoso (1470–1524)

A man from Genoa must be mentioned among the contemporaries who saw things as did Machiavelli, if we can rely on the annals of the city of Genoa. He is Ottaviano Fregoso, who wrote these words:

> Private individuals and the state are not judged by the same standards. Private individuals are called wicked when they break their word or fail their friends, and frivolous and untrustworthy when they change their minds and opinions—but these things are accepted in the case of the state when they are of use to the country, and are considered honest when they are essential to the safety of the state and of its citizens.[251]

The Machiavellian distinction between private and public morality could not have been more clearly expressed.

7 Francesco Guicciardini (1492–1540)

Guicciardini is an exception to those who read but did not understand Machiavelli.

He was Machiavelli's contemporary, but younger by ten years, that is he came to a world that was older in experience by ten years. He was a witness, after Machiavelli's death, of the final outcome of many earlier disasters that Machiavelli witnessed. However, his mind was of a different stamp from that of the Florentine secretary, less subject to illusion and hope. He started from the same principles: an awareness of the shams and dissimulations of politics, a belief that the state is force; and he desired virtually the same things: freedom of Italy from barbarians, and from the clergy; but he knew that this was a dream. He felt that it was better to remain within the limits of reality and the attainable, and to fulfil the duty that is dictated to a man of honour by his own feelings rather than by divine law or human customs. Guicciardini possessed a more subtle and controlled mind than did Machiavelli. He was wealthy in comparison to Machiavelli, and occupied a socially superior position that allowed him to enter into the field of active politics. He could use his own judgment in making decisions and, unlike Machiavelli, he was not forced to await word from his superiors.

All scholars of the two men have made a study of their relationship. In some ways they are opposites, but in a certain sense they complement each other like the two sides of the same medal. Guicciardini's judgment of some of Machiavelli's ideas is basic and stands up even today. The fundamental point of divergence is in their interpretation of history. Guicciardini does not believe that history repeats itself, nor that it is possible to formulate laws or even maxims of practical politics. To him, politics is a matter of intuition and subtlety in sizing up situations that forever vary. It is a question of judgment (we would say *art*), and not of science. It cannot be applied—it must be solved at the moment new situations arise. Of course there are suggestions to be made, and Guicciardini gives us some excellent ones in his *Ricordi*,[252] but they must always be interpreted with reservations.

Despite these differences, the correspondence between the two Florentines remains a great document of political intelligence, refinement, reciprocal respect and mutual comprehension. Guicciardini treats Machiavelli as an equal, and Machiavelli knows how to respect the confidences of his friend without taking advantage of them. We see Guicciardini in these few moments of his life when he permitted himself to joke; this is perhaps the greatest influence Machiavelli had on him. Guicciardini, whom a biographer states was never seen laughing, laughs with Machiavelli; he jokes about the monks of Carpi, and even about government matters, and at that moment at least he was more interested in the comedy *Mandragola* and the actress Barbara, who was in love with Machiavelli, than in state affairs. As far as Guicciardini's influence on Machiavelli is concerned, there is none worth mentioning. Their letters to each other deal with the prevailing political situation and with forecasts, but not with principles.

In a letter of 1521, Guicciardini makes an appraisal of Machiavelli that must have been common at the time and was even accepted by Machiavelli himself. Guicciardini expressed it to his friend in these words: "You have always been (*ut plurimum*) to the utmost greatly removed from the common opinion; you are an inventor of new and unusual things."

Knowing Guicciardini's philosophy, it is clear that this is a criticism, although veiled in a eulogy, of some of Machiavelli's counsels which at times savoured of Utopia (like the proposal of drafting an army for the Pope in the Romagna district). Nevertheless Guicciardini must have had respect for Machiavelli's practical judgment inasmuch as he consults him about the purchase of a villa and a farm and about the marriage of his daughter. In any case the letters reveal no dissension on matters of political theory. This is only seen when Guicciardini, like Machiavelli and Castiglione before him, is removed from active political life because of the change in the leaders, and retreats to a life of contemplation and to writing. It would take too long a time to show, point by point, where Guicciardini differs from Machiavelli, and it would also be a complicated affair, because at times he differs in part of a maxim and not in another part, and at times in the consequences drawn by Machiavelli, or in the principles themselves. But the important thing is that both men belong to the same realistic school of thought. To put it in Guicciardini's words, they do not deal with theoretical states "which are governed by philosophical theories—but with those which are, as a point of necessity, governed according to the common usage of this world. If states governed by philosophical theory could exist, they would be weak, oppressed and trampled on by neighbours." Machiavelli would have subscribed to this dictum.

8   Brucioli and Luigi Guicciardini

Machiavelli's personality left a mark, and some reverberations and echoes in Florence, but usually the image was weak and garbled.

In the *Dialogues* of Antonio Brucioli (who died in 1556) Machiavelli emerges as an important character, and some of his ideas are expressed. The one where the Prince is the surgeon of the Republic, or the arguments in favour of a national militia seem taken from a work of Plato rather than from one of Machiavelli, and the theory of defensive warfare does not correspond to his thought at all.

It has been said that in the dialogue, *De libero arbitrio dell' huomo* ("On man's Free Will") that F. Gilbert (Journal of the Warburg Institute, 1937–38, I, 163) attributes to Luigi Guicciardini, one of the characters whose name is Nicolò represents Machiavelli. According to a letter of Guicciardini of May 30, 1533, he chose Machiavelli to portray one who "questioned everything, the things he was expected to believe, as well as those he could laugh about". This would be a satisfactory enough picture; but in this dialogue we find expressed the opinion of Machiavelli as one who praises and exalts poverty, and denounces and condemns idleness. Luigi Guicciardini makes the character who is supposed to be Machiavelli say:

> I still don't know how virtue comes from the one (poverty) and vice from the other (idleness).

He also makes him ask:

> I hope it does not annoy you to have us ask once again why necessity is called the mother of virtue rather than of vice.

This is in *complete* opposition to one of the most fundamental, uncontested, and reaffirmed beliefs of Machiavelli. If this is a picture of Machiavelli, it is like an upside down photographic negative.

9   Bandello

Another accusation was levelled at Machiavelli by one of his younger contemporaries, Bandello (1485?–1562?), that he was a theoretician, and didn't know what he was talking about. The accusation is directed only at Machiavelli as author of *The Art of War,* but was taken up again by others and became one of the many Machiavelli legends. Those who could not actually contradict Machiavelli's theories, enjoyed themselves at his expense by recounting the anecdote of Bandello where it appears in the fortieth story of the first part of his *Novelliere.* The anecdote is the following:

Machiavelli, having one day been invited on the parade grounds to arrange the soldiers as he had indicated and prescribed for the Roman Legions in his *Art of War,* unsuccessfully tried to do so, until the captain, who wanted to go to lunch, took over the command himself. With a couple of commands, to the tune of drumbeats, the captain put everything back into order. At lunch, Machiavelli, in trying to make up for his failure, is said to have tried to amuse the guests with a story in the vein of Boccaccio. The anecdote of Bandello is long and drawn out, and very little remains of the spirit and style of Machiavelli.

In the following century, that quixotic personality Gerolamo Cardano (1501–76) made use of the ancedote in this way:

> We are men and always subject to errors. It is easier to preach than to act, as is shown by Nicolò Machiavelli who had often and with clarity written many things about the military discipline of Roman soldiers, but who did not succeed in forming even a cohort offered to him by the *Signore* of Urbino.

Later the anecdote passed down to Bayle and to the Encyclopaedists. Finally it is found again in modern novels and historical biographies. Dmitri Merezhkovsky has Borgia recount the anecdote to Leonardo da Vinci:

Did you ever hear tell of the Macedonian phalanxes? Well, listen. Once Nicolò was explaining right from his book on warfare to my Marshall Bartolomeo Capranica and to other officers the method of forming the troops according to the order of the phalanx. He spoke with such eloquence that everyone wanted to see it actually done. At the parade grounds Nicolò was to give the orders. Well, he wore out 2,000 soldiers for three hours, exposing them to the cold, the wind and the rain, but he couldn't succeed in forming that phalanx. Finally Bartolomeo lost patience and he, who had never read a book on military art in his whole life, took the troops under his command and in a flash arranged them as he wanted. This is the difference between practice and theory, but be sure not to remind Messer Nicolò of this unfortunate experience.

Thus, with the passing of centuries, legion became phalanx, but it was always the same story of Bandello.

VI

MACHIAVELLIANISM

1 Machiavellianism or the real life of Machiavelli:

For many thinkers their real life begins after their death. This is true of Machiavelli who exists in his works. Machiavellianism came into being when Machiavelli died. While he was alive his doctrines did not elicit either astonishment, nor hatred, but only a slight murmur. The leaders of his time did not acknowledge him as their spokesman, and during his lifetime his career was no different because of his having written *The Art of War,* the *Florentine Histories* and *Mandragola;* nor was he censured for what he wrote. The church leaders and princes would probably have burnt him at the stake if they had read his books or understood his ideas. It was only when he stepped out of his own time that he became the big bad wolf. Contrary to what has been said, he belonged to the future, and made only a slight impression on his contemporaries.

Even Guicciardini, who seemed the most qualified among his contemporaries to judge him and who was the most interested in his doctrines, looked down on him from the heights of his different experience. When he writes on Machiavelli he seems to be somewhat on the defensive, because Machiavelli wanted the Italian leaders to be heroes and redeemers and Guicciardini knew this wasn't worth the trouble of even thinking about.

Machiavelli's reality consists not of what he left in writing, but of what readers of his works think of them. What is a book that remains unopened? What truth printed on a sheet of paper exists, if there are no readers to keep it alive? All literary and philosophical criticism should be renewed on the basis of the principle that only what is in men's spirit has reality. As Berkeley said, *esse est percipi*—only what is seen by man is real; reality acquires its value from the spirit of man. The real life of an author emanates from his readers, disciples, commentators, opponents, critics. An author has no other existence.

We have seen that the so-called forerunners of Machiavelli began to live—insofar as they were forerunners—only after Machiavelli's thought was instrumental in searching them out. But even Machiavelli began to exist only from the time that eyes and minds were concentrated on the printed words he had left, when people of imagination took an interest in him, and currents of thought were initiated with Machiavelli as a starting point. Thinkers have created Machiavelli in their own image, they have used him and even when they have avoided him, they were forced to follow a trail blazed by him. This then is the true Machiavelli.

The doctrines, sometimes in embryo and sometimes developed, that he expounded have not always been acknowledged as his by his interpreters. Blindness when reading him and deafness at the sound of his dramatic expressions might be surprising if this were not so common in the history of all ideas.

Some ideas of Machiavelli—the *raison d'état,* for example— were immediately understood and still continue to be disputed and to trouble men's souls. Others were only hinted at but for the most part remained dormant for years and even centuries, like his placing the love of country above all else, or his advice to establish a national militia. At certain moments of history, some of his phrases became the battle cry of a faction, like "the stiletto for tyrants", carried down from the School of Monarchomachs to the Mazzini group of the Italian Risorgimento.

There are some observations that advance political thought in general, like the one made by Bacon, that Machiavelli described the customs of political leaders as they are and he cannot be held responsible for their actions. There are also important judgments of Machiavelli, like that of Guicciardini, which remained buried in family archives until 1860 and when it came to light was found to be as full of vitality and vigour as the seeds of grain recently found in Egyptian tombs. On the other hand, certain interpretations of Machiavellianism, like the one that Machiavelli wrote *The Prince* only to overthrow the Medicis, have had no importance in the history of thought. At the most they have served as a shield to protect Machiavelli, or as a sign of sympathy for him.

Can it be said that all centuries, all thinkers, all schools of thought, all political crises have twisted, strained, hidden and mutilated Machiavelli's thought? Is there a "real Machiavelli" to set against the falsifications of centuries?

Every time that Machiavelli is discussed, something else is really at stake. For instance, the divorce of Henry VIII of England, the influence of Catherine of Medici on the French government, the consolidation of the domination of Cosimo in Tuscany. Later we have the independence of the state from the church in Naples, the French oppression of the Germans after the Napoleonic war, and the burden on Italians of Austria's occupation. Later still we have the rights of the Bolshevik revolution against the feudalism of the Russian ruling classes. The stand for or against Machiavelli is taken with a view towards some political end, or to satisfy some antipathy. Machiavelli always seems timely. His very vitality and therefore his truth consists in this.

But what about Machiavelli's actual words? No text has ever offered insurmountable obstacles to those who wanted to interpret it in their own way, or to those who, because of the profound irrational forces that are dominant at the time, want to adopt his theories to suit their own purposes. Just think of the Gospels being interpreted to allow free love as well as castration by hundreds of denominations in which men of good will will abound who find in the Bible a basis for their strange creeds.

Machiavelli's actual words have been known since 1530, in the separate editions of his main works. To the Testina edition—with the false date of 1610—modern philology has not been able to add important variants as far as the sense is concerned. However, knowledge of Machiavelli's life began to improve considerably from Fossi's edition on, that is from the time of the publication of his letters and the reports that revealed his personality and his activity. This was truly the discovery of Machiavelli, and took place from the middle of the eighteenth century after the new manuscripts were found.

This knowledge of personal documents and of the Florentine environment rectified the legend that had grown around him, a legend which started with his famous dream. Shortly before his death, Machiavelli was said to have had a dream which he related to four friends who came to see him. In his dream he was taken to a place where there were poor, wretched and sick people and he was told they were the poor in spirit, who, the Gospel says, would inherit heaven. Then in another place he was shown dignified and noble people who were discussing state matters. When he was told they would never have salvation because they were pagan, he asked if he could join them because he wanted only to discuss things that were of interest to them. This dream has not been historically verified, but it can be traced to a maxim in his *Life of Castruccio Castracani* and to some of his other maxims. It is more in harmony with his spirit than many interpretations of historians weighed down with documents like Villari and Tommasini. In the dream there is an echo of Dante's limbo, or perhaps the reminiscence of a death-bed saying of an Italian humanist. It may not be true, but in any case it was well invented.

It is an important dream, because Machiavelli's death inaugurated his second life as a thinker. This is the beginning of that travesty which is a sign of an author's vitality. Let it be clearly understood that this sketch of the history of Machiavellianism does not intend to decide who understood and who has not understood him, or of opposing the "real" Machiavelli to the "false" one. Rather it seeks to discover the "real" life of Machiavelli which begins after his death. It has as a premise that his doctrines elicit continuous reactions, interest, torment, admiration and are used by factions and by political, religious or moral forces in a crescendo that increases to our own day. Naturally if at times I use the phrase the "real Machiavelli", or imply it, this is just a manner of speaking. For me, the interpretations of Machiavelli were justified at any stated moment, and possessed a grain of truth, if they satisfied that superficial but constant need of men and social institutions to justify their own actions by means of doctrines.

The excellence of a work does not consist so much in what the author said, or what he wanted to accomplish or express with it, as much as in what humanity has added to it with comments, derivations, substitutions, modifications, interpretations. If a work serves only its own time, and does not speak to a later period, it dies with its own century. Therefore the author himself and his contemporaries, while they are the best witnesses of some point of detail, know less than we who come later about the significance, and the total value of the work itself. "The author didn't mean to say this", commentators tell us—and this may be true. But we understand it in this way and now the work belongs to us and we have the right (who can deprive us of it?) to make it say what we want to make it say. What keeps authors alive is not their books, but the imagination of those who read them. No book has ever been able to check an imagination which is spirited and sharpened by desire. And each wave of imagination and desire that has enveloped a work and has bestowed on thinkers its will to live, has also modified and reconstructed the work. This will not end while the human mind is capable of using its imagination, desiring and reaching towards the future, seeking reasons and logic which provide it with a permit to go on; and this will continue as long as the mind remains human.

2 The universal hatred for Machiavelli and its origin

Save for a few exceptions, Machiavelli was universally hated for a couple of centuries. What is the origin of this hatred?

If we examine the first documents of denunciations against him it is fairly clear that they stem from three principal currents of European thought: Catholic, Protestant, and Republican (or Liberal). The exceptions are a few independent thinkers. The three currents from which originate the first condemnations of

Machiavelli are political currents, representing political minorities crushed by the formation of the great national states in Machiavelli's epoch.

The leaders of the first denunciation were Cardinal Pole for the Catholics; Councillor Gentillet for the Protestants; and the exile Busini for the Republicans. These three individuals were very dissimilar; and very different were the reasons for thier denunciation. Yet they all have in common the fundamental tendency to attribute to the Machiavellian doctrines the misfortunes of their political parties, which in the case of all three are those of a minority that was expelled, or conquered, or subjugated. They were all maimed, wounded or defeated.

This was the period of the formation of the great national unities under the leadership of the ruling families who, in order to attain their goals, combated without mercy the aristocracy in England, France and Spain, but not in Italy. Machiavelli was aware of this historical phenomenon and he was sorry that his country did not participate in the movement. Even today many historiographers believe that Machiavelli realized the termination of the autonomies, the disintegration of medieval civilization and the end of regional self-determination. In France, England and Spain it took place on a large scale; in a smaller way it was about to happen in Florence and Tuscany. The end of the Commune of Florence, which for many romantic historians like Sismondi also marks the end of Italian freedom, inaugurates the beginning of the modern state (when politics is actually more democratic than the Commune, inasmuch as it puts the subjects of the state on an equal footing and is not founded on the predominance of one city and its merchant citizens over other cities and the surrounding countryside). The period of tyrants, when all the citizens were *subjects,* followed that of the oligarchies and these in turn gave way to the modern democracies.

The adversaries of Machiavelli responsible for the stigma that was not to be shaken off for two centuries, all came from families that the monarch or prince had eliminated by death, by confiscation of their goods, or by the absorption of their feudal privileges. The hatred for Machiavelli stemmed from the feudalism that was dying. When the individualistic formation of the Middle Ages began to lose ground, the power of the states became concentrated in the hands of a reigning family that had a centre, the capital of the country, wherein was concentrated all the wealth. The capital—London, Paris, Madrid—imposed its customs and language on the rest of the country. With Rome, Italy alone did not have a capital whose court set the tone for the rest of the country.

But in a secondary city of the peninsula there is found the isolated intelligence of Machiavelli who formulates political doctrines which can serve to justify the rulers' abuse of power, with the unsuspecting consent of the plebeians, against those amazing autonomies of citizen and lordly privileges, the Ultramontane French clerics or some classes of workers. The new dominators are not tyrants who govern for their own personal interest, but Kings who impersonate the interests of a vaster group of people, held together by the natural characteristic of the countryside, by a common language, and sometimes by an enforced religious unity. The adversaries of Machiavelli represent the conservative party of the old order.

The leaders were not aware of the forces they were unleashing to bring about this great transformation, and in order to justify their aggression they mumbled vague terms of religion, justice or honour. Their enemies were always considered traitors. And sometimes they really were, as when they preferred a foreign dominator to a native one, whom they would accept only as a "first among equals" but not as a sovereign.

To these new rulers the doctrine of the State offered by Machiavelli seemed a justification of their deeds. To their adversaries, instead, the same doctrine seemed the negation of their rights. And from then on, until the modern state was affirmed in its purest form, as a national democracy, the leaders read Machiavelli in secret, the aristocracy denounced him openly, and the Church, which had always feared the rivalry of the State, condemned him as the worst of enemies. And in truth he was.

3   The first enemy, Cardinal Reginald Pole (1500–1558)

It was Cardinal Angiolo Maria Quirini who pointed to Pole as being the first denouncer of Machiavelli. His works up to that time had elicited some murmurs of disapproval, but they were published with the imprimatur of the Roman Curia without causing any scandal. As Quirini pointed out:

> In any case, Pole is worthy of the highest praise because he was the first to sound the trumpet-call against the impious and evil doctrine of Machiavelli, first in Florence, then in England where Machiavelli's follower Cromwell was denounced by Pole as meriting public indignation.[253]

As a youth, Pole admired Henry VIII and his minister Thomas Cromwell (not the more famous Oliver), but later he became their most bitter foe. This occurred when Henry VIII, who wanted to divorce his wife but could not obtain the sanction of the Church, left Catholicism and caused a schism. Or perhaps Pole's change of heart was also brought about by the king's increasing power, which Pole sensed as a diminution of the power of the aristocratic classes to which he belonged. It is significant that in the conflict between the Tudor monarchy and the English aristocracy, Pole left England and sought refuge in Italy where he heard of the arrest of his two brothers—one of whom was beheaded, when the other brother denounced him. His mother, who was accused of being a traitor to the king, was also beheaded. To this justifiable aversion for Henry VIII and for Cromwell, Pole added a third person—Machiavelli.

His knowledge of *The Prince* and of Machiavelli's life is a subject of discussion and interpretation and remains a bit mysterious. It seems he was summoned by Thomas Cromwell for a private consultation on the problem of Henry VIII's divorce. Cromwell started out by asking him what he thought of the duties of counsellors of kings. Pole answered that among other things, the counsellors should point the way along the path of honour as well as of the country's interest, according to the laws of virtue and reason. Cromwell observed that these were good enough notions for schools and pulpits but of scant value to the "Cabinets of Kings". (This phrase later served a popular anti-Machiavellian pamphlet.) Cromwell pointed out that the position of counsellors was not an easy one to fill, because often it was not possible to discover the king's desires which lay hidden under different appearances. The aims of kings were never regulated by religion or other virtues. A king would willingly listen to such advice from his confessor, but would not tolerate it from his political counsellors who were forced instead to help a king attain his aims without allowing him to break off completely with religion or other virtues. In this way the counsellors would succeed in "reconciling the appearance of virtue which the king did not abandon gladly, with the essential interests of the State". Pole is said to have answered without contradicting him directly, although he realized that those maxims would have justified Nero's murder of his mother. Cromwell felt his disapproval under his reserve, and told him that he (Pole) had little experience in public life inasmuch as he read about such things only in scholastic manuals, but that if he (Pole) would permit, he could learn from another book based more on experience than on speculation.

Pole reports on what Cromwell told him:

> There is one book by a most acute modern author who did not write about his own dreams as did Plato, who devised a plan for a Republic which could not be put into practice; but had instead formulated maxims and observations of which daily experience confirmed the truth—and if I would give him permission and a promise to read that book, he would send it to me.[254]

There is no doubt that this is a clear enough description of *The Prince*, above all in that particular detail of "realistic politics" opposed to those of Plato. Pole was soon in such open conflict with the king that he had to flee from England, but first he procured the book described in those stimulating words of Cromwell. And he tells us:

Reading it, I found all the stratagems [*Stratagems of Satan* was the title of an anti-Machiavellian book] by means of which religion, justice and good will were invalidated and through which all human and divine virtues would become a prey of egoism, dissimulation and falsehood. It was written by a certain Machiavelli, native of Florence, entitled *The Prince*—and it is such a work that if Satan himself had had a son for a successor, I don't know what other maxims he could pass on to him.[255]

Prof. Van Dyke wonders whether Pole was in good faith or had a poor memory when he recounted this, because *The Prince* was not published until 1532 and the talk with Cromwell took place in 1527 or 1528. But this is not only a matter of Pole's "memory" but of his faith. If he forgot, he also filled that *lapsus* in his memory with very precise inventions. His *Apologia* (I, 138) has a fairly long analysis of *The Prince* that shows an attentive reading of Machiavelli, especially of chapter XVIII.

One thing is certain—Pole's hatred for Machiavelli as the theoretician and inspiration of a diabolic phenomenon, the "tyrannical" prince (that is, the destroyer of the medieval autonomies). Pole's writing marks the start of accusations that persisted for centuries directed against Machiavelli as a counsellor of tyrants.

Pole felt that Cromwell would not have been as he was if he had not read Machiavelli. Pole's importance today is that he gave the initial impetus to that type of hostility towards Machiavelli. In his own writing is clearly visible the origin of this hatred.

After Pole came other Catholics who had greater influence on the official condemnation of Machiavelli by the Church, which took place in 1559. Among others there was the Dominican, Ambrogio Caterino Politi (1487–1553), with his book *De libris a Christiano detestandis et a Christianismo penitus eliminandis,* published in Rome in 1552.

Bishop Gerolamo Osorio (1510–80) in the third book of *De Christiana nobilitate* (1552) opposed only one point of Machiavelli's doctrine—the accusation that Christianity destroyed the grandeur of spirit and power of the Roman Empire. On behalf of Innocent IX, who did not live to see the result, a priest of the

Order of the Oratory, Thomas Bozius, at the end of the sixteenth century published four large volumes *Adversus Machiavellium* against Machiavelli.

Needless to say Machiavelli's works outlasted these bitter, heavy, literary, rhetorical and stupid accusations which attempted to show that Christians—or rather Catholics, as they became during the course of the book—were the best of warriors; or else that virtuous kings always won out (or almost always) and evil kings (almost always) were defeated, with an amazing erudition of all the official histories of that time. Machiavelli is pictured as a Circe who administers foul beverages to men to remove virtue and truth from their minds, thus reducing them to beasts—the very opposite of what Machiavelli advocated, who tried to turn human beasts into heroes.

4 Gentillet

After Pole, whose political rancor blurred his memory, we come to Innocenzo Gentillet, the Huguenot of France, who denounced the doctrines of Machiavelli as instigating the Night of St. Bartholomew, the political massacre by which Catherine of Medici freed herself of the Protestant minority hostile to the concentration of political power in a French central monarchy. Gentillet is the first Protestant foe of Machiavelli and, like Pole in the Catholic field, he had great influence among his own people. His *Discours sur les moyens de bien gouverner et maintenir en paix un royaume, ou autre principauté. Contre Nicolas Machiavel florentin,* was published in 1576, four years after the massacre. The principal themes of the book, large in format but poor in essence, are two: religious vengeance and national pride. He accuses Machiavelli of having planted in the mind of Catherine of Medici the idea of the massacre and of having introduced foreign methods—in this case Italian—in the policies of the Kings of France.

What is Gentillet defending? The French nobility against the absolute power of the sovereign—in complete opposition to what is most modern in Machiavelli. He is long-winded and a falsifier. He quotes fragments of Machiavelli out of their original context, puts together two passages giving them a completely different meaning, and he also invents. He adopts the viewpoint of Natural Right, of Christian precepts, of the laws of states that should limit the absolute power of the prince or leader. Machiavelli's new point of departure—which implicitly makes *tabula rasa* of Natural Rights and advances the belief that only force counts—eludes him. Gentillet's book is full of banalities (for example, a tyrant cannot last for a long time; honesty always ends up by being triumphant; God punishes the wicked). He should not be considered in bad faith, because he had the ingenuousness of a person of faith and does not mind leaving obvious traces of his manipulations. It was thought that Gentillet's book, translated into English in 1602, had tremendous influence on English public opinion. However, various manuscript-copies of English translations of *The Prince,* made before the first edition was published, have been uncovered; and when someone called attention to the great number of upper-class Englishmen who travelled in Italy and who received Italian books, it was no longer believed that Gentillet was solely responsible for the seven hundred and more malicious quotations of Machiavelli to be found in Shakespeare and other English tragedians. But even thus reduced, Gentillet's influence on the English and Protestant public was noteworthy.

5   Busini

The third of Machiavelli's early enemies was G. B. Busini (1501–1574?), a Florentine exile when the Republic party was forced to yield to the Medicis in 1530. He wrote a letter on January 23, 1549, many years after this defeat, and gave us the first hints of a new Machiavelli legend, which is part of the aversion to his political doctrines:

After Florence was freed, Machiavelli left Rome and came here (Florence) in 1527. He tried desperately to take up again his work with the Ten. Zanobi and Luigi (Buondelmonti and Alamanni) were greatly in favour of him but Messrs Baldassare and Nicolò di Braccio opposed him as did the majority because of his book *The Prince*. The wealthy considered it a document written to teach the Duke how to take away their possessions and the poor felt it was written as an encouragement to take away all their freedom. By the Piagnoni (followers of Savonarola) he was considered a heretic, by the virtuous dishonest, by the scoundrels a greater scoundrel and cleverer than they were—so that everyone hated him.[256]

The passage is well written, I would almost say in the vein of Machiavelli. Here we have a new element of hostility, that of social classes—the wealthy and the poor. This is the first affirmation of a *general* aversion.

The letter degenerates into gossip, but it is important because it shows the opinion of Machiavelli held by the Florentine exiles. It is made up of some true statements mixed with a tissue of partisan assertions. This "liberal" Busini is not satisfied to condemn Machiavelli's doctrines; he succeeds in impugning his personal honesty. This is the same line taken by the Medici historians who came later: Varchi, Segni, Nerli, and Nardi.

6 The Florentine Historians

The Florentine historians, after the Church's condemnation, are torn between patriotic pride and fear of disobeying ecclesiastical authority. They all read Machiavelli, and sometimes quote him directly, or copy him. They seek to preserve a glory of Florence by praising his genius but condemning his doctrines, or lauding his work and deploring his immoral life. This holds true for the literati as well as for the historians. And when the historians, as narrators of events that took place, are forced to speak of him, they skim over his name with great circumspection.

Nerli is the closest to Machiavelli. In his *Commentaries* he quotes some verses from Machiavelli's *Decennials* in order to revive Capponi's answer to Charles VIII and he makes frequent use of this same work. In recounting the Conspiracy of 1522 against Cardinal Medici, he dares to boast of being a most intimate friend of Machiavelli:

> Having spent much time with a group of young literati of great promise in the courtyard of Rucellai, while Cosimo Rucellai, who yearned for the literary life, was still alive (he died very young), a frequent member of the group was Nicolò Machiavelli. I was a great friend of his and of the others too and I often talked with them. This group discussed literature, but principally lessons of history. Making use of these discussions as a foundation, Machiavelli composed his book on the discourses of Titus Livius and also the book of those treatises on war.

In addition, Nerli copies one of Machiavelli's most severe judgments on Soderini, and on the mediocrity of men in general, but Nerli limits it to the "heads of Republics":

> And often the first citizens, that is the heads of governments, cannot make up their minds to be either good or evil.[257]

In other points too (compare Book V, 110, with Machiavelli's *Discourses* III, 3 and Book XII, with *Discourses* III, 6 on conspiracies) his thought follows the ideas of Machiavelli, but always at a safe distance, with reservations, in diluted form.

Segni (1504–58) knew Machiavelli's works as we can gather from his explicit declarations, from frequent imitations of his concepts and from his attempt at copying Machiavelli in the structure of his *Histories,* where the narrations of the different periods are preceded by general considerations which refer to themes of Machiavelli and at times to those of Aristotle. And what was unusual for that time, Segni noted the similarity between the two, or rather realized that Machiavelli's ideas had their origin in Aristotle. Segni translated Aristotle's *Politics* (1549) and at a certain point makes these observations:

From here [Aristotle] our Machiavelli in his *Discourses* derived that maxim of universal value, that the man who has made another great, will himself come to ruin.

Machiavelli in his book, *The Prince,* took many things from Aristotle on conspiracies.

But as Füter has observed, when Segni deals with this point in his *Histories* he quotes Machiavelli rather than Aristotle. He felt closer to his Florentine countryman.

Nardi too (1476–1563) mentions Machiavelli in connection with the conspiracy:

> Around him [Cosimo Rucellai] there gathered the friends already mentioned above, especially Zanobi Buondelmonti and Luigi Alamanni, for whom Machiavelli had already written and to whom he had dedicated his *Discourses,* certainly a work with a new idea, and as far as I know never before attempted by anyone else. Because of this book Machiavelli was greatly loved by them and was also helped financially by them and they delighted in his conversation, esteeming highly all his works—so that as far as their thoughts and deeds were concerned, Machiavelli was not without blame.[258]

It is clear that the Florentine historians wanted above all to point out the importance of the writer, and at the same time confess that the man was not without fault, that his works might be considered morally responsible for deplorable deeds.

More important than the other three is Varchi (1502–65). As a youth he had known Machiavelli at the meetings at the Orti Oricellari (Varchi, *Lessons on Poetry,* 1590) but he was convinced, or at least he said so in order to save appearances, that there was a clear-cut distinction between Machiavelli's genius and his morality:

> If to his intelligence in respect to state affairs and to the experience of things of this world, Machiavelli had joined an honourable viewpoint of life and a sincerity in describing customs, in my opinion he could be compared to ancient men of genius.[259]
>
> He [Zanobi Buondelmonti] had gained a great deal from Machiavelli without assuming any of his vices.[260]

In Varchi more than in the other historians is seen the formation of a Machiavelli legend which was to invade Europe. It starts with his death, which popular legend attributed to his learning that another person was chosen to fill his position as Secretary of the Commission of the Ten:

> This unexpected election was believed by many [as far as what is still said and believed] to be the cause in part at least, of Machiavelli's death, inasmuch as he tried, after his return with Guicciardini, to do all he could to get his old position of Secretary, but despite the support of Luigi Alamanni and Zanobi Buondelmonti, his greatest friends, he was replaced by Giannotto. Machiavelli, who could be called unlettered rather than literary, felt more suited than Giannotto for that office and realizing how much he was hated by everyone, he became sick and died. The reason for this great hatred was his obscene speech, and his not being very upright in his personal life. Because of his low social position he should not have written the book which he entitled *The Prince,* which he dedicated to Lorenzo di Piero di Lorenzo who he hoped would become the tyrannical Signore of Florence. This work, really ungodly and reprehensible— a book to be destroyed, as Machiavelli himself tried to do before it was printed after the upheaval of the state—to the wealthy seemed to advocate taking away their wealth, to the poor taking away their honour, and to both their liberty. [Here Varchi copies Busini.]
> At Machiavelli's death there occurred a very unusual thing: the virtuous as well as the wicked rejoiced—the wicked not only because they realized he was more wicked than they were, but also because he was cleverer than they were. Nevertheless, it was a pleasure to listen to him talk. He was thoughtful of his friends, a friend of good men. Nature should have given him either less genius or a better ethical sense.[261]

Revealing is Varchi's half-criticism of Machiavelli: "unlettered rather than literary". This was typical of the time in which literary ornaments served as screens to conceal absence of thought, and to express adulation towards social superiors. The historians that came after Machiavelli are superior to the chroniclers, but only because Machiavelli came in between and pointed the way towards modern interpretations of history, but they still remain far behind Machiavelli. They seek consolation for their lack of ideas by adhering to the rules of grammar and rhetoric, knowledge of which had made great strides at that time. In Italy, weakness of thought, cowardice and servility have always gone hand in hand with fastidious and over-refined writing.

7 Writers and Mannerists (Literati)

Florentine wits, literati, and playwrights continued to follow in the footsteps of Machiavelli and tried at least to preserve its artistic value despite his condemnation by the Church.

Lorenzo Strozzi in his *Second Comedy* (Ms. Ashburnham 606, Laurenziana Library, quoted by Tommasini, II, 420) shows that he remembered the *Mandragola*:

> In this world, in my judgment, it is more necessary to *seem* rather than to *be* good.

And more precisely the playwright of comedies, G. M. Cecchi (1518–87) says:

> However, as Machiavelli has already said, if men should return as do events, it might be possible that every hundred years we would come back. You know the old proverb: he who wants to know what will occur must look at what has happened.[262]

Doni, famous for his wit, (1513–74) often quotes Machiavelli and mistakenly attributes to him the comedy *The Secretary*. He edited a story written by Machiavelli, *Il Belphagor,* and in the *Marmi* he cautiously states that Machiavelli's works were "beautiful, but they teach things I don't like".[263]

Gelli (1498–1563), a Florentine shoemaker who wrote comedies, owes a great deal to Machiavelli; it is said his *Sporta* was based on Machiavelli's notes. (But who has ever seen these notes?) His *Circe* is an imitation of the *Cricket* of Plutarch, but also of Machiavelli's *Golden Ass,* and his *Error* comes from *Clizia:*

From this don't you see that man is never content with what Nature has given him (or so I think). There is always so much confusion, and many dangers and evil deeds abound everywhere so that no place can be found where there is no hostility. It would be best to live in the most bitter and abandoned solitude, and among the cruellest animals in existence, rather than in any well-governed province among men.[264]

But what is of special interest to us is the recurrent interest in Machiavelli despite his condemnation. Playwrights of comedies copy the vivacious dialogue of *Mandragola*, politicians the maxims of *The Prince*, historians the tales in the *Discourses*. Each one takes only what especially appeals to his own nature, what he understands and then quotes with discretion what he can use, at times even in opposition to Machiavelli's ideas (*The Cautio* of Possevino). Machiavelli the Florentine writer, the convivial and irreverent character, is more popular among other Florentines than Machiavelli the man of thought.

Donato Giannotti (1494–1563), Secretary of the Republic after Machiavelli, in one of his letters to Pietro Vettori, uses one of Machiavelli's witticisms at the expense of monks:

Like Machiavelli, I will tell about that monk whose head was split open by a crucifix that fell on him while he was praying. When urged by the other monks to forgive the crucifix, he answered he would but that it should attend to its own affairs and he would attend to his.

Later in full Counter-Reformation, animated by local pride, Poccianti collected a list of Florentine writers in a book entitled: *Catalogus scriptorum florentinorum omnis generis, quorum et memoria extat atque lucubrationes in literas relatae sunt ad nostra usque tempora,* 1589. In this list he has no intention of omitting the name of Machiavelli and he heaps praise on him:

He worked so hard in literature, he was so greatly appreciated for the light of his intelligence, and so resplendent were the subtleties of his inventions, and he was so stimulating and so varied and abundant that rightly all decided to call him an orator full of erroneous judgments, but a most amusing and instructive comedy writer and a most renowned and serious historian.

But naturally he had to add that because of Machiavelli's opposition to Christian faith and to the Catholic religion, the Council of Trent condemned all his works.

A great help to the spread of Machiavelli's ideas were certain authors' works in which some of his maxims were incorporated, at times literally, at times adulterated and at times sweetened, like the celebrated one of Francesco Sansovino (1521–83) that has been translated in many languages, *Propositioni, overo considerationi in materia di cose di stato sotto titolo di Avvertimenti, Avvedimenti civili et Concetti politici,* Vinegia, 1583; see, for example *Pensiero* XLI:

> A war that is necessary is just, and those arms are holy, where there is no other hope except in arms.

This concept, literally taken from Machiavelli (*Florentine Histories,* V 8, 505), is contrary to the Catholic doctrine of a "just" war. Thus *Pensiero* CCCXLIV:

> Men and arms can find money and bread, but money and bread cannot so easily find men and arms.

But Sansovino mixes in these things the notes of Guicciardini and others and everything becomes watered down in his style.

Later, from the testimony of the writer Magalotti, we learn that in the Florence of his time (1637–1712) there were still some followers of Machiavelli and he notes that "the presumed original manuscript of *The Prince* . . . is in the hands of a certain Jacopo Lippi, a very great Machiavellian".[265]

This local tradition of Machiavelli continued for a time but was founded not on his principal ideas, but on his having been Florentine. Even in the eighteenth century it persisted among the Tuscan Jansenists, and we have them to thank for the edition of his works published by Cambiagi, the first that was openly permitted.

8 Giovio

Of all the historians, the one who had the greatest influence on the legend of Machiavelli was Giovio (1483–1552), both because of the popularity of his work and also because three of the other above mentioned histories were not published until the eighteenth century.

Giovio was considered untruthful and corrupt even in his own time. He was certainly hostile to Machiavelli because of religious motives, parochial reasons and his turn of mind. Giovio is really not a historian but, as Croce aptly described him, "a curious type and collector of odd bits of classic lore, to whom one can turn for unusual information".

It is clear he did not learn the art of writing history from Machiavelli, inasmuch as his historical works are composed in the old humanistic manner of a series of biographies. His biography of Machiavelli served as a starting point for the origin of the Machiavelli legends that were beginning to form and that continued unchallenged until well into the nineteenth century. His biography sought an equilibrium between praising the man of natural genius (without schooling) and condemning him for his heretical and immoral ideas, which are mysteriously adumbrated:

> Machiavelli was so endowed by nature that although he hardly knew Latin he almost succeeded in attaining a good style of expression.

Of Machiavelli's works he knew the *Florentine Histories*, *The Prince* (although he does not mention the title), *The Art of War* (always through hearsay) and perhaps the *Discourses*. He is the first to mention the light works, like the *Mandragola*, along with the serious ones:

> But we admire the Etruscan (Tuscan) puns, like those in the comedies of ancient Aristophanes and especially in Machiavelli's comedy, Nicia (*Mandragola*).

But today we would say he only knew these books from their covers. The value of the works is so distorted that it is clear he had not read them carefully. In certain assertions he is positively untruthful.

Giovio reproves Machiavelli for having accepted writing the history of Florence for the Medicis, and for having praised Brutus and Cassius, and thus being responsible for the conspiracy in which Diacceto lost his life. Giovio confirmed the legend that Machiavelli's death was caused by a restorative tonic and that he died mocking religion (a mocker and an atheist). It is strange that later the atheists and French deists among the Encyclopaedists hung on the lips of Giovio, a false historian, a false priest and a false moralist.

9   The Plagiarists

The history of the plagiarism of Machiavelli's *The Prince* is well known, but it has not been examined from a psychological and historical angle.

Machiavelli had no sooner written the greater part of *The Prince* than he feared that some one would take advantage of that concentration of contemporary experiences and ancient readings that had been distilled by him. On this matter he wrote to Vettori:

> I have talked with Filippo about this little work of mine that I have spoken of, whether it is good to give it or not to give it; and if it is good to give it, whether it would be good to take it myself, or whether I should send it. Not giving it would make me fear that at the least Guiliano will not read it, and that this rascal Ardinghelli will get himself honour from this latest work of mine.[266]

It seems incredible but a few years later, not Ardinghelli, but a stolid, loquacious and undiscerning professor of Aristotelian theories sought fame with a book that was four-fifths a paraphrase, and in some places a literal copy of *The Prince*. It was published on March 26, 1523 but had already been printed on October 3, 1522. The author was Agostino Niphus da Sessa (1474–1538 or 1545, see Naudé, *Opusc.* 1645), professor at the University of Pisa. He has left in all 44 volumes, which no one has the courage to tackle. One of these is his plagiarism of *The Prince*, entitled *De regnandi peritia*. He had already published a book on the problem of the prince (*De Principe*), and later in 1526 he published another, *De rege et tyranno*, both remote from Machiavelli's ideas which he appropriated for his *De regnandi*, written and published between the other two. It is important to note that in Niphus' book, the last chapter of Machiavelli's *The Prince* is missing (the liberation of Italy as the final goal of the prince) and he has substituted a fifth book, which is as banal as his other works and a bit in the vein of Aristotle: "In the fifth book I have shown the method of ruling in an honest way"(!)

The first person to denounce the plagiarism was Giuseppe Ferrari in what is still considered his best work, *Corso sugli scrittori politici italiani* (1862), and he did so with his characteristic vehemence:

> A brazen plagiarism of Machiavelli which he copied word for word without using any quotation marks, and then prostituted his larceny by dedicating it to the Emperor.[267]

But probably Giunta, Machiavelli's first publisher, was aware of this plagiarism. In his preface to the edition of Machiavelli's *The Prince* of 1532 he stated he was driven to publish it because: "Already there have been people who have translated it in Latin and have had it published as their own."

And Blado, in his preface to Machiavelli's *Discourses* of 1531, said: "Like the famous crows of Phaedrus who adorned themselves with peacock feathers, some writers have appropriated as their own the works of Machiavelli in order to gain glory."

There have been controversies on this subject and some scholars have even affirmed that Machiavelli copied Niphus. A definitive study accepted by all serious scholars was made by Nourrisson:

In truth one is amazed and can hardly believe one's eyes to find in the work of Niphus all the substance of Machiavelli expressed in the same words, transposed one after another, abbreviated, divided or copied wholly. Without doubt, in the *De regnandi peritia,* the maxims of *The Prince* have lost some of their poisoned wisdom, and of their morbid colouring, somewhat like poisonous plants picked at the summit of the Alps which become discoloured and dried in a herbarium. But the origin is no less recognizable, and consequently one is led to ask how such a theft could have been perpetrated, especially without eliciting any protest.

Nothing more need be said; nor do I think the recent study of Valletta has added anything to the conclusions of Nourrisson.

10   The purge and the Tuscans

With the Counter-reformation, Machiavelli became one of the authors most strongly rejected by the Church.

Much more notable is the esteem of Tuscan writers for Machiavelli based on patriotic solidarity. The condemnation of his ideas was accepted by them without any conviction and resulted in their unsuccessful attempt to republish him in an expurgated edition as was being done at that time with many authors, like Boccaccio.

Despite their obedience to the Church, the Tuscans did not willingly seem to accept the condemnation of a writer who was such a paragon of the highest traditions of the spirit of Florence, a region of Italy whose natives are noted for their independence and free and irreverent use of the language.

The first idea of making an expurgated edition comes, as I believe Sorrentino has shown, from the writer Gerolamo Muzio, born at Padua in 1496, who owed his nickname, Giustinopolitano, to his origin in Capodistria. He became acclimatized, and lived mostly in Tuscany where he died in 1526. With a greater spirit of inquiry than Toffanin has given him credit for, he saw clearly the poison in this saying of Machiavelli and realized it was not at all Christian:

> Among all men, those are worthy of praise who have been leaders or founders of religions.[268]

Machiavelli put on an equal footing a pagan like Numa Pompilio, Moses, Mahomet, and Christ—to him they were all human and all founders of religions. But after having denounced this heresy against the divinity of Christ, Muzio states:

> *Eug.* What do you really think of that book of his?
> *Nob.* That it is a good and useful book, from which many things pertaining to civil life can be learnt—but there is in it also too much that poisons men's minds. And I would think it an excellent idea to expunge it and to publish it expurgated—so that everyone could read it. And this can be done by removing a very few pages, and here and there a few lines. In the chapter where I have noted those audacities, by changing it or rather by removing fewer than ten lines, everything would be in order—because the rest of it is indeed a beautiful chapter.[269]

In 1572, at the instigation of the Commission of Cardinals charged with the revision of the Index, an edition was prepared under the supervision of two cousins, Nicolò Machiavelli and Guiliano de' Ricci, and of a theologian. The text still exists. But the two descendants of Machiavelli, above all Giuliano de' Ricci, to whom we owe the preservation of many of Machiavelli's papers, did not want to have the name of the author substituted by another name. (This occurred with *The Art of War* in Spain.)

This expurgation met with the approval of the Tuscan writer Pier Vettori, who in one of his letters to Cardinal Guglielmo Sirleto (*Prose fiorentine*, Vol. IV, 32–3) written in 1578, tells him that the two descendants of Machiavelli had with great diligence read and re-examined the works of their great forbear and had expurgated them considerably.

11 The Jesuits

The Jesuits were too cultured, intelligent and loyal to the Pope not to note immediately in Machiavelli's works an enemy of Christianity and Catholicism. And they were among the first to denounce him, oppose him, and have him placed on the Index Librorum Prohibitorum. Yet almost immediately afterwards many Europeans were to accuse them of being Machiavellian, and in Protestant countries a popular equation between Jesuitical and Machiavellian was reached. The sentence, "The end justifies the means", which at least literally is not found in either the Jesuits or in Machiavelli, was attributed to both of them.

But in general it can be said that the Italian Jesuits who saw the danger in Machiavelli's works and denounced him, did not understand him. Above all, they never brought forth any positive or serious arguments to refute his doctrines. Famous, for example, is Antonio Possevino (1534–1611) eminent diplomat and colourful personality of the time, who wrote a *Judicium* on four heretical writers, the last of whom is Machiavelli (he also includes Gentillet, from whose works he learnt all that he knew of Machiavelli):

> Beware of the works of Machiavelli, as well as of those written against him by an Anti-Machiavelli without signing them.

This notice to readers begins with a sort of eulogy of Machiavelli:

> We have said elsewhere that there was no lack of genius and perspicacity in Machiavelli, but of religion and of practical matters, and whoever lacks these things, if he should try to fly, would inevitably fall.

But the rest is a series of phrases, some taken from Machiavelli, some attributed to Machiavelli by Gentillet, whose refutations do not indicate great intellectual ability— as when Possevino makes use of many historical examples to show that the princes who upheld Christian truth were helped by God to win: "No Catholic prince (leader) who followed God in his soul was ever conquered by the enemy."

For many years editions of Machiavelli's works were published with the addition of this *cautela* of the Most Reverend Possevino, like a passport. Perhaps this was not from conviction, the intention of the publishers being to sell books.

12   Paolo Paruta (1540–98)

Along the path cleared first by Guicciardini, but with less vigour in thought and style, is the Venetian Paolo Paruta's criticism of Machiavelli. When you read his *Discourses,* where he discusses in an academic manner which of two people is more important, or what political action is more beneficial, the lesson to be reached is never positive but dubitative. An exception is the case of the politics of Venice, where Paruta's thought is purely apologetic. He seems to say that inasmuch as history is always different, it does not teach anything and no rules can be drawn from it. Paruta is opposed to the idea of extracting from experiences of the past maxims of action for the present, and he conducts a continuous polemic against Machiavelli, but it is tacit, since this name

already famous for the strangeness of the problems he wrote about in his *Discourses,* and now condemned by the Apostolic See to perpetual oblivion, cannot even be mentioned.

Paruta defends governments that have not increased their territory, like Venice, which have however endured as long as Rome and have given greater happiness to their subjects— assuredly a thought that is extraneous to the bellicosity and heroism of Machiavelli. Notwithstanding his mention of the Holy See, Paruta's historical concept is not profoundly Christian. It has been justly noted that in his work God is equated with Fortune, which dominates human affairs. He saw in the balance of power of the various princes in Italy a hope for tranquillity and a peaceful Italy. His style was well suited to this vision of life.

13   Botero, Boccalini, Sarpi and others

In the seventeenth century many writers made use of Machiavelli and referred to his ideas, but they did not dare admit they had read him. In his study of the period, Curcio writes:

> This Machiavellianism of the anti-Machiavellists, one of the most characteristic aspects of political thought during the Counter-reformation, is found everywhere—in followers of Livy and Tacitus and in secular and clerical writers. It consists of hating Machiavelli on the surface, without even mentioning him. . . . It is the real key to the Counter-reformation and to the new politics.[270]

In a special way, as Toffanin has so well shown,* Machiavelli's name and his ideas are hidden behind quotations from Tacitus. Salvator Rosa (1615–73) in his own way was right when he noted (in verse form) that "with Machiavelli we see the transformation of the *raison d'état* into dogmas, notwithstanding the Gospels of Matthew, Mark and John".

It should be kept in mind, however, that the political thought of the seventeenth century leaned more heavily on Machiavelli's ideas regarding the "preservation" of states than their "establishment". In the latter category were the "lions", whose Italians who arose from the plebeian class to conquer a state and establish a new one by means of *virtù*. But the era of the lions was over; foxes rather than lions were developing. The most outstanding theorist reflecting the new tendency was Botero (1540–1617). Through Botero's work the phrase, *raison d'état*, became famous:

> The state is a continuous dominion over people, and *raison d'état* instructs how to establish, preserve and enlarge a dominion thus secured. . . . It seems that (this instruction) embraces preservation rather than the other two; and of the other two, enlargement rather than establishment. In fact, the *raison d'état* presupposes the Prince and the already established state, the former almost as a craftsman and the latter as his material.[271]

* G. Toffanin, *Machiavelli e il Tacitismo*, 1921.

The language of this passage is completely Machiavellian; even the Prince is considered as a craftsman and the people as material. Yet three times out of four Machiavelli's examples show that he is thinking of those who have established, or taken possession of, a state. He invariably set his gaze on the initial phase, which seems the least important to Botero. Botero goes on to say:

> It is more difficult to preserve than to enlarge a state. A state is acquired by force and is preserved with wisdom; force is common to many, wisdom to few.[272]

Machiavelli sees the Christian religion as an enfeeblement of mankind. On the other hand, Botero and perhaps also Castiglione, recommend an alliance between governments and the Christian religion as an aid in the enslavement of subjects:

> Among all laws, there is none more favourable to princes than the Christian one; because it subjugates not only the body and the wealth of the subjects, where it is needed, but even the emotions and thoughts. It stipulates obedience to an undisciplined as well as to a gentle prince; and holds that injustice can be resorted to in order to maintain peace.[273]

In other ways, Botero did not lack a certain theoretical Machiavellian courage. He well understood the completely selfish nature of politics:

> Princes, as Polybius teaches [in this case, Polybius and not Tacitus replaces Machiavelli], are made in such a way that they have no friends—nor enemies, in an absolute sense; but towards friends and foes they act in a way that is to their own advantage.[274]
> Raison d'état is little else than selfish reason.[275]

Whereas Botero's work is gloomy and suggests prison bars, another Italian, Boccalini (1551–1613) presents a carnival of fables, masks and jokes, in the form of epigrams, pungent witticisms, admonitions, apologies and quotations. He revives, in a more lively way, an aspect of Machiavelli's doctrine. People are pictured as sheep who let themselves be shorn but who have "sharp teeth" with which they can defend themselves. Here is found the apology for the northern people Machiavelli so greatly admired—the Swiss, Germans and Dutch. It is a mixture of Machiavellianism and anti-Mechiavellianism, the latter sincerely felt, as in his aversion to using religion as an instrument of the state.[276] It must be said that he had a precise idea of Machiavelli's fundamental problem when he invents a competition for the best definition of *raison d'état* and gives the prize to the following:

> *Raison d'état* is a useful law for states but is contrary to the law of God and of mankind.[277]

In Botero, Machiavelli's thought became a gloomy swamp; in Boccalini it was a series of sparkling brooks which made Europe curious and impatient to know more about the subject. Strangely enough this was especially true in Spain, despite his anti-Spanish cast of thought.

A practical politician of this period, also an intellectual, become impregnated with Machiavelli's ideas, above all for the independence of the State from the Church: Fra Paolo Sarpi, a theological defender of the rights of Venice against Rome. He made expediency and politics identical, and his thought could not have been expressed in a more Machiavellian way than in the words of his Advice to the Republic of Venice:

> Under the title of Justice one must put everything that refers to the service of the state; because the Prince [Sarpi means the head of any state, even of a Republican one like that of Venice] has no greater justice than to remain Prince and to keep the state under his control. Some broaden this reason to include all that makes it possible to increase the state, but in this it is not possible to avoid events that might destroy rather than maintain the quality of justice. Therefore to speak if not with absolute truth at least with likely truth, we always say that we consider justice to be the quality that is required for the preservation of the state.[278]

To Botero goes political credit for having indicated the supremacy of politics with those fear-inspiring words, *raison d'état*. Though the term had been used earlier by Della Cosa (1503–1556), as Rodolfo De Mattei has shown, it became famous only through Botero's work. For a long time the phrase *raison d'état* seemed, especially to liberals, to be the quintessence of the shrewdness, trickery and rascality that tyrants were advised to make use of. The acceptance of *raison d'état* by such Catholic writers as Botero also shows the difficult situation in which the Church found itself regarding the Machiavellian doctrine that evil is necessary in politics. Catholics interpreted *raison d'état* as universal reason.

This is at the root of the fact previously noted that, during the seventeenth century, Machiavelli even though unnamed is always present. The great number of books and reflections on the *raison d'état* which appear from this century on (to disappear in the nineteenth century, at least under that name) show that Machiavelli's thought remained like a thorn in the side of those concerned with the art of politics.

"We all have it on the tip of our tongues," says Scipione Ammirato (1531–1601) in referring to the *raison d'état*. He belongs to that group who waver between accepting the evidence of the thesis and a desire not to accept it. He defines *raison d'état* as:

Infringement of ordinary law for public benefit, that is, in place of a greater and more universal law.[279]

A representative poet of the time, Torquato Tasso, was to say: "For faith, for the good of one's country, everything is legitimate." But no one is able to show how this principle is in accord with Christian precepts, and all writers try to conceal this contradiction from their readers.

In other parts of his work it seems as though Ammirato were in agreement with Machiavelli's dreams for an Italian national militia:

We can surely believe and hope that in our time a man may arise to put in order the old militia. A gleam of hope for this reorganization was offered by Giovanni dei Medici, not a prince but of the nobility, who was able to form an exemplary group of soldiers who were for a long time unquestionably an asset to the Italian militia. At Giovanni's death the soldiers wore a black band of mourning and were thus known as "Soldiers of the Black Band".[280]

That Machiavelli's spirit was alive and in force in the seventeenth century is also seen in the collection of writings entitled *Politicians and Moralists of the seventeenth Century,* published by Benedetto Croce. It contains extracts from books by Famiano Strada, Ludovico Zuccolo, Torquato Accetto, Antonio G. Brignole Sale, and Virgilio Malvezzi. They follow, teach, and ignore Machiavelli (without quoting or denouncing him) and ascribe the kernel of his thought to Tacitus. The soundest thinker is Zuccolo, who makes a distinction between *raison d'état* and politics:

> Politics seems to aim principally at the public good, the *raison d'état* more at the good of those who are heads of governments; as a consequence the former has an honest and pious appearance, whereas the latter very often seems wicked and impious.

Sèttala follows him and dilutes his thought. They all smother the little they learnt from Machiavelli under a great deal of Aristotle. Some who have more lively minds, like Malvezzi, appear enlightened, as in this observation:

> All states, even tyrannies, are governed by élites. When magistrates do not form the government, officers of the state do; and most governments are republics.

This statement makes him a direct precursor of Pareto and Mosca. In all these writings, the *raison d'état* appears in a sinister light as a doctrine to keep the state under the power of the prince, in violation of moral law. There abounds in these writers knowledge of a multitude of psychological motives that are certainly absent in Machiavelli.

14 The Utopians

The importance of Machiavelli's thought can better be appraised if we compare him to his contemporary, Thomas More (1478–1535). Almost at the same time as *The Prince,* More wrote his

Utopia (1517), which named and described an entire series of political dreams that are not yet ended. They fulfil a need, irrepressible in mankind, to transform irrational reality into an ideal. *You will dream,* seems to be the fate of humankind, *and yet you will never attain your dream.* Machiavelli was considered the arch-enemy of these authors of Utopia. Yet this need is so deeply ingrained in man that even Machiavelli paid tribute to it when he set about forming a perfect constitution for Florence. He describes in great detail the most minute devices needed for the "perfect constitution" which he is designing, completely aware of following in the footsteps of Plato and Aristotle, whom he had criticized, and upholding the following:

> If Solon and Lycurgus were not able to establish a civil life, this was not due to their ignorance but to their inability to put it into practice.[281]

Reading about Machiavelli's blueprint for the perfect Republic led Burckhardt to call him a "watchmaker".

It is likely that Machiavelli knew this little book of More's because it is mentioned in the correspondence between him and Vettori. Machiavelli's work on the Florentine Constitution must not have been considered Utopian in his time, inasmuch as it sought to fashion a constitution for Florence suitable to the customs and spirit of his people. The Utopians never took reality into account at all. Even Machiavelli did not realize that in these terms he was his own critic; while considering in what way "the constitution could endure", he wrote:

> It will always be obeyed when each man has a part in its management, and when each one knows his duty and in whom he can confide; and when no citizen, either for fear of losing his position or for personal gain, becomes ambitious.[282]

This resembles the political solutions of present-day pacifists who say that men *only* need to love one another, or that *if* all people understood their own interests, wars would cease. Very true indeed, except for that *only* and that *if*.

Among the Utopians there is one who occupies a special place in the history of Machiavellianism—Tommaso Campanella (1568–1639) author of *The City of the Sun*. His is an interesting case, inasmuch as he is more anti-Machiavellian and at the same time more Machiavellian than all the other writers who side for or against the author of *The Prince*. In his works there abound maxims that are completely Machiavellian. He was to say: "It is right to lie, if by doing so good is accomplished."[283] This, however, he could have taken from Plato. In one poem he dreamed that Christ returned, armed: "If you return to earth, oh Lord, come armed."[284] This is a reference to Machiavelli calling Savonarola an unarmed prophet.

Campanella is an intellectual and puts his faith in the subjugation of matter and of history to the power of the human mind. He believes in reason and he combats Machiavelli because the latter interprets politics as an art which leads men to religion in the following way:

> The art of drawing men to religion through fear of God, as buffaloes are drawn by a ring in their nose.[285]

The doctrine of the political use of religion is the one at which Campanella aims his darts most frequently in his attacks on Machiavelli. His dream is not satisfied by a Utopian island or city (even though he writes *The City of the Sun*), but reaches towards the realization of a monarchy and an illuministic theocracy which would dominate the world. He feels that Machiavelli's nationalism is the real obstacle and therefore he fiercely attacks it, along with all schismatic movements. He calls Machiavelli "impious", "sad", "pig", "sheep", "most ignorant of sciences", "vial of God's wrath", and denounces him as a bad cook who prepared infernal dishes for princes which will end by bringing ruin on them. He is not a hypocrite like Botero, who continuously drinks from the Machiavellian well and then writes over it "poisoned spring". In his arrogance, Campanella does not realize that his plan to destroy politics can only be Machiavellian. He had no more respect for people than did Machiavelli, and at times had a greater contempt for them than Machiavelli ever had, as in his saying:

> People are like beasts, fickle and gross, who are unaware of their strength.[286]

It is clear that Campanella contradicts himself at every turn. He is a disciple of Galileo and a believer in astrology; a supporter of the universal rule of the Church and of that of the King of Spain; a universalist and also a nationalist; opposed to political exploitation of religion, but ready to make use of it. He belongs in the movement against Luther, but actually his dream surpasses his time. He belongs to the Counter-reformation in appearance only.

All the Utopias ever written are in opposition to Machiavelli's thought, and contribute nothing to the knowledge of man and of politics. But all consist more or less of realistic elements of the time, combined in a fantastic manner and revealing a criticism of the prevailing conditions of the life of their time. Later Sorel in his theory of myths saw in the Utopias a creative and moving force of mankind that Machiavelli did not acknowledge. Machiavelli placed self-interest above ideals.

MACHIAVELLI
AND THE PHILOSOPHERS

1 *Francis Bacon* (1561–1626)

All the philosophers of the seventeenth century evolved from Galileo, but in two separate currents: the rationalists, like Descartes, made use only of the mathematical method, and this continued up to Spinoza; the empiricists utilized only the experimental method, beginning with Bacon and ending with Hume. The inheritance of Galileo was thus split in two. It is felt that here is something missing in both heirs, although in their fields each advanced with logic and an admirable and productive courage.

For a long time it was believed that Bacon had paid a single but very important tribute to Machiavelli, when he touched upon one of the most fundamental aspects of his thought. Bacon says approximately this:

> We must be grateful to Machiavelli and to authors like him, who write about what men do and not about what they should do. It is not possible to join the wisdom of the serpent to the innocence of the dove, if we do not know all the characteristics of the serpent—his meanness, his dragging his belly, his slipperiness, his inconstancy, his malice, his poison: and all the rest—that is, all the forms and aspects of evil. Because without this knowledge, virtue is vulnerable and defenceless. On the contrary, honest people could not even redeem evil ones without the help of the knowledge of evil. Men of corrupt minds believe that honesty is characteristic of a simple soul.[287]

Bacon here cleverly defends Machiavelli in the same way as did his first publisher, Giunta, who said: "The doctor must also know about poisons."

In the Latin version of the text, Bacon adds another eulogy of Machiavelli when he says that, in order to attain this necessary knowledge of evil, it must be *"aperte et indissimulanter"*. Here he is acknowledging one of the characteristics of the spirit of Machiavelli, "open and without dissimulation".

To Professor Orsini goes the credit of having brought to light, by comparing the English text and the Latin one, many points in which Bacon made use of Machiavelli's thought. Orsini maintains also that Bacon was responsible for the progress of Machiavellianism, in his application of the science of the state to the personal fortunes of men, thus making Bacon a precursor of Gracian.

Bacon then was drenched in Machiavellianism and it must be added that in this he is an exception among Englishmen of his time. He was also unusual in openly quoting him and praising his opinions, and for having a broad knowledge not only of *The Prince,* but also of the *Discourses,* probably of the *Florentine Histories* and even of the *Picture of Things in France.*

2 Descartes (1596–1650)

After having read the *Discourses,* Descartes admitted not having "remarked anything bad" in them. His objections, which are out of focus, refer to matters of details:

> Machiavelli has not made a distinction between princes who have acquired a state by just means, and those who have acquired it by illegitimate means; and he has generally given to all of them precepts which are only applicable to the latter.[288]

The essence of Machiavelli's thought eluded him. For Machiavelli all politics being immoral, he had already recognized the difference between a legitimate and an illegitimate prince.

3   Thomas Hobbes (1588–1679)

What can be said about Hobbes, if not that he seems the closest and yet the farthest from Machiavelli? It is true that for Hobbes a man without a state is a beast, who lives in a condition of perpetual war with his neighbours:

It is manifest, that during the time men live without a common Power to keep them all in awe, they are in that condition which is called warre; and such a warre, as if of every man against every man.[289]

But in Hobbes the state is an artificial state that came into existence from an agreement between men to save themselves from this eternal war. It is not a living animal (a mixed body), as it is for Machiavelli.

Men, for the attaining of peace, and conservation of themselves thereby, have made an Artificiall Man, which we call a Commonwealth; so also they have made Artificiall chains, called Civil Laws. . . .[290]

Hobbes' thesis is based on physical sciences, Machiavelli's on biology and history. Hobbes tends to justify the absolute power of the King of England, Machiavelli a doctrine of politics that deals with all the forms of government. Hobbes is a utilitarian, and makes the state spring from a contract between men, with the motive of fear, while Machiavelli has a keen sense of the moral problem; and the power of heroism and ambition pervades all his pages. In Hobbes the state is born of calculation; men do not seem free. He proposes not growth and conquests but stability and welfare, comforts and amusements. The state is a shelter, indeed an escape, from the ravages of war, not a path leading towards other conflicts. Machiavelli's state springs from force, not from fear; men create it with their own *virtù*, and it is imposed by great minds on lesser ones. His image of the state is that of an animal-being. For Hobbes the image is that of a watch, a mechanism that cannot create other lives. To put it briefly, Hobbes is English and

Machiavelli Italian. Perhaps when Hobbes wrote *homo homini lupus* (man is wolf to man) he remembered a phrase Machiavelli put in the lips of Ciompi of Florence:

> From this we see that men eat each other up and the weakest are always the losers.[291]

Unless he had in mind Bacon's *homo homini draco* (man is a dragon to man), Hobbes may have remembered Plautus: "A man is not a man but a wolf, to those who do not know him." Or perhaps his own observation of life made him draw the same conclusions.

4   *Spinoza* (*1632–77*)

The quotations of philosophers are rare in Spinoza and they bear witness to a special appraisement. For that reason many eyebrows are raised when they read a sentence in his *Political Treatise* (but who reads it any longer?) in which the name of Machiavelli appears. He is praised as being "most acute" and "most prudent". Hs is also spoken of as a "prolix writer", which is contrary to everyone else's opinion. Machiavelli has always been most commonly praised for his concentrated style.

A prince, dominated only by the desire to command, was inconceivable to Spinoza and since he admired Machiavelli he imagined he wrote *The Prince* to warn people against dictators:

> Perhaps Machiavelli wanted to show that a free people should by no means entrust their own safety to one man who, unless he is conceited and thinks he can please everyone, must fear traps set for him at all times.[292]

As to the general laws that compare political and physical bodies, and find the reasons for their dissolution in their atomistic growth and death, he is in complete agreement with Machiavelli.

> The primary cause for the dissolution of such states is the one noted by that most acute Florentine that from time to time the state, like the human body, needs a cure.[293]

A scholar (Pollock) has fairly well seen what beliefs united Machiavelli and Spinoza: first, the state must be the master in its own house and cannot tolerate rivals, in Spinoza's as well as in Machiavelli's times, such as those who with a pretext of a spiritual mission assumed an absolute power over men's consciences (this is the anticlericalism of free thinkers); second, affairs of state must be entrusted to competent people; third, human actions are generally determined by selfish motives rather than rational forces; for that reason, the legislator and statesman must take into account so-called "base" motives rather than those which are usually called "altruistic". Some of these propositions might be applied at the present time to threats of a different kind of government; for example, in America capitalistic forces and monopolies of the unions limit the freedom of the state.

5 Vanini (1585–1619)

In the writings of that bungler named Julius Caesar Vanini, composed in large part of quotations and plagiarisms, Machiavelli is mentioned. Vanini seems on the surface such a saccharine apologist for Catholicism as to make one think that he was not serious and was trying to spread incredulity by pretending to combat it (he was found to be a heretic and was burned at the stake).

In the preface to his *Amphitheatrum* the sect of "Machiavelli-politicians" takes first place and to them Vanini attributes the spreading of atheism among "Christian Catholics". For him Machiavelli is the *prince of atheists*. Perhaps Vanini takes pleasure in saying that Machiavelli thought that religions were lies invented by statesmen in order to make the underlings respect laws, and confirmed this by quoting from no less a person than St. Augustine: *"Expedit in religione civitates falli*—People must be deceived in matters of religion."[294] But this quotation of St. Augustine was misinterpreted by Vanini. It gives the opinion not of St. Augustine but of a pagan, "the most learned pontifex Scevola". St. Augustine states that paganism advocates lies rather than the truth.

Even Pascal used this passage of St. Augustine in a sceptical manner:

> The wisest legislators said that for the good of mankind one must often delude them; and another, a good politician, said: *"Cum veritatem qua liberetur ignoret, expedit quod fallitur*—He who does not know the truth that frees, must be deceived."[295]

Pascal quoted St. Augustine from Montaigne and modified it. Something similar could have been found in St. Thomas (*Summa*, I^a, I^æ, qu. 9, art. 3).

Vanini refers to the strange praise of Machiavelli for St. Francis and St. Dominic, who saved the Church which was almost destroyed. Then adds: "But how could the Church fall if it was instituted by the will of God?" We don't know whether Vanini was in earnest or trying to implant a doubt.

He uses an odd designation for *The Prince* (to be repeated by Leibnitz) and called it a Gordian Knot. In any event it is interesting to see that Machiavelli appears in Vanini not as a representative of a political theory, but as a materialistic philosopher.

6   Leibnitz (1646–1716)

What else could possibly be expected of Leibnitz except that he completely misunderstood Machiavelli? He was the philosopher of logic and of a universal language; he believed that the world was "the best of all possible worlds" and that the plan of Bernardin de Saint Pierre for peace among nations was attainable in his lifetime:

> I am convinced that such a plan is generally feasible and that its execution would be one of the most useful things in the world.[296]

In politics he was Aristotelian: "The political writings of Aristotle cannot be praised enough," but he did not seem to realize how much Machiavelli had taken from the Master. Politics for Leibnitz was "morality":

Politics is nothing more than ethics.[297]

He realized that for Machiavelli the criterion of politics was expediency. And here and there in referring to some of Machiavelli's maxims, he agreed with them and at times appropriated them for his own purposes: "True is the saying that arms, not wealth, are the sinew of politics."[298]

He used the same phrase of Vanini when he said that in *The Prince* Machiavelli had constructed a Gordian Knot that could never be untied but had to be cut. He did not understand Machiavelli. As he said, he admired him "although I condemn the school of thought of Machiavelli".[299]

MACHIAVELLI
AND THE EIGHTEENTH CENTURY

1 Alfieri (1749–1803)

Alfieri is to be mentioned only because of his unbounded enthusiasm for Machiavelli whom he called "great", "divine
genius", and "beholden to no one". He also "illuminated the
world and eviscerated the nature and the rights of man". Also "in
his *Prince* here and there can be found some immoral and tyrannical maxims. These are brought forth . . . only in order to reveal
the ambitions and shrewd cruelties of princes, rather than to
teach princes how to make use of them."

Typical of the slant of Alfieri's observations is the twisted and
strange picture he presents of Machiavelli, stressing only one
aspect of the Florentine, his republicanism. It would be like
drawing a picture of a man with the thumb so large that the rest
of the body is hardly visible.

The people Alfieri admired became heroes *ipso facto,* and
Machiavelli is one of his heroes. In his *Of the Prince and of Literature*
(1778–86), Alfieri borrows the title of his final chapter and its ideas
from Machiavelli's *Plea to rid Italy of foreigners.* This humanistic
concept—unchanged from the time of the Romans, from Petrarch
to Carducci, from Alfieri to the young Leopardi—is that the
Italian peninsula was destined to dominate the world. Alfieri starts
the reduction of Machiavelli, from one who had laid the foundation for an understanding of a profound human problem into
an apostle of the national independence of a European country.
This idea persisted and set the tone of the Risorgimento period.

2 Giuseppi Baretti (1719–89)

Baretti, who was a better critic than Alfieri, was devoted to Machiavelli and published his complete works in London (in Italian). This edition was an understandable source of irritation to the Tuscans because of the preface, and perhaps also because of its competition with the edition they were preparing for the publisher Cambiagi in Florence. Baretti saw in Machiavelli only a writer who was not bombastic, and who expressed himself clearly.

Baretti's judgment of Machiavelli comes out by fits and starts and while at times it is electrifying, it is never profound. He leaves no appreciable mark on the history of Machiavellianism, any more than did Alfieri.

MACHIAVELLI IN FRANCE

1 Corbinelli

Jacopo Corbinelli, who was born in 1535 and who published many Italian books in France towards the end of the century, is credited with making Machiavelli known to the French Court.

His copy of Machiavelli's *Discourses,* with marginal notes in his own handwriting, is in the National Library of Paris. These notes show that Machiavelli's real meaning escaped him and became, in his limited mind, only the purveyor of political expedients which were relevant to his own time.

2 Hostility of the French

In general Machiavelli did not like the French and the French did not like Machiavelli, with a few exceptions of course. As Pintard writes:

The conclusion of all research made on the influence of Machiavelli in France is that if he was considered the best-known political theoretician in Court during the sixteenth century, he was also the most detested and the most scorned. He was approved, or so said his rabid adversaries, by the princes [rulers] and the courtiers, but was opposed by the Huguenots, the humanists of the Evangelical order, lawyers, judges, the Catholics who were mystics, and the Preachers of the League. His name was on everyone's lips but there was hardly a decent man who did not consider him an object of horror. The weight of his influence on the contemporaries of Montaigne and Charron, of Bodin and of Juste Lipse, was very light. In twenty works he was bitterly combated, in four or five credited

226

with an idea, an example, a formula—but even in these he was denigrated. Only the translators very timidly took it upon themselves to defend him. Can you imagine that under these conditions anyone would dare take him for a model or a guide, or meditate line for line on his teachings, or adapt them to the political condition of their times, in brief, would anyone attempt to inject into French soil a seed of this Florentine plant?[300]

And yet the knowledge of Machiavelli's writings was more general in France than in other countries. More of his works were translated and were probably more generally read because of the similarity of the two languages and the affinity between the two literatures. But the knowledge of his ideas certainly was not profound.

Usually it is held that the opposition between the logical spirit of the French whose national genius is to consider political problems from a purely intellectual viewpoint, and the historical spirit of some Italian thinkers was the main reason for this hostility to Machiavelli which ranged from Catholics and Protestants to unbelievers.

But it might be more accurately said that in France Machiavelli was very well known, greatly imitated (literally so), attacked or defended (as a thinker) but that he never penetrated French thought. He remained alien even when he seemed to be accepted. There were no developments of the Machiavellian spirit in France as there were in England (Bacon) or in Germany (Hegel).

But in addition to the anti-historic spirit of the French, rivalry between the two nations and French chauvinism played their parts. From the start Machiavelli was considered the foreigner who introduced new political systems in France. This motif began to appear in Gentillet and in such Huguenots as Agrippa d'Aubigné (1552–1630), in his work entitled Les Tragiques (1511), and in Henri d'Estienne (1531–98), who accused Catherine of Medici of having filled the Court with the worst Italian elements who were inspired by Machiavelli. In his poem Monitrix Musa, d'Estienne attempted to refute The Prince.

However Machiavellianism bore fruit, even in France, in the

form of discussions about the *raison d'état*. It is seen in the work of Jean Bodin (1520–96). He attempts to create the conscience of the modern state, from a viewpoint different from Machiavelli's, inasmuch as it does not spring from human nature but from law. He is a man of politics, as he was called in his time, a supporter of the sovereignty of the State against the Church. (About these men who accepted the *raison d'état* and who however condemned Machiavelli, see Meinecke.)

Gabriel Naudé (1600–53), exposer of the iniquities of rulers, sceptic and Italophile Frenchman, apologist of the Massacre of St. Bartholomew, praised Machiavelli in this way:

> This excellent and prodigious mind, greatly esteemed in Italy, whose ideas were defended by Gaspare Scioppio, a foe of the Jesuits. . . .[301]

But what did Scioppio understand of Machiavelli? And elsewhere Naudé mentions Procopio and Machiavelli as those who

> uttered in public the secrets of rulers, the occult frauds and wickedness of state officials, and all those things that in a country's administration should be kept hidden. It would be like exposing the sacred rituals of the Eleusian Mysteries, and presenting Diana unclothed to the public gaze.[302]

3 Montesquieu

There is only one exception to the infertility of thought in France regarding Machiavelli, and it is the important one of Montesquieu. He was certainly stimulated by the Florentine. The first person to be aware of this was Voltaire, who was horrified when he read Chapter II, Book X of Montesquieu's *The Spirit of Laws* which states:

> Among societies the right of natural defence at times necessitates an attack as when one's own country, because of a period of peace, is in danger of being destroyed by neighbours who have prospered.

Voltaire exclaimed:

> If this were Machiavelli addressing these words to the bastard son of the abominable Pope Alexander VI, I would not be at all shocked.
> ... But that this maxim comes from such a man as Montesquieu makes it hard to believe one's eyes.

Montesquieu's thought (so easy to understand when one thinks of the U.S. and Pearl Harbour) irritated Voltaire to such a degree that he came out with an amazing statement:

> If, unfortunately, what Montesquieu said is true, this truth must be combated even if it is supported by facts.[303]

This surprising sentence shows the power of emotion over reason, even in such a sceptic as Voltaire who tried to combat religion with reason.

Later, little by little, the derivation, quotations and the influence of Machiavelli on Montesquieu were discovered and studied. It is interesting to note that the above-quoted saying of Montesquieu is still timely. Even today political moralists protest against the idea of a "preventive war" and perhaps one day will be destroyed by those who will not heed such a protest.

Montesquieu knew Machiavelli well, admired him (he called him "great"), often made use of his ideas but was always very careful not to quote him except on special occasions, as in his *Grandeur and Decline of the Romans* (1725). Montesquieu was a humanitarian, and the spirit that animated him was different from Machiavelli's. The problem of the unavoidable immorality of politics eluded him. Montesquieu took from the historian Machiavelli the determinism of natural forces, but the life of the states was not the supreme good in his eyes. And in every other way he was in complete accord with French tradition.

An almost complete documentation of the passages of Montesquieu which are similar to Machiavelli's is found in E. Levi-Malvano, *Montesquieu and Machiavelli* (Paris, 1912); and a detailed evaluation of the historicistic position of Montesquieu is found in Meinecke's *Historismus*.

4 The French translators

The French translators of Machiavelli were more favourable to him than the scholars, perhaps because they were forced to read him more attentively. Especially enthusiastic was Amelot de la Houssaye, a French diplomat at Venice who translated *The Prince* in 1683. But he too seeks refuge behind the name of Tacitus:

> The *raison d'état* alone forces the hands of rulers who cannot consider morality; so that if Tacitus should be read by those who want to learn the art of governing, Machiavelli is no less important. The former teaches how the Roman Emperors governed, the latter how one must govern today, so that it is not possible to listen to or condemn the one without the other.

5 Richelieu

Perhaps the best of Machiavelli is found in politicians, pure and simple. They do not theorize or worry about the *raison d'état,* but are aware of the nature of their activity. Such a person was Richelieu, who realized that the morality of the State is one thing, and the morality of individuals another.

> In the conduct of state affairs it [morality] is not the same thing as in other matters. For the State, action and possession are imperative; for other matters recourse is made to law.

And he understood the burden of government:

> Great men who are put at the helm of government are like the accused who are sentenced to torture with this difference only, that whereas the latter are condemned because they are guilty, the former are condemned because of their merit.

He knows how little is the importance of individuals in comparison to the security of the State: "The loss of individuals is not comparable to the public safety." Finally he seems to translate into French that famous Italian saying, *cosa fatta, capo ha* (what's done cannot be undone), in referring to matters of State: "Many things are prohibited, but when they are done they are accepted."[304]

At Richelieu's instigation, Canon Louis Machon wrote an *Apology for Machiavelli in favour of Princes and State Officials* (1643, in ms. form studied by R. Céleste 1883, and K. T. Butler, 1940). It was written for a special occasion, and upon order, and is without any philosophical aim. It attempted to justify the *raison d'état* of France, especially against the Church of Rome (Gallicanism). The *Apology* starts by maintaining that Machiavelli was a Christian spirit:

> He hates irreligion and rejects disloyalty. He could not tolerate dissolute ambition and condemns above all else vice, cruelty and tyranny. He raised religion and piety above everything; he made it the basis and the sole support of States. In brief, there was no religion in morality, nothing holy in politics, nor anything sacred or reverent in men that he did not preach and that he did not counsel with fervour, justice and piety.

This is another travesty of Machiavelli, heeding only the literal meaning of many of his sayings without considering the whole work.

Machiavelli must have been greatly read in Europe, because there were many editions of his works and all the cultured people read Italian. We find secondary authors, like Jean de Muller (Swiss historian and diplomat, 1752–1809), mentioning him:

> I have just re-read Machiavelli's *Titus Livius* and his *Prince*, something I had not done for twenty-four years. This *Prince* is a classical book, one can even say an antique—nothing but pure gold. Experience enlightened by the most vigorous intelligence, nothing chimerical, nothing exclusive or partial, nothing sterile. All genuine political wisdom, but one must know how to grasp it. How many suggestions we could gather from it![305]

MACHIAVELLI IN ENGLAND

1 The diabolic legend

Fundamentally, English opinion of Machiavelli consists of verbal condemnation of Machiavellianism, accompanied by its practical application behind a mask of hypocrisy. With a few exceptions, this has continued from the moment of the first relations between England and Italy to the present day.

The English felt a mixture of admiration for and moral repulsion from Renaissance Italy, as one might from a beautiful but corrupt woman. The sons of the rich roamed the continent, and remained in Italy to study the classics and learn elegant manners and court etiquette. Back home nationalistic satires and indignant spokesmen for burgeoning Protestantism treated these travellers in the land of the Pope with contempt; according to pamphleteers and preachers of the time, these poor disillusioned creatures returned from Italy "with corrupted mind, upset stomach and empty purse". Despite this invective, English students continued to travel and live in Italy, attracted to the huge museum which Italy was becoming, where even guides and guards gave evidence of a legacy of friendliness.

For the English, Machiavelli became the proverbial prototype of the diabolic legend, personifying this ambivalent attraction of Italy—a country that seduces and corrupts. Mario Praz, who devoted one of his finest books to this theme (*Machiavelli in England*, Florence, 1962), states that Gentillet's book "contributed towards popularizing the concept of Machiavelli as a scarecrow and towards establishing the characteristics which became traditional—but (in England) the soil had already been prepared". There was a national disposition on the part of the English to identify Machiavelli with the worst corruption attributed to Italians of that time.

Machiavelli was considered an atheist, a devil, a descendant of the devil, a poisoner, an assassin, and a traitor. His name became synonymous with sodomy, treachery, lying, seduction, cruelty. It was associated by the anti-Semitic poet and playwright, Christopher Marlowe, with what he considered the worst characteristics of Jews in his powerful drama, *The Jew of Malta*. Little by little this feeling even caused the word "politics" to change meaning from the science or activity of life in the state, as in Latin, to the art of deceit and of the teaching and practice of astuteness and fraud.

In contrast to the popular aversion of the English for Machiavelli, there was a cold and calculated appreciation of his doctrines shown by individual Englishmen, some of whom would not admit it, or confessed it only in their notebooks (see Milton, below), or who even plagiarized him in secret political reports but condemned him in print. This practice was indeed a perfect example of Machiavellianism, in line with the worst legends.

While for the large majority Machiavelli was labelled as a political deceiver, among serious writers his name stood for resolution, speed and efficacy in political action. In a certain sense this represents a splitting of the double image of the lion and the fox, in whose union Machiavelli had defined the perfect prince. The large religious and sentimental majority saw only the fox; political men and thinkers saw only the lion.

2   Edmund Spenser (1552–66)

Spenser is one among many English writers of that period who knew and imitated Italian literary styles, and is an example of how deceptive literary influences can be. He knew Machiavelli well, as did all the members of his circle. In Spenser's poem, *Mother Hubberd's Tale* (1591), inspired by a medieval French poem, the main character is a Fox, and Machiavellianism is in fact interpreted as the art of egoism, atheism and deceit. The Fox, who has very carefully studied "Matchavell", is a counsellor of irreligiousness, cruelty and hypocrisy.

Yet in 1596, when Spenser had occasion to offer a political opinion to the Queen on how to dominate Ireland (*View of the present state of Ireland*), he did nothing more than make use of Machiavelli's ideas on how to deal with a state in the provinces "different in language, customs and laws"—which was the situation of Ireland with respect to England. As the scholar Edwin Greenlaw has written:

> In its general theme, the *View* follows *The Prince* very closely. . . .
> The entire tract is a development of this idea, except that Spenser
> includes the difference in language in his discussion of the customs of
> the Irish, and stresses the variation in religion. . . .[306]

In order to obtain peace in Ireland, Spenser advised using strong medicine and violent means—the same measures for which Machiavelli was censured when he recommended them for Italy. Lord Grey's cruel régime in Ireland, which was defended by Spenser, can easily be compared with Borgia's treatment of the Romagna region.

It would be useless to dwell on Spenser's hypocrisy—the important thing is to note his double standard. He condemns Machiavelli ideas in general, but makes use of them in practice. Whenever the English proclaimed the politics of integrity, which was almost always, they realized that in practice it was impossible for a state to endure and prosper by means of verbal honesty alone. The denying of their words by their deeds is a confirmation of their being arch-Machiavellians.

In England, Alberico Gentili (1552–1608) in his *De Legationibus* maintained that Machiavelli was a rabid promoter of democracy and that, born, educated and honoured by a Republic, he was considered the greatest enemy of tyrants. Machiavelli's intention, according to Gentili (in *The Prince?*), was to reveal the mysterious secrets of the life of tyrants to poor, oppressed people! This was not the English view, but then Gentili was Italian.

3 Walter Raleigh (1552?–1618)

Machiavelli was subjected even in England to a partly literal and partly transformed plagiarism. An example of this was the *Cabinet Council* (1658) of Sir Walter Raleigh, published posthumously by the poet John Milton. Raleigh was one of the great minds of imperial England under Elizabeth, and the first to write a world history. He was a statesman, poet, colonizer of Virginia, a favourite of the Queen (at times), and all in all a fine type of adventurer and versatile writer. The maxims he appropriated from Machiavelli are mixed with others he took from Guicciardini Sansovino, Bodin, Lipsius and perhaps even from Aristotle, and are set forth in his *Cabinet Council*. However, he repudiates and condemns the same ideas in other works of his, especially in *The Prince, or Maxims of State* (1642), composed in prison.

Although his maxims or observations did not spring spontaneously from his own mind, he read Italian authors with open eyes and with more freedom than other English writers. He paraphrased what he borrowed and presented a picture of politics as it is in reality. This can be seen in his statement that treaties, although founded on written pacts or strengthened by an opportune marriage, are not as binding on a sovereign as force or necessity; that mercenary troops are dangerous; and that states endure by means of systems which can be considered cruel. However, he always remained fundamentally English in that, although he thought that certain things had to be done, he also thought it best not to say anything about them. Thus the title of his book, *Cabinet Council,* seems to imply matters to be kept locked up in a cabinet. A study, not definitive, of the sources of this work was made by Nadja Kempner in *Raleighs Staatstheoretischen Schriften: die Einführung des Machiavellismus in England* (Leipzig, 1928, Beiträge zur Engl. Philol. VII). See also the additions in V. Luciani's "Raleigh's *Cabinet Council* and Guicciardini's *Aphorisms*" (Studies in Philology, 1949, 20–30).

Mario Praz advanced a possible hypothesis as to the date of the *Cabinet Council* in his essay, "An English Machiavellian, Sir Walter Raleigh".

4 The dramatists

Perhaps the strongest and deepest impression of Machiavelli in England was the one to be found indirectly in the many plays written during the flowering of Elizabethan and Jacobean drama. A list has been made of quotations in which he is vilified and damned; they comprise hundreds of lines. Although playwrights of this period always condemned Machiavelli, they created memorable characterizations of generals, tyrants, conquerors, rebels, invaders—all supermen of some kind or other—derived from Machiavelli's historical or idealized types. This is especially true of Marlowe and Shakespeare. For detailed comment see Mario Praz, *Machiavelli in England,* pages 173–194.

5 David Hume (1717–76)

No less strange than Gentili is the attempt made by the philosopher Hume to whitewash Machiavelli's personal ethics. In another connection ("On Civil Liberty") he termed Machiavelli "a great genius".

> Machiavel himself discovers a true sentiment of virtue in his history of Florence. When he talks as a *Politician,* in his general reasonings, he considers poisoning, assassination and perjury, as lawful arts of power; but when he speaks as an *Historian* in his particular narrations he shows so keen an indignation against vice and so warm an approbation of virtue in many passages, that I could not forbear applying to him that remark of Horace, That if you chase away nature, tho' with ever so great indignity, she will always return upon you.[307]

Hume considered it important to point out that Machiavelli's errors stemmed from his mind (his thinking) and not from his soul. Elsewhere Hume was to say that Machiavelli had lived in an era of humanity that was too young to be able to offer an interpretation of political truth. It almost seems as if the English philosopher wanted to redeem Machiavelli so that his name could be mentioned in good company. As a philosopher Hume did not have recourse to such superficialities, but as a historian even Machiavelli was to be placed in the category of a gentleman.

Plenty of examples of a similar interpretation of Machiavelli could be given. English writers were surprised to learn that the real Machiavelli was not as he had been pictured. For instance, Lord Bolingbroke (1678–1757) wrote:

> This very Machiavel has written a whole chapter concerning the religion of the Romans, in which he mentions that Rome was more obliged to Numa than to Romulus; in which he shows that her grandeur and felicity were owing to her religion, nay, he asserts in general, that as religion raises commonwealths, so the contempt of it must ruin them. "Good God, is this talking like Machiavel?"[308]

All this is very superficial, as a reading of the opening section of this book should indicate.

6 John Milton

In his studies on Machiavellianism in England, Orsini has called attention to the fact that Machiavelli "furnished well-defined ideas on both arguments (the relation between sovereigns and subjects; and between church and state)" to Milton. In fact in a notebook of Milton's which came to light only in 1876, are found annotations on many of Machiavelli's thoughts. They picture a very different Milton from the generally accepted one. For example, he copies from Machiavelli's *Discourses* the famous passage:

> Against a bad ruler there is no remedy but the sword. To cure the ills of the people, words are sufficient; to cure those of the ruler, the sword is necessary.[309]

Elsewhere Milton made a summary of the thought of Machiavelli and interpreted it in this way:

> Machiavelli greatly prefers a democratic state to a monarchy and gives his reasons, which are not without merit.[310]

But does Orsini realize that Milton expressed his views only in his private notebooks, which he kept secret? It took centuries for them to appear in print. When it came to quoting Machiavelli openly in print, Milton took great pains not to defend him from the current erroneous opinions; indeed he accepted them, as when he wrote:

> Yet Beza's opinion is that a politick Law, but what a politick Law, I know not, *unless one of Machiavel's,* may regulate sin; may bear indeed, I grant, with imperfection for a time, as those Canons of the Apostles did in ceremoniall things: but as for sinne, the essence of it cannot consist with rule; and if the law fail to regulate sinn, and not to take it utterly away, it necessarily confirms and establishes sinne.[311]

This holds true in other passages where he used the adjective "Machiavellian" in the same derogatory sense as his contemporaries. Milton learns from Machiavelli and uses him in secret, but condemns him in public. The case of Milton can be coupled with that of Spenser, in that both are typically English.

7   The romantics

Later even England, little by little, followed the current which throughout the eighteenth century lead towards the vindication of Machiavelli in the nineteenth century. Even in such a poet as Edward Young (1683–1765) we find the concept that Machiavelli could not be considered guilty for men's actions, and that actually he was naïve in teaching men what they already knew when they reasoned:

> Poor Machiavel! who laboured hard his plan,
> Forgot that genius need not go to school;
> Forgot that man, without a tutor wise,
> His plan had practised, long before 'twas writ.[312]

March 1827 is an important date that marks a change in the consideration of Machiavelli. An article by the historian Macaulay appeared on that date in the *Edinburgh Review*. It had an enormous circulation in Europe, not because it contained anything new or unusual, but because of the different tone employed in examining Machiavelli. It was translated into Italian, and even reached Russia and Spain. For Lord Macaulay, Machiavelli is a tissue of contradictions and can be understood only by a study of the Italians of that period:

> The whole man seems to be an enigma, a grotesque assemblage of incongruous qualities, selfishness and generosity, cruelty and benevolence, craft and simplicity, abject villainy and romantic heroism.[313]

We can say that despite the fact that Machiavelli's works were widely read in England (many translations were made, and moreover there was a general knowledge of Italian, French and Latin among the educated classes), and despite the fact that some Englishmen understood Machiavelli very well, the theoretic contribution to the fortunes of Machiavelli by the English amounted to practically nothing. English political doctrines did not profit from Machiavelli's ideas. Except in Bacon, there is no English development of Machiavellian thought, as there was in Italy with Cuoco or with Pareto and Mosca, or in Germany with Hegel, Treitschke and Meinecke.

The English romantic writers always quoted Machiavelli with a measure of respect, but they never actually penetrated his thought. Wordsworth read him attentively and called him a "great statesman" (*Letters,* Oxford, 1937, II, 748). Coleridge memorized a passage of Machiavelli. Southey has More judge him, in his "Sir Thomas More or Colloquies on Society":

> Machiavelli is always sagacious, but the tree of knowledge of which he had gathered, grew not in Paradise; it had a bitter root, and the fruit savours thereof, even to deadliness.[314]

Machiavelli takes part in the imaginary dialogues of such a fine writer as Walter Savage Landor (*Machiavelli and Michel-Angelo, Machiavelli and Guicciardini*), but it seems to me that the only interesting observation to come forth here is the one about the anti-Italian style of Machiavelli; and even this is not completely valid: "The great merit of Machiavelli, in style, is the avoiding of superlatives."

Byron is filled with rhetoric when viewing the tomb of Machiavelli in the Church of the Holy Cross in Florence; it suggested to him only this line: "Here Machiavelli's earth returned to whence it rose." And his friend Hobhouse, commenting on this passage, finds nothing better to say than that Machiavelli was an adversary of the Jesuits, and a libertine.

Naturally Shelley too admired Machiavelli and places his books among the best in the world, alongside the Bible! And for Keats, Machiavelli is a "great man"—but in the same category with Aretino and Sannazzaro!

The contrast between Machiavelli's style and that of other Italians in general is constantly referred to. Robert Browning has this to say:

> How *slow* (to the ear and mind) that Italian rhetoric is: a language for dreamers and declaimers. Yet Dante made it for action, and Machiavelli's prose can walk and strike as well as float and faint.[315]

8 The moderns

All things considered, the greatest English contribution to Machiavellian studies, as regards facts as well as interpretation, was made by Arthur L. Burd. He is to be respected for his painstaking research into the sources of *The Art of War* and *The Prince* (ed. 1891). Burd had learned this method of study from the Germans.

An example worthy of note in recent years is the short essay by the poet T. S. Eliot in his *For Lancelot Andrewes*. It is full of uncertainties about Machiavelli; yet it offers a glimpse of the truth:

> And yet no great man has been so completely misunderstood. He is always placed a little askew. He does not belong with Aristotle, or with Dante, in political theory; he attempted something different. He does not belong with Napoleon and still less with Nietzsche. His statements lend themselves to any modern theory of the state, but they belong with none.[316]

The most original point is where Eliot says: "But Machiavelli was no fanatic; he merely told the truth about humanity ... Lord Morley intimates that Machiavelli saw only half of the truth about human nature. What Machiavelli did not see about human nature is the myth of human goodness which for liberal thought replaces the belief in divine grace."[317]

MACHIAVELLI IN SPAIN

1 A positive anti-Machiavellianism

Whereas in France the Machiavellian seed fell on sterile soil, in Spain it generated the strongest and, for that era, the newest type of opposition.

For a short time before his works were placed on the Index, Machiavelli enjoyed a certain amount of success in Court circles in Spain. It was said that Charles V always carried *The Prince* around with him. A Florentine banker, Giovanni Lorenzo Ottevanti, published his own Spanish translation of Machiavelli's *Discourses*. Moreover, a Spanish book, almost a copy of *The Art of War* was published by Diego de Salazar (*De re militari*, Alcalà, 1536), with no credit given to Machiavelli. No one realized it was simply a translation of Machiavelli's book. This is another example of the plagiarism of Machiavelli, to be placed alongside the one by Niphus. An illustrious Spanish general and bibliographer, Don José Almirante y Torrolla, who apparently did not realize it had been plagiarized, said this of de Salazar's book:

> The *De re militari* represents a true levelling rod in the military literature of Spain. It epitomizes the system of the Great Captain, which at the beginning of the XVI century inaugurated the revival of the militia in all of Europe, with the restoration of the famous infantry, which for nearly two centuries was the terror and the model of our enemies.[318]

After his condemnation by the Church, the purely political works of Machiavelli elicited a different type of reaction. They gave rise to a doctrine of the State in opposition to Machiavelli, that is still in force today. As the German historian, Dempf, wrote:

242

The strong reaction against Machiavellianism and the cult of Tacitus took place in Spain from before to the end of the reign of Philip II. King Philip II was actually the real adversary of Machiavelli, and of the theories of territorial politics.[319]

Pedro de Rivadeneira (1527–1611), with his *El Principe cristiano* (Madrid, 1595); Francisco de Suarez (1548–1617), with his *De Legibus ac Deo legislatore* (1595); Juan de Mariana (1536–1624), with his *De Rege et regis institutione* (1599); Juan Eusebio Nieremberg (pseud. Claudio Clemente), with his *Dissertatio christiano-politica ad Philippum IV regem catholicum in qua machiavellismo ex impietalis penetralibus producto et jugulato* (1636), are all involved in the Machiavelli controversy. They attempt to formulate a doctrine opposing Machiavelli's, the doctrine of a State based indirectly on religion.

Secondary works of the same type are numerous. *La politica de Dios,* of the historian and diplomat Francisco Gomez de Quevedo y Villegas (1580–1645); *El Gobernador Cristiano deducido de las vidas de Moisés y Josué,* by the Augustinian monk Juan de Marquez (1564–1621); *Cien empresas o Idea de un principe politico cristian,* by Diego de Saavedra Fajardo (1584–1648); and the very popular *El Sabio, instruido de la naturaleza con esforzos de la verdad, en el tribunal de la razón alegados en quarenta y dos maximas politicas y morales contra la vanas ideas de la politica de Machiavelo,* by Father Francisco de Garau (1640–1701), where Machiavelli appears only in the title. By combating Machiavelli's weakest point, morality and religion, they sustain the principle of a "true" *raison d'état* in opposition to a "false" one. By the latter they mean a *raison d'état* in accord with the doctrine of Catholic sovereignty, and they are all in favour of the supremacy of religion:

> They [the politicians] want to use religion for the sake of appearance, in order to fool and divert the people. ... We want the princes [leaders] earnestly to serve true religion.[320]

Amidst outbursts of rage and contempt aimed at Machiavelli, the "wicked man and minister of Satan", there appeared in Spain at the end of the sixteenth century the image of a prosperous, peaceful and conservative state, with no desire for conquest. This image is still as popular today with Christian Democrats as it is with Socialists and Liberals—that is, with all political parties in which moral concepts transcend political. For Catholics, states should provide man with a religious life; for Socialists and Liberals, the State should furnish material welfare. The states are never ends in themselves. Hence, in addition to the positive governmental programme (headed by a so-called Christian prince or leader), in opposition to the concept of Machiavelli, the Spanish Jesuits advanced many suggestions and propositions of an economic and international modern nature. This was especially the case with Father Francisco de Vittoria (1483–1546).

2 Juan de Mariana, S.J.

In this medievalism and Aristotelianism which accompanied the new Scholasticism, the doctrine of modern democracies appears in the work of a talented, inspired and original writer, the Jesuit Juan de Mariana (1535–1624). He stipulates that power should come from the people. According to him it is right, indeed imperative, to kill the sovereign who is a tyrant, or who becomes one through an illegal seizure of power. His writings have been, and continue to be, the cause of violent controversies.

The first question that Mariana explores is the origin of the State. It is interesting to note how this fervent Catholic reconstructs the origin of organized human society without ever mentioning God or Providence. For him, as for Machiavelli, society is formed through untamed human nature, for purely human motives. While in Machiavelli the nucleus of society is force, which is then taken over by the cleverness of a single individual who is stronger than the others, in Mariana society comes into being after a period of happiness (similar to the golden age of the pagans), when men felt weak and in danger. For that reason they "associated" and entrusted themselves to one leader who derived his dignity from men who were "moderate, honourable and virtuous":

> At the beginning, men roamed the world like beasts. Inasmuch as they saw that their lives were constantly endangered, and also that kinsmen abstained from violence and assassination when they were united, those who felt oppressed by the powerful started to unite. They focused their attention on the one who could be expected to prevent all kinds of private and public violence, to establish equality, to control affairs by means of laws equally applicable to inferiors and superiors. The rulers derived their dignity not from intrigues or gifts, but from men of moderation, honesty and other virtues.[321]

For Machiavelli force and cleverness are at the root of the origin of the State; for Mariana weakness, poverty and fear. Mariana does not explain what caused primitive men, who formerly lived in a state of innocence and happiness, to feel weak and unprotected. Machiavelli is more explicit and logical: he postulates not an ideal situation but a bestial condition which is transformed by force into order and justice. It seems to me that Mariana, whose thinking usually gives evidence of a powerful logic, here amalgamates residues of his classical culture (the golden age), his adherence to the Aristotelian doctrine (man is social by nature), and his desire to postulate a Christian antithesis to the Lucretian naturalism of Machiavelli. For Mariana, the good man is chosen for leader. In many other ways he also differs from Machiavelli. To those who say, "In the interest of the Republic it is sometimes necessary for the Prince to lie and deceive," he answers that in the long run truth hurts less than a lie. This is, after all, a purely utilitarian thought, without relation to history.

Logic played a nasty trick on Mariana. He never made as many terrifying statements as Machiavelli but because of one, he was violently hated, denounced and condemned. This one was his apology for tyrannicide; it did not shock the Spanish kings, but made a very unfavourable impression on the French. It is interesting to see that even the words used by Mariana tally with those of Machiavelli, when he suggests iron (sword) for the tyrant:

And if circumstances demand it, if in no other way it is possible to save the Fatherland, the prince should be killed by the sword as a public enemy. . . . In this case, not only does authority rest with the people, but the individual (who does the killing) who does not run away after his deed, and places his life in danger, is acting for the good of the Republic.[322]

What is amazing in these pages of Mariana is not the doctrine, which is as old as classical antiquity, but the warmth and sincerity with which he expresses himself. At the end of the chapter he seems to give vent to his inner feelings and explains to the reader why he was so bold and daring: "This is my way of seeing things."

In a careful examination of Mariana's doctrine, we note discrepancies. He does not always speak of the Fatherland, but sometimes of the Kingdom, and once he places religion above everything: "When even the sacredness of religion and the welfare of the kingdom are put in jeopardy . . .",[323] whereas Machiavelli speaks only of the Fatherland, or the State: "When the welfare of the State is in question, injustice, pity, cruelty must not be taken into account."

Still more important than the coincidence of terms in both Machiavelli and Mariana, is the latter's affirmation of the doctrine of the necessity of evil in politics. The Christian Mariana realized that in order to save the State it was impossible not to violate Christian morality. Murder is permitted if the end for which it is committed is to "save one's country". Mariana agrees with Machiavelli on other things. He insists on the religious unity of the State and on a national militia: "His armies should always be composed of his own subjects, and never of foreigners (mercenaries)."[324]

In this group of Spanish Jesuits we find the first positive objection to Machiavelli. It is an attempt to construct a distinctive value in opposition to and superior to the State, which rules the State itself and takes into account the limitations of the State. As we can see from the writings of these Spaniards, this superior value is the Catholic Church. It is always considered inviolable (see the chapter in Mariana on the king who cannot legislate in matters of religion and cannot seize ecclesiastical goods). The Church is therefore considered by these writers as a super-state.

3   The Machiavellists: Barrientos

Among Spanish statesmen there are some examples of theoretical Machiavellianism. These are the authors of writings in harmony with the political realism of Machiavelli as opposed to the *"arbitristas"* or Utopians. They examine political problems in a scientifically objective manner, with the sole purpose of preserving the State. Very notable is a report of 1598, published several times with various titles, presented to Philip III. For a long time it was thought to be the work of the statesman Antonio Pérez, but now it seems more reasonable to attribute it to Baltasar Àlamos de Barrientos.

At the beginning of his "opinion", Barrientos makes some distinctions between the various states of the king of Spain which greatly resemble those at the start of the Prince:

> The Kingdoms of your Majesty are divided into inherited and conquered . . . inherited I call one, conquered I call the other. . . . And I make this distinction because with those that are conquered by force against their will, it is necessary to make use of deceit. . . .[325]

He knows that "conquered states always desire the restoration of their original condition", and this accounts for the perennial enmity of the conquered people of Italy and of Flanders towards the oppressor, the Spanish monarchy. He also knows that gratitude does not exist in politics and that, when the debt is too great, the debtor desires the death of the creditor—*"los muy cargados quieren ver muerto al acreedor"*. Like Machiavelli, he composed general maxims; and in his pessimism regarding human nature, he even goes beyond Machiavelli. He knows and uses the *raison d'état* and he also knows how to make use of it in a malicious vein by drawing examples from the Bible. He defends hypocrisy, "as David did with Joab", and adds that David "was a very wise king". When cruelty is resorted to, it should not be prolonged, but used quickly and all at once—the same thing that Machiavelli advised. It seems to me that Barrientos must have had Machiavelli in mind in that tragic utterance that sons remember more the loss of a patrimony than the death of a father:

> Sons will forget more easily the death of their parents and relatives (which after all occur all at once and then their sorrow ends), than the confiscation and loss of their farms, which they miss every day.

Barrientos asks, What is the good of history if it does not teach leaders how to act? Indeed, in an almost Vico-like manner, he adds that this is the only knowledge man can have, because God alone can have total knowledge. His words are very similar to those of Machiavelli for what concerns foreign affairs of a nation. He warns princes that they will have enemies, friends and neutrals among other heads of States, and urges them to remember that neutrals are ready to become enemies and to want a part of the spoils. And he tells them never to count on peace or alliances with other countries, but only to trust in their own power and judgment:

> Never should princes trust peace and treaties with others, but they should put their trust in their own power and preserve it by means of their own strength.[326]

Leaders of neighbouring states should be treated as friends but be considered as potential enemies, because they can become so from one day to another:

> It is wise to treat neighbouring princes as friends, especially the more powerful during times of peace and treaties, but it is best to be on one's guard with them in the event one day or another they become enemies.

In these counsels, the papacy is considered an elective temporal power whose interests lie in being surrounded by a great number of powers but with no desire to be under the protection of any one king:

> And finally the papacy, as a temporal and elective power, seeks always to have a great many princes surround it, but never wants to be under the protection of any one prince.[327]

Machiavelli's expression *new prince* appears only in an hereditary sense in Barrientos, because the Italian adventurer who became the leader of a country did not exist in Spain. The position of a "new king" was always threatened by medieval autonomies and the rights of the various states; and since force was not enough, the king must use judgment (*prudenza*), that is, cleverness:

> The new prince who assumes the administration of a defeated kingdom, who is fearful of more enemies, and not being able to rid himself of all of them, nor possessing enough strength to conquer them, must make use of cleverness, bargaining with some, bribing others, attacking those who are weak and easy to conquer.[328]

The author always trusts in the lessons of antiquity and, as was the habit of Machiavelli, the old example is accompanied by the modern one, as for instance when he couples Philip of Macedon with the Venetians.

He pays lip service to religion "to be respected more than any other thing in life", but hastens to add the *raison d'état* which advises keeping priests on one's good side:

> It is wise to treat priests well in following the *raison d'état,* because they are in the majority in the republic, and with relatives and friends the majority can cause trouble, or be a help to the kingdom, according to the respect shown them.

He believes the clergy can be put to good use as spies:

> Through them [the priests] finally, the general inclinations of the provinces can be known, a knowledge that is of much importance.[329]

He speaks of states as "human bodies" which have "bad humours", and of provinces which are far removed from the "head" and "heart" of the State, a condition that is a great peril to a new prince.

All things considered Barrientos, although at times reverting to the anti-Machiavellian language of the difference between the good and the evil *raison d'état*, is totally immersed in a Machiavellian way of thinking. His political calculation is always based on "forces" of humanity and on their conflicts, and his counsels are objectively determined by the interest of the State—that is, of the leader. In certain points he goes beyond Machiavelli and is even more coldly detached. Even though he didn't quote Machiavelli, he had certainly read him. He is honest enough not to combat or repudiate him. He uses his ideas, and follows in his footsteps, using a style that for clarity from start to finish could serve as a model for a modern scientific report.

4 Setanti

Less distinctive but nevertheless appreciable is the imprint of Machiavelli on a collection of thoughts written by Joaquim Setanti, entitled *Sparks (Scintille)*. This work, published posthumously in Barcelona in 1614, was openly opposed to Utopian political dreams. Even the priests, who had to consent to its publication, remarked on its anti-Platonism: "Long and beautiful discourses of Plato and others, who wanted to depict republics and rulers as seen in dreams."

The books is made up of 500 maxims, some dealing with politics and some with the private life of man, with a realistic sentiment that does not exclude a tribute now and then to Christianity. Some of these maxims sound a bit like Guicciardini (for example, 428, "to understand the how, the when and the how much", or 18, "to cure the ailing body of the State and to maintain it in health, an ounce of practice is worth more than a pound of theory"). The author dislikes Utopians who "speak with wonder of the State but like the poor, who dream of being wealthy, they awake and become beggars" (385). Without copying him, as did Barrientos, some of Setanti's maxims are very similar to Machiavelli's:

The faith and the word of a king are in accord with the good of the State. (216)
Women with oil and ointments or other palliatives of their own invention should not try to cure the bad humours of the body of a State. Experience, know-how and a man's hand to administer purges, bloodletting, sweats and cauterization with fire are needed. (300)
Secrecy is the soul of political treaties. (312)
The kings and republics (states) that are approached for help should first be convinced of the justice of the one who seeks help, and must never lose sight of their own interest. (333)

Setanti is convinced, as was Machiavelli, that internal strife leads to a state's ruin because outside forces take advantage of the situation. To make soldiers fight, nothing is as good as to convince them they can be saved only by the sword (337). See also Ramon Ceñal, *Antimaquiavelismo de los tratadistas politicos españoles de los siglos XVI y XVII,* in "Umanesimo è scienza politica", Marzorati, Milan, 1951; and also George Uscatescu, *De Maquiavelo a la Razón de Estado,* Madrid, 1951, especially Chapter IX, "El pensamiento politico renascentista en el mundo hispanico".

5 Gracian

A little later Spain was to give the world a most original work, still reprinted and read, composed of 300 maxims which became famous in the nineteenth century. It is *The Art of Wordly Wisdom* (*L'Oraculo manual,* 1647) by Baltasar Gracian y Morales (1601–1658). These maxims have been called Machiavellian as well as anti-Machiavellian. But Machiavelli's influence is seen through the eyes of other Italian writers like Guicciardini, Botero and Boccalini, whose realism is not so violent as Machiavelli's. As G. J. Andreu has written:

The Machiavellian formation of Gracian—common phenomenon in the majority of Spanish writers—is found more than in the writings of Machiavelli himself, in those of his benefactor Guicciardini, and in those of the great politician Giovanni Battista Botero.[330]

However, with Gracian Machiavellianism passes from politics into everyday life, from the principles of states (where he is condemned) to principles for the conduct of individuals. Gracian accepts the idea of evil in life and therefore of the inevitableness of acting counter to Christian morality. "Life is a war against the malice of men."

At times Gracian's ideas are similar to those of Machiavelli or of his classical source: "If you cannot put on the coat of a lion, wear that of the fox." "Hope has a good memory, gratitude a poor one." His first work, *The Hero* (1637), is thought by some people to have been written to combat Machiavelli (J. Hurtado de la Serna y A. Gonzalez Palencia, *Historia de la literatura española*, 1943, 736; A. Coster, "Baltasar Gracian", Rev. Hispanique, 1913, 469–70). One of his definitions of fortune seems to come directly from Machiavelli: "Not only is fortune as fickle as a woman, but as frivolous too in making fun of young men."[331] But its origin is in that lesser Machiavelli, Botero: "Fortune is a wicked woman who only accosts young men."

The purpose of *The Hero* is to depict a great Christian, "who always knows how to take advantage of the situation in order to succeed in the world". Although he adds that to succeed in the world is nothing and what is important is to succeed in Heaven, the tenor of the book is completely worldly and not Christian. It is Machiavellianism reduced to problems of everyday practical life, and his is a hero without heroism.

It is ironic to see that another of Gracian's heroes is King Ferdinand the Catholic, whom Machiavelli on various occasions pointed to as a model of the greatness and hypocrisy of a real statesman. For Gracian, Ferdinand is the "artist of the wordly wisdom" of the *raison d'état*:

The true and masterly policy was that of Ferdinand, secure and firm, which was not destroyed by fantastic quarrels; useful because it allowed him to reign for years, honest because it earned him the Catholic coat of arms. He conquered kingdoms for God, crowns for His Cross, provinces for fields of faith, and finally, he was the one who knew how to unite earth and heaven.

Machiavelli is openly attacked by Gracian in his *Criticón,* where he is represented as a charlatan of the marketplace, treated as a "false politician" who tried to peddle his "false aphorisms", Gracian calls them nothing more than "sweepings" and adds a pun that must have greatly amused his contemporaries—"not of the State but of the stable".

There is no way of knowing how many of these insults were sincere or dictated as a precautionary measure meant for the eyes of the Church. Common to both Machiavelli and Gracian is their pessimism, and the acceptance of evil as a means of action. But their destination and aims are very different, and so is their style of writing.

MACHIAVELLI IN GERMANY

1   Acceptance by the Germans

Even in Germany there were anti-Machiavellists (besides Frederick the Great, whose thought and collaboration with Voltaire should be linked with the Encyclopaedists), but the first open defence of Machiavelli and the most important modern development of his ideas come from that country. Germany's contribution to Machiavelli studies, even in recent times, is greater than that of any other country with the possible exception of Italy. In Germany, especially at the beginning of the nineteenth century during the period of the romantic and national reawakening, there are thinkers who understand him, and who add to the further development of his thought.

Not without reason the national-religious reforms of Luther and of German Protestants have been compared to the doctrines of Machiavelli, even by such non-German scholars as the Englishman Figgis, and the Swiss Von Muralt. This comparison may seem strange, but there is something to be said in its favour.

Although the translations of Machiavelli into German came later than those in English or French, the Germans, along with one scholar from the Netherlands, were the best translators of Machiavelli into Latin—thus making him available to the large reading public of that day. The first defenders and admirers of Machiavelli were these very translators who were forced to read the text with great attention, and perhaps also because of an affinity with the author, inasmuch as a person ordinarily selects a book to translate that he likes. In the Latin translation of *The Prince,* which appeared in 1648, the preface (perhaps by the translator Vogel) calls Machiavelli a man of highest genius, an expert in history and a master of practical politics. He confronts national examples with foreign ones, the present with the past, with future events, and people who are in the same situation in various countries—a method that often enabled him to predict events.

This eulogy, although showing signs of a pompous and generalized literary form, revealed an understanding of certain points of Machiavelli's thought, especially where it is pointed out that, when Machiavelli describes the Roman *virtù*, he does it with the express purpose of advocating its use in his own time. After an appreciation of Machiavelli's dry style, which he calls *compact*, the German critic goes on to say that if the actions described and the counsels suggested seem wicked, the fault is not Machiavelli's but of that period of Christianity where those vices required such remedies: "Assuredly, the greater the sinner, the more conspicuous the vice."

Germany, which gave Machiavelli as it were a second life, can be called his second fatherland.

2 Justus Lipsius and Gasper Schoppe

We might begin with Justus Lipsius (1547–1606) who was moderately Machiavellian in his books on politics (*Politicorum . . . 1599*) wherein he finds certain "baffling dilemmas" in political activity, such as is found in the saying of Thucydides that "the most stupid rule the state better than the most acute". This saying reeks of Guicciardini, whom Lipsius does not mention, and is in opposition to the thought of Machiavelli. However, Lipsius calls him "most acute", but an unfortunate counsellor of Caesar Borgia.

We are indebted to a learned German for one of the first affirmations of Machiavelli's thought: Gaspar Schoppe, a Protestant who was converted to Catholicism but opposed the Jesuits. His philo-Machiavellianism is linked to his anti-Jesuitism. The importance of the defence of Machiavelli by Schoppe is not in his two books, inasmuch as one was never published (*Apology for Nicolò*

Machiavelli, 1618) and the other, *Paedia politices,* published only in 1623, was not widely read. In the midst of the usual arguments of little value, common to writers who try to save Machiavelli either by saying he did not expound the doctrines attributed to him (which he really had), or try to make his ideas fit into Catholic orthodoxy, Schoppe affirms the important Machiavellian principle of the separation of morality from politics: "Everything that is extraneous to politics, even if it is right and true, must be put aside and removed."[332]

It is strange that Schoppe should assume that the Church in 1618 would allow the publication of a work praising Machiavelli. Although it was not published until later, it seems certain that Campanella knew the *Apologia* and combated it in his *Atheismus triumphatus.*

3 Conring, Althusius, Christ

In 1660 Conring (1606–81), who published a more precise Latin translation of *The Prince,* was the first to denounce Possevino for having judged *The Prince* not directly from the source, but through Gentillet's erroneous text. (The fact that Possevino repeated what Gentillet had said about the book being divided into three parts proved that he did not have a first-hand knowledge of the text.) Conring thus came to the defence of Machiavelli and added in his preface that the majority of those who had condemned Machiavelli had really never read him, or had not even seen the book.

Judge Johannes Althusius (1557–1638) shows an inclination for Machiavelli's thought in a realistic and anti-legalistic sense typical of the Florentine. He also shares with Machiavelli a rather pessimistic vision of mankind: "The stupidity, ignorance, forgetfulness and indolence of men are notorious."[333] However, we can see from this passage that Althusius' thought is more Augustinian than Machiavellian.

Althusius accepts the *raison d'état* and assents to the use of fraud when employed to save the state from rebellion and defeat. He is a pragmatist and political utilitarian and, as did other Machiavellians, he takes his example from the Bible (David's use of a spy to quell the revolt of Absalom). But what is really striking is the same contradiction in the thought of both Althusius and Machiavelli: a faith in the use of rational means in order to dominate political situations, joined with a profound conviction of the general irrationality of human behaviour.

There is general agreement that the work of John Frederick Christ (1700–56) marked the first step in a change of opinion of Machiavelli on the part of cultured Germans. It is entitled *De Nicolao Machiavello libri tres, in quibus de vita et scriptis, item de secta huius viri, atque in universam de politica nostrorum post instauratas literas temporum, ex instituto disseritur* (1731).

The work, in the form of a defence, was favourably received in cultured circles. This can be seen from the review of the book in *Bibliothèque raisonnée des Ouvrages des Savants de l'Europe* (Amsterdam, 1733), which added also the name of another defender of Machiavelli (Henningius Arniseus) to those given by Christ (XI, 329–375).

The affect of this change can also be seen in the influential work of Brucker, *Historia Philosophiae* (1744), an informative handbook, gigantic even from the standpoint of our own time, where the controversy centring around Machiavelli is traced from its beginnings with a vast bibliography, where Christ's work is mentioned as containing all that was to be said in defence of Machiavelli: "He set forth the 'question' of Machiavelli and in order to defend him brought forth all possible evidence."[334]

Bruckner considers Christ Machiavelli's greatest defence attorney and refers to his "most erudite" work. And always in the form of an impartial bibliography he adds that Machiavelli cannot be blamed for suggesting methods that have been in use since the beginning of time, not only between nations but even in private life:

Those same methods were always in use in courts of law, public assemblies, church conclaves, public life, museums, taverns, among individuals, where Machiavelli was never even heard of.[335]

4 Gottfried Herder (1744–1803)

The harbinger of the historicist century, Herder, is the first to place *The Prince* in the century and environment of its author. Herder does not share Machiavelli's mechanistic vision of history; history for him is a continuous revelation of personalities and groups of people who are bound together spiritually, and not mechanically through cause and effect. But this more complicated vision enables him to see more deeply into *The Prince* than preceding commentators. For Herder *The Prince* is "a pure political masterpiece composed for princes of that period, in accordance with their tastes and their principles, written to free Italy of barbarians", an aim which Machiavelli stated only at the end of his book. According to Herder, Machiavelli "considers history as a tale of natural events, and a prince as a creature of the species whose customs, inclinations and instincts are close to his own".[336]

5 Fichte and Hegel

Fichte (1762–1814) or better still Hegel (1770–1831) carried Machiavelli's thought into a superior climate, into a veritable rarefield atmosphere. Around it they created a new structure and in it they found a distant relative of Germany and discovered one of their own ancestors. These "descendants" chose Machiavelli as their Ur-vater.

They were inspired by the situation of a Germany occupied by the troops of Napoleon and a battleground for foreigners, and by the romantic movement which at that time encouraged expression of all people and no longer upheld only Greek and Roman classical authors. It has been said that Germany at that time discovered Machiavelli.[337] Machiavelli becomes the subject of constant study in Germany between 1802 and 1818. What Machiavelli had hoped for the Italy of his own time became the ideal of the German patriots of the period.

Many countries even in our own time have been similarly inspired and have passed through such a phase. When they rid their own land of foreigners, they in turn tried to penetrate the lands of others and were delighted when they could destroy those who had tried to conquer them. Liberty is a strong emotion, but perhaps reprisal is equally strong.

But in Fichte and Hegel there is more than this. Their defence of Machiavelli is not concerned with the petty problem of whether or not Machiavelli had taught the art of betrayal, or whether he was a supporter of tyranny. It is transported to the larger problem of the state. For Fichte, the state is in the creative process, for which it is worth fighting; for Hegel it is a process already perfected, to be maintained. The conflict between the individual and the state no longer exists for these thinkers, who consider liberty and law identical. In this way they resolve the problem with a new synthesis of which Machiavelli certainly had no idea. This placed him on a high pedestal and his works, in the light of these two German philosophers, were to be read with profit by Europeans.

The necessity of evil in political action becomes a superior ethics which has no connection with the morals of an individual. The state swallows evil. Hegel says: "The state is lifted above all this, and evil becomes reconciled with itself."[338] In order to express this position of the state beyond good and evil, he makes use of almost the same words as Machiavelli's.[339] For him the state is the pure and simple absolute spirit, with no limitations except those given by the state itself, and therefore it has "no concept of good or evil, of shame or abjection, of wickedness or deceit".[340]

As a starting point, Hegel (as well as Fichte or Herder) makes use of a Machiavelli placed against his historical environment:

With cold judgment [Machiavelli], saw the necessity of saving Italy by uniting it. There was no choice of means. When poison and assassination were common weapons, it is not possible to make use of other sweet counter-remedies. The putrefaction of conditions necessitated a reorganization by means of energetic measures.

But in Fichte, who probably had in mind the last detractor, Frederick II, the vindication of Machiavelli from the petty defamations of the preceding centuries assumes a personal tone that is moving. With Fichte it was a matter of "giving an honourable burial to an honest, intelligent and worthwhile man", to vindicate "a noble Florentine", a writer who was "wise, consistent, truthful, honest, who once he had postulated a truth had the courage to follow it through to its final consequences". This is a funeral oration and a warm rehabilitation of an honest man. "May my words have favourable results!" exclaimed Fichte at the end. Fichte feels close to Machiavelli, and sees Italy in the same position as Germany. The most important and animated part of the essay is where he applies Machiavelli's standards to "illuministic" Germany at the beginning of the nineteenth century.

In Fichte there is a certain amount of ambiguity about the historical position of Machiavelli, and about his theoretic absolute affirmations, which are applicable to all times. In certain passages it seems as though Fichte saw *The Prince* as nothing more than a book destined to advise and sustain that very prince who wanted to provide a certain stability to the vacillating political situation of Italy. In other passages it seems that Fichte believes *The Prince* can be applied to all political dominions.

But in the fundamental concepts, Fichte ferrets out Machiavelli's most secret thought. For him too the state is force and compulsion (*Zwanganstalt*) and the sovereign a strong ruler (*Zwingherr*). And if in the state there are moral rights, they are not to be observed in the case of international conflicts:

> In relations between states, there is no law or right except that of the strongest, and these relations . . . place the prince [leader] above the laws of individual morality, in a superior ethical atmosphere

whose material context lies in the words: *Salus et decus populi suprema lex esto.*[341]

Fichte sees clearly the necessity of imperialism innate in any living state:

> The territory of a state must not only be defended but it is necessary to keep one's eyes always open to observe all that can influence the situation of a country. The sphere of action must not be interfered with by other countries and every favourable occasion must be taken to enlarge the territory. It must always be remembered that a state which does not expand and grow, while others are doing so, is diminishing.[342]

It has even been noted that in the same way as Fichte hoped that Germany would one day be freed through the King of Prussia, so at a certain time Italian patriots pinned their hopes on the King of Piedmont who would unify the peninsula and give it independence.

From Fichte, almost a prophet and temperamentally close to Machiavelli, we turn to Hegel (who began to write about Machiavelli even before Fichte). With him there ceases to exist the opposition between reality and Utopia, between the ideal and the real, because "what is real is also rational"—that is, not only good but evil also functions in favour of reason. This bastard "evil", says Meinecke, is legitimized by history.

The outlook of Hegel is more impersonal and stern than Fichte's, but he too sees the historical similarity between Germany and Italy:

> The course of Germany's destiny runs parallel with that of Italy, with the difference that Italy, already in possession of a culture, saw its destiny follow the course of its natural development more rapidly than Germany.[343]

But from a special condition he goes on to a general one. From the condition of Italy in Machiavelli's time and from that of Germany during his own time, he goes on to the conditions of all States in all times:

When the founding of a state "is a necessity", Machiavelli set forth the essential requirements for its foundation.[344]

The importance of this German moment in the history of Machiavellianism is clear. Those thinkers wanted to solve the contradictions in Machiavelli's thought in a superior optimism, in an acceptance of the arts of the state as a necessity. However, they made use of Machiavelli for their own national ends, by drawing the destiny of their country close to that of the Italians as described by Machiavelli.

6 The historians

To follow the path of Machiavelli in Germany from that time on would be too arduous a task—and the intinerary has already been traced. There are two fundamental moments: the romantic period of the national formation of Germany, and the despair of Germany after the defeat of the First World War. In these two moments of its history, Germany turned to Machiavelli for consolation.

G. G. Gervinus (1805–71) in his text (*Florentinische Historio-graphie* of 1833) speaks of Machiavelli as a genius to be read especially in his (Gervinus') own time and he insists especially on the unity, even on the unilateralness of his spirit. He adds that in the historian Machiavelli is seen the statesman, and in the states-man the historian, and in both the man and the poet.

And how many eulogies in Friedrich von Schlegel:

> Unique not only among Italians, but also among the Moderns, and the first among Antiquity.[345]

And he does not agree with those who find Machiavelli immoral; the explanation is in his patriotism.

In Ranke too (1795–1886), a Catholic who really hesitated before that tremendous problem of immorality in politics, there is found that same redemption of Machiavelli:

The condition of Italy was so desperate that Machiavelli did not hesitate to offer poison as a remedy.[346]

Among later historians the powerful voice of Treitschke (1834–1896) was raised in tribute to Machiavelli as a "companion in arms" of Luther.

What is most striking in his doctrine is not found in the immorality of the suggested means, but in the lack of moral content of his state which exists only to exist. Of the aims of domination, there is hardly any mention which justify the conflicts. The dream of the unity of Italy appears only slightly, here and there. Machiavelli is Luther's companion in arms. In the political thought of the two men the same destiny is realized and with it the necessary conflict of the two great civilized countries of central Europe—which, idealists among nations, one through knowing and constructing, the other through the reformation of the State and the Church, have opened the doors to a new history.[347]

The inaugural speech of Prof. E. W. Mayer (*Machiavellis Geschichtsauffassung und sein Begriff "virtù"*, 1912) is important in Machiavellic studies because it focused attention on Machiavelli's vocabulary.

7   The diabolic in politics

During Hitler's time, in its preparation and its defeat, numerous works on Machiavelli appeared, in some of which is seen the concept of the "diabolic" in politics, resuscitated from the time of the first Christians. (Tillich, P. *Das Dämonische, Ein Beitrag zur Sinndeutung der Geschichte*, 1926; Ritter, G., *Machtstaats und Utopia. Vom Streit um die Dämonie der Macht bei Machiavelli und Morus*, 1943.) But the titles promise more than is found in these books.

Special mention must be made of the fundamental work of Meinecke, *Geschichte der Staatsräson,* and that of Leonhard von

Muralt, *Machiavellis Staatsgedanke* (Basel, 1945), the latter dia-metrically opposed to the present work, but worthy of respect and admiration. The book of Meinecke sprang from a study of the Treaty of Versailles, and that of von Muralt from a study of the Hitlerian system.

Machiavelli will probably continue to reappear in Germany. And in more recent times, Switzerland, a country that had heretofore neglected him, is in the process of dedicating to him works of local historical research (Schwartz, D., *Die Schweig in Denken Machiavelli,* 1943; Kaegi W., *Historische Meditationen* which contains a study on the faith of Machiavelli and interesting information on Tegli's edition; F. Scorretti, *Machiavel et les Suisses,* Neuchatel, 1942, a good summary of preceding works).

PERIODIC REBIRTH
OF MACHIAVELLI

1   Ferrari, Joly and others

Mainly in France and in England and for at least two centuries, publications appeared, which brought Machiavelli back to life, mostly by anonymous authors who placed him in the role of a judge of contemporary events. At times he is pictured as having a superior and crafty mind, often he appears as a sinister image. And almost always he is depicted as a fox. It was a sort of "conviction" in reverse. "If Machiavelli counsels it," these booklets seem to say, "who knows what evil is involved." "Machiavelli would do it, therefore it is reprehensible." These books did not flourish in Italy (with the exception of the one by Boccalini) because, despite his condemnation, Italians thought of Machiavelli as a national figure, or in Germany because there he was considered too serious a person, whose tragic utterances were well understood.

Typical of the first type, where Machiavelli's superior mind is praised, is *Machiavel juge des revolutions de notre temps,* (1849) of Giuseppe Ferrari; of the second type, where he is pictured as a sinister figure, is *Dialogue aux enfers entre Machiavel et Montesquieu, ou la politique de Machiavel au XIX siecle par un contemporain* (1864) supposedly anonymous, but by Maurice Joly. The importance of the latter, which is a bibliographical curiosity, consists in the fact that the thirty dialogues contained therein advocate a secret plan on how to skirt around the freedom of the press and how to place parliamentary freedom at the service of a clandestine and sinister foreign power. Later, a great deal of the material contained in them served as a basis for a notorious anti-Semitic booklet, *The Protocols of Zion* (1905), which was published over and over again and kept making periodic appearances despite clear proof of its having been a fabrication. Joly's book shows an understanding of Machiavelli's thought far above the average for that period. This is proven by what he has Machiavelli say:

My only crime was to tell the truth to people as well as to kings. Not the moral truth, but the political truth; not what it should be, but what it actually is, and what it will always be. I am not the inventor of the doctrine that has been attributed to me—it is the human heart.

Have you ever seen a single State act according to the principles which govern private morality?

What happened to Napoleon during the French Revolution and the Empire period was repeated during the Second World War in the case of Mussolini who was said to have been inspired by Machiavelli, as was supposedly proved by a thesis on the Florentine he presented when he was awarded an honorary degree by the University of Bologna when he was at the helm of the Italian government.

It has been said that during the Irish civil war even such a devout Catholic as De Valera asked for a copy of *The Prince* while he was in prison and then urged his followers to read it. More than once this was charged against him in the Irish Parliament (Grattan Freyer, in Hermathena, 1940–41, vol. 56, 166). And perhaps it is even true that he read Machiavelli and encouraged his followers to do likewise.

The same accusation of having been the inspiration of successful politicians keeps on being levelled at Machiavelli. It dates back at least to the time of Catherine of Medici and of Gentillet.

2   G. B. Vico

According to Croce, Vico (1674–1744) plays a significant role in the history of Machiavellianism because of all philosophers up to the time of Croce, Vico is the first and the only one to understand, and at the same time to correct, Machiavelli's system. He is also the first and the only one up to Croce's time to develop Machiavelli's thought further. Machiavelli was the first not to discover but to place on a scientific footing the concept of politics as utility. Vico completed this concept with that of ethics. A statesman can only act in a utilitarian way—but above this necessity there is, in the complete historic life of a man, the ethical action which includes and perfects the political one. (B. Croce, *The Philosophy of G. B. Vico; Ethics and Politics; Historiography and Moral Idealism*.)

Assuredly the weakest point on the Machiavellian doctrines is the religious one, interpreted by him intellectually, as we have seen. That is, religion is a deception employed by a few clever people to generate in the majority (the innocent) a complete observance of social laws, which force alone could not succeed in doing.

In Machiavelli's writings is found that very story and myth of the government of Romulus, through which untamed men "in the state of nature" become capable of social co-existence through the courage and determination of a hero, and of the government of Numa Pompilio, who followed Romulus, bringing to his domain of pure force the help and persuasion of religious reverence, by simulating a talk with a Divinity in the woods.

For Vico, on the other hand, religion is not a deception practised by wise and clever men, but a natural sentiment of reverence on the part of man, an integral and natural part of his humanity, which transcends primitive bestiality:

> Hence the conclusion is easy, that in refuting the utilitarians and the theorists of force, Vico was at the same time recognizing and absorbing the need which they represented, his only mistake having been that they developed this need in an abstract and one-sided way. His "state of nature" is in some respects like that of Hobbes, with the difference that mankind transcends the latter owing to the recognition of utility, the former owning to the religious and moral consciousness.
>
> (Croce, *The Philosophy of G. B. Vico*, London, 1913)

With Vico there came into being that new modern religiosity which is called immanency, which substitutes philosophy for religion in the domain of thought. It is clear that to philosophize is always a religious exercise; religious reverence is inherent in all learning.

In a history of Machiavellianism it is well to remember that this "progress" of Vico made no impression on his time, nor did it do so later until Croce came along. Vico was superior to the philosophers of his time, and his words were above their heads.

Croce's reconstruction of the thought of Machiavelli and of his connection with Vico is aesthetically beautiful. The *New Science* of Vico resembles a baroque church because of his turgid, and what has been called his forest-like (*selvoso*) style. Croce, extracting from his book only the basic elements and omitting the many ornamental devices reconstructed a classical and rational edifice which is a feast to the mind. However, Vico would not recognize it as his.

Moreover, it can be questioned if the philosophy of Machiavelli actually served as a basis upon which Vico was able to erect his system. Machiavelli insisted on the fact that every organized human group adopts a different morality from the Christian one; it is concerned only with survival. He tried to establish scientific laws—but these mean that the life of the state is that of a superior animal (a "mixed body", as he called the state) which struggles for existence and which, if it were to follow the precepts of Christian morality, would be weakened and destroyed by other "bodies" that surround it. An ethical system is already inherent in this vision and it is not Christian.

How can we call Vico's thought a progress over that of Machiavelli, as does Croce, or an integration of it, as Russo does? I believe that there is instead a contradiction between the thought of the two men that cannot be reconciled. For example, Machiavelli certainly believed that it was important for a state to be made up of people bound together by the same language, religion and tradition, and that such a group facilitates the proper functioning of the state, and probably helps it to last a long time. For him a state in the process of acquiring territories made up of people with different customs and languages has to struggle and resort to expedients in order to dominate the various populations. These are common-sense observations. Machiavelli always speaks of states, and recognizes no other unity than that of the state. Unlike Vico, he does not mention the concept of a nation, which is not a very clear concept in any case. Or better still, he implicitly subjugates the nation to the state. All the better if it is a national state, but the state exists even without the nation.

What then is the nation? Who knows where it begins and ends? Vico is responsible for having given birth to this obscure romantic concept. The state is something that is well-defined. I would say it is classical: it is that territory where the police force is in operation and where it can make use of force to maintain order. But the nation? How could the nation be a more integrated and perfect concept than that of the state? The nation is provided by fortune and chance; one is born into a certain nation and nothing can change this fact. But we can change states by an act of will. Machiavelli's thought is clear, Vico's is confused. In the concept of the nation there is an element of uncertainty; it cannot be considered a progress over that of the state.

From the point of view of the history of Machiavellianism it seems to me that Vico's greater importance is found in his implicit criticism of Machiavelli—and in his having substituted nations for Machiavelli's "great men". In the universal history of Vico, Machiavelli's great personalities, heroes and founders of states and religions are replaced by nations. The consequences of this substitution are strange.

I would say that Machiavelli has an aristocratic concept of history, made up of the few. Vico has a democratic concept, because for him history is made up of nations, that is of people, or as we now call them, the masses. For Machiavelli the few lead the many; for Vico the few are essential representatives of the many.

The Soviets have always admired in Machiavelli the theoretician of dictatorship, in Vico the apologist for the obscure sense of the masses.

For Vico the actors of history are nations, or peoples, each nation with its own characteristic and its own life-cycle already inherent in its own inner nature, destined to unfold in accord with a type of ideal model, thus fulfilling its life-cycle, independently of others.

This is a new concept of history in which "great men" are no longer the autonomous forces animated by the Machiavellic *virtù*, but only indexes to the degree of social development. Vico says:

> In the human race there first appears the huge and grotesque, like the Cyclops; then the proud and magnanimous, like Achilles; then the valorous and just, like Aristides and Scipio Africanus; nearer to us, imposing figures with great semblances of virtue accompanied by great vices, who among the vulgar win a name for true glory, like Alexander and Caesar; still later, the melancholy and reflective, like Tiberius; finally the dissolute and shameless madmen, like Caligula, Nero and Domitian.[348]

But what are the consequences of such a view? What credit can be given to Alexander the Great, and what blame ascribed to Caligula? They are merely "necessary" performers in the history of a people unfolding in accordance with the law of life—which postulates infancy before adolescence, adolescence before maturity, and maturity before old age. Can we praise a youth who is an ardent lover, or an elderly man who is a wise temporizer? They deserve as much credit as having a black beard or a head of white hair. It is only what is to be expected of them or what we expect from that phase of life through which they inevitably must pass. I seem to hear in Vico's "win a name for true glory" a certain irony.

If Vico has any connection with Machiavelli it is only where he opposed him, not where he supposedly accepted him as a part of his moral system. Vico is an opponent of materialism, and for that reason he placed the philosophy of Plato in opposition to those "dregs of Romulus". Unlike Machiavelli, he does not believe the "dregs of Romulus" are innately in human nature in all political action.

It thus seems to me that the political philosophies of Machiavelli and Vico travel along two different routes and in opposite directions. The nature of a moral system is very clear in Machiavelli: it is a fact of grandeur and, by implication, it includes all political activity. It does so in this sense: affairs of state are the most important in a world that does not continue in the hereafter (*Florentine Histories*, I, 379b). Gian Paolo Baglioni was considered by Machiavelli to be a vulgar criminal, because in killing his relatives his motive was a personal one—to obtain for himself the domination of Perugia. But if he had slaughtered the Pope and the Cardinals in order to rid the country of their power, and had done this for the glory of the country, then he would have been a hero and his action moral.[349]

The fact that Vico's history is controlled by a Providence makes it impossible to be linked with Machiavelli's. I don't believe that Vico ever accepted Machiavellianism and certainly if he alluded to it as the "dregs of Romulus", as Croce tells us, it is clear that he was contemptuous of it. For Vico, the drama of history is animated by a meaning and a design.

Machiavelli is a fatalist. He believes all societies are destined to end, and that human liberty is limited to the small field of political activity close to the individual (a passenger on a ship is free to move around the ship, but if it is shipwrecked his sphere of activity ends). Vico too is, after all, a fatalist inasmuch as nations for him are motivated by an inner fatality (paying tribute to Catholicism, he calls this Providence). But in Machiavelli history is a movement of forces which unite and separate without reason or scope. In Vico, it is a growth dictated by a Providence, made one with the action of growth itself.

That men and philosophies are composed of contradictions is seen in both Machiavelli and Vico. Side by side with Machiavelli's atomism, we find in him a strange faith in the courageous individual who arrogantly pits his *virtù* against Fortune, the ultimate dominator of the world. Although he does so in a limited way, Machiavelli allots this *virtù* a certain amount of importance and a field of action.

Vico, who is so serious and truly religious, and who gives birth to a doctrine that can only lead to contemplation, interprets the affairs of the world in an ironical manner. Historicism, which originates with Vico, teaches that the movement of history takes place through the enterprise of a Providence which makes use of the illusions and powers of individuals, in order to make them fulfil its own ends (see Meinecke, *Der Historismus*). But this view goes back to St. Augustine.

Individuals, according to this concept, strive, combat and make sacrifices to reach the fulfilment of their ideals. Instead the Providence that animates history directs their efforts, their tragic conflicts and their sacrifices towards other ends which are those of history and not of individuals. In a certain sense History (and it should be spelt with a capital letter because it is the same as the God of St. Augustine, Bossuet and Luther, whose motives cannot be questioned), instead of acting in a miraculous way by intervening from the outside on the course of events, has perfected the Christian system and makes use of deception and illusions to make men act. With Hegel this principle is, in fact, called the "cleverness of history", although it is not easy to demonstrate that there is reason in history, any more than to prove that there is reason in the will of God.

Men at times wonder why they should struggle, engage in conflicts and make sacrifices for ends which to them seem important when History, through deception, makes them attain ends other than the ones they desire. Thus History treats them as children who expect to attend a game but are deceived into just taking a walk because it is supposedly good for their health.

Naturally historicism remains a philosophy for the few, and not a conviction of the many. Even historicists, as individuals, have given evidence of being blind, or acting childishly in the matter of political passions, and capable of being carried along a popular wave by the turn of events. However, historicists have erected this idol they call History and have perpetrated its cult. Like the rest of humanity, they muddle their way through to attain their own ends, but sanctify their defeat when it is the will of their idol.

It is not a very different system from that of Christianity, which is resigned to the will of God. The difference between the Christian God and History is that the Christian God is a person with whom man in his imagination enters into a relation of love, while it is hard to see how the divinity of History can have compassion for man and forgive him his errors. It can only castigate. No historicist has had the temerity to say that History loves mankind.

With Vico the circle which Galileo had started to describe is completed. It takes away from man all hope that the cosmos participates in his needs and moral aspirations. With Galileo the world of the firmament was shown to be absolutely extraneous to man's fate, and indifferent to his requests for justice and peace. With Machiavelli and with Vico even the panorama of history has been revealed in its true nature as not concerned with the events or desires of humanity. The world perhaps makes use of men for its own ends, but it is not a world made in man's image, nor one able to satisfy the moral needs of mankind. Unless there is a belief in another world, where reasons for the struggles and sufferings of this one are revealed, nothing remains for man except to despair and to reach the same conclusion as Leopardi: "I think perhaps it were better never to have seen the light of day."[350]

MACHIAVELLI
AND THE ENCYCLOPAEDISTS

Machiavelli represented an enigma to the Encyclopaedists, or rationalists of the eighteenth century. They could not understand an author who was so profoundly convinced of the baseness of human motives. On the other hand, they felt he was their ally inasmuch as he was the first to maintain the superiority of the State over the Church and was the originator of the doctrine—which they cherished and which appears so often in their works—that religion is a deception practised by a few crafty individuals to fool the majority of people. But they could not swallow his acceptance of the evil nature of man, and his thesis of the necessity to force and deceive men in order to make them function in a political manner. Their optimism and rationalism always exceeded their hatred of Christianity. We are faced therefore with a strange spectacle: almost all the Encyclopaedists condemn Machiavelli in the name of honesty and virtue. It is understandable that Hegel should have used the Encyclopaedists' lack of understanding of Machiavelli as the starting-point of his defence of the Florentine.

1 Bayle (1674–1706)

Bayle was largely responsible for the attitude of the Encyclopaedists, as is seen in his *Dictionnaire historique et critique* which Faguet called "the arsenal of all philosophisms and the storehouse of ideas from Fontenelle to Volney."[351] Bayle wrote his article on Machiavelli with seemingly unintentional malice, making use of an accumulation of contradictory facts. The general tone, so light, so French, is set at the very start:

Machiavelli, native of Florence, was a man of great wit who possessed a beautiful pen.[352]

For the facts of his life, Bayle turned to the most legendary sources, like Giovio, or even to a vicious one, like Varillas. We are shown a Machiavelli who is a counsellor to Caesar Borgia and who influenced Catherine of Medici:

This is a book [*The Prince*] of which Catherine of Medici made a special study and which she placed in the hands of children.[353]

His Machiavelli even corrupts children, something really unexpected. This can be understood if we remember that Bayle came from Huguenot stock, heir to the animosity of that political party so that it is natural for him to say:

The maxims of this author are very wicked: people are so convinced of this that Machiavellianism and the art of ruling tyrannically have become synonymous terms.[354]

If he quotes Amelot de la Houssaye and Boccalini, who were somewhat favourable to Machiavelli, he only does so to attribute to princes the iniquity of which Machiavelli is only the historian. He adds:

This does not justify Machiavelli at all; he propounded maxims that he did not condemn; but a good historian who shows what these maxims are in practice condemns them. This is the real difference between the Florentine's book and a book of history.[355]

He becomes malicious when he pretends to be shocked to find that some of Machiavelli's maxims (really Aristotelian) are found in St. Thomas:

He has appropriated these maxims from the Angelic Doctor, the great St. Thomas d'Aquinas.[356]

And he reports that Pope Leo X had the *Mandragola* produced in Rome, and recounts various versions of Machiavelli's dream in which the Florentine appears as an unbeliever.

Bayle's article is tendentious and of great importance because almost all rationalists of the eighteenth century appropriated material and comments from it. At that time in Italy the official and personal letters of Machiavelli were beginning to be published, an event which could have effaced the legend formed around him, yet none of the French philosophers bothered to examine his case in the light of new documents. Bayle was to remain the poisoned fount of their culture.

2   *Voltaire and Frederick II*

As for Voltaire (1699–1778), when his method of treating Machiavelli is examined, everything is a little askew. He never grasps fundamental problems. For Voltaire, Machiavelli is a military writer:

> He taught Europe the art of war. Wars had been waged for a long time, but no one knew how to wage them.[357]

This is simply not true. He repeats this on three separate occasions, and again in some secondary quotations in an article in his dictionary ("Bataillon", in *Remarques diverses sur l'histoire de la France*), and in a letter to Algarotti where he writes with less common sense than Bandello:

> I believe as you do that Machiavelli would have been a good army general.

But immediately after he makes another quip derived from the legend of the Machiavelli who advises the use of poison:

> But I would never advise the enemy general to dine with him in times of truce.[358]

This theme of the Machiavelli-Borgia legend is one that Voltaire enjoys; he repeats it again in his *Essai sur les moeurs*.

Although he admired the *Mandragola,* and made use of and

translated the *Golden Ass,* he did not know how to become reconciled with a thought he could not understand:

That Machiavelli is indeed a strange man![359]

Along with his superficiality and perplexity, Voltaire was also servile. He modified his admiration or his doubtful opinion of Machiavelli to please Frederick of Prussia. At an early age, before he was on the throne, Frederick initiated a collaboration with Voltaire, which became famous:

I find your history of the century of Louis XIV charming. I only wish you had not placed Machiavelli, who was a dishonest man, among the other great men of his century. Whoever teaches not keeping one's word, oppression, injustice, were he otherwise the most distinguished of men because of his talents, should never occupy a place reserved only for those who possess admirable virtues and talent. You are too upright a man to put in a place of honour the dishonourable character of a detestable rascal. I feel sure that you have only shown Machiavelli from the angle of his genius.[360]

From that moment on, the French philosopher enters into the service of the King, encourages him and contrasts his beautiful soul with that of the princes of Machiavelli:

It was the Borgias, father and son, and all those petty princes who, needing crimes in order to advance their own position, studied these infernal politics; a prince such as you would detest these politics.[361]

There is no doubt that as a flatterer Voltaire knew a thing or two. On March 22, 1739, Frederick informs him of his intention to write a refutation of *The Prince,* and he tells Voltaire how he can help him:

I am thinking about a work on *The Prince* of Machiavelli; it is all still very confused in my mind and I need the help of some divinity to bring order out of this chaos.[362]

The product was a work as famous in the eighteenth century as that of Gentillet in the sixteenth, and with the same title, *Antimachiavel.* Voltaire took an active part in it. He started to re-read

The Prince in order to discover new flaws and in a letter dated October 18, 1739, calls Frederick's attention to what he considered the most repulsive part, and would make the attack even more popular:

> I have re-read Machiavelli in the little time that my ailments and studies allow me. I have the temerity to think that the most revolting thing in this author is his chapter on Cruelty . . . but above all Chapter XVIII.

After having thus located the forest for this inexperienced hunter, Voltaire teaches him how to shoot. Pretending to correct the French of his student, he changes some typical Prussian expressions, shows him errors of logic, shortens some chapters that were too long, deletes repetitions and takes great pains to compress and refine the argument. He removes useless insults, blue-pencils rhetorical phrases, and even warns Frederick against certain passages which might one day be compromising. Who knows, some foreign power might be angered—it's better to omit it. At the end, he offers to write a preface and have the book published.

What is the meaning of this sudden animosity towards Machiavelli? This work is not so much an attack on Machiavelli as it is a glorious monument to Frederick, an ideal prince who, once on the throne, would show what a disciple of philosophers was capable of doing. Voltaire's enthusiasm even suggests to him a kind of dream-apology, very much in the spirit of the times. It might almost be called Jesuitical:

> I saw you on a large silver throne which you had not erected yourself, and which you mounted more in sorrow than in joy. . . . The Antonys, Tituses, Trajans, the Julians descended from the sky to witness this triumph. They ordinarily attended only an election of the Pope, but these Cardinals and the Holy Ghost are not made for the Tituses and the Marcus Aureliuses. The Truth, which these heroes loved, is never at the Conclave but only near the silver throne.
>
> Truth knows well that even the throne is no longer a place for her and that this poor exile could not expect such an honour. But Frederick reassures her as he would a personal friend.

The Florentine Machiavelli,
Seeing this daughter of Heaven,
Returns as fast as he can
To the bottom of the infernal
Region with a Cardinal,
A Minister of State and an old Jesuit.

But Frederick would not let Machiavelli appear before him until he had made honourable amends to humankind in the person of his protector. He makes him get on his knees:

And the Italian, embarrassed,
Made public penitence,
Declaring that Truth
Is the best politics.[363]

Voltaire was to become disillusioned with Frederick, as is seen in his correspondence (t. XXXV, 83, 8 July 1741). In his memoirs (*Oeuvres* I, 17–8) he tells of the fascination exerted over him by Frederick in very human and believable terms: "I never tired of feeling charmed by him, because he had wit, grace and above all, because he was a sovereign, a great seduction in the face of human weaknesses." A sentence then escapes from his pen that became justly famous; it destroys the entire book written in collaboration with the young king:

If Machiavelli had had a prince as a disciple, the first thing he would have done is to urge him to write against him.

The actions of Frederick as a prince belied his book, and Voltaire had had time to realize this. However, the book was very popular. It does not represent progress in an understanding of Machiavelli, but it is a typical expression of the optimism of the eighteenth century and of the naïve faith which men had in the power of reason over princes who would benefit humanity. This is the most significant aspect of this work, which contains a new and celebrated definition of the functions of a sovereign:

The sovereign, far from being the absolute master of the people under his domination, is none other than the first servant.

And better still, he was later called "the first servant of the State"

(Meinecke, *Idee der Staatsraison*, 387). This formula is modelled on that of the Popes of the Middle Ages (Gregory I, 590–604) who were, however, servants of servants of God, not of the State.

3   Diderot (1713–84)

Denis Diderot, the principal compiler of the Encyclopaedia, also acts in a holier-than-thou manner with respect to Machiavelli when he writes about him in two articles, *Machiavellianism*, and *Politics*. More sincere than Voltaire, he puzzles over the contradictions he finds in Bayle, who is his principal source. He realizes that Machiavelli

> was a man of a profound genius and of a varied erudition. He knew languages, ancient and modern. He knew history. He dealt with morality and politics. He did not neglect literature. He wrote some comedies that are not without merit.

But in these words one feels a lack of direct contact with Machiavelli's works, as if he were speaking from hearsay. In the list that he gives of Machiavelli's works, relying on Giovio, he attributes to him "four books on the Republic" (!), "treatises on the Prince and on the Senator" (!), and calls him "one of the most ardent defenders of monarchies" (!). He also seeks refuge in the interpretation then common (but which made its way around Florence at the time of Cardinal Pole) that *The Prince* was a warning and a suggestion to people to show them how to preserve their liberty:

> As a matter of fact, it was the fault of his contemporaries if they misconstrued his aim: they mistook a satire for a eulogy.

By the time Diderot wrote the article on *Politics,* he had read more of Machiavelli—perhaps the *Discourses*—because he praises him in this way:

> He didn't follow in the footsteps of authors of his time, nor did he fill his books with all those details that make their books so tasteless

—but because of his superior genius, he grasped the meaning of the real principles of the constitution of states, clarified the mechanisms with finesse, and explained the causes of revolutions—in a word, he blazed a new trail and probed the depths of politics.

Diderot's ideal always remained the Voltaire who saw in Frederick the Platonic Prince who would bring happiness to his subjects. Diderot was not only original but a man of genius, but here he did nothing more than compound the prejudices of others.

4   Rousseau (1712-78)

Because of his fame and the exceptional position he occupied in his century, Rousseau's judgment of Machiavelli had an importance that it would not otherwise have had. Though not an Encyclopaedist, he was one of their allies in the conflict against the Church. He was a revolutionary, not a reformer, and amidst those ultra-civilized rationalists, he appears as a madman. The Encyclopaedists did not understand Machiavelli, nor did Rousseau who, by means of his powerful personality, put words in Machiavelli's mouth that he never uttered. He also attributed irony to them, as an attempt by Machiavelli to mask his real meaning. This has lead critics like Culcasi to think that an influence over Rousseau was exerted by Machiavelli whose doctrines "are to be kept in mind as among the most important sources of Rousseau's *Contract*".[364]

An approach to Machiavelli might be found in Rousseau's theory of the political function of the Church:

> Therefore the legislator who cannot use either force or reason must of necessity turn to another kind of authority which can succeed without violence and convince without conquest. . . . This sublime reason which rises above the comprehension of the vulgar common man is the one by which the legislator places decisions on the lips of immortals, in order to influence, by means of divine authority, all those which human wisdom cannot persuade.[365]

But this is merely a superficial similarity, because for Rousseau religion is a living force which is found in men's hearts and not a deception practised by wise men.

Not knowing how to reconcile his interpretation of Machiavelli with *The Prince*, Rousseau contrasts the *Discourses* with *The Prince*, which he interprets as a warning to people:

> He pretended to instruct kings, instead he taught the people a magnificent lesson. *The Prince* is a book for Republicans.
>
> The choice itself of his hateful hero shows clearly his secret intentions and explains the opposition of the maxims in his *Prince* to those in his *Discourses* and in the *Florentine Histories*. It is clear that this profound political writer has only had superficial and corrupted readers.[366]

5 Helvétius, Condillac, Morellet Verri

Other Encyclopaedists who often quoted Machiavelli were Claude Adrien Helvétius (1715–61) and Condillac (1714–80); but they refer especially to his *Florentine Histories*, which they use to attack the nobility and the Church. They neglect *The Prince*, which produces in them a feeling of uneasiness:

> Machiavelli says the nobility in a Republic is the vermin which corrodes the foundations of a State. (Helvétius, *Pensées et reflexions*.)
>
> Gentlemen, says Machiavelli, are those who live from the product of their lands in abundance and in idleness. Such men are the ruin of a Republic—but the most pernicious are those who have chateaux, fortresses and feudal castles. (Condillac, *Oeuvres*, vol. 17, 147.)

Sometimes they make Machiavelli say what he never said:

> Man, says Machiavelli, has the right to think as he pleases, to say and to write what he wants, but not to impose his ideas on others. (Helvétius, *De l'homme*, sect. IX, ch. 7.)

However, they refer to Machiavelli as an authority without questioning him. They do not see that his thought is in opposition to theirs. The critic Meda was right when he said: "All or almost all philosophies of the eighteenth century were anti-machiavellian."[367]

Sometimes these ideas were contagious among the so-called Italian Encyclopaedists, like Pietro Verri, who should have been capable of understanding Machiavelli better:

> What other country besides ours has produced a Machiavelli and a Fra Paolo Sarpi, two monsters in political ideas whose doctrines are so atrocious that they are false, and coldly demonstrate the advantage of vice because they do not know those of virtue?[368]

Only one Encyclopaedist took it upon himself to study Machiavelli seriously, and apparently read *The Prince*. This was Morellet (*Mélanges de littérature et de philosophie du XVII siècle*, Paris, Lepetit, 1818—*Du Machiavélisme*). Yet he puts a little twist in what he translates from Machiavelli. For example, he says Machiavelli's prince (and Morellet adds *any* prince) "must confiscate the lands and homes of the old inhabitants and give them to those who will help him attain his ends", but he does not add that Machiavelli was referring to provinces "dissimilar in language or customs", advising the prince to go and live in this new province. The advice to give lands and homes to those who could help the prince is simply not found in Machiavelli.

6 Galiani

The slaughterhouses of the French Revolution and of the Napoleonic Wars provided the reveille for these dreams of the Encyclopaedists. Thus later the Second World War was the result of the pacifistic frenzy of Wilson. In Machiavelli's sense, all optimistic and pacifistic doctrines inevitably lead to war. The countries subscribing to these doctrines end up by becoming weak and offering an opportunity to be invaded and subjugated. Machiavelli would have advocated never leaving a void; although he did not know modern physics, he knew politics.

In the century of the Encyclopaedists it was not noted, but today we hear with delight the laughter of a witty Neapolitan who lived among them in Paris, who admired their talents but in a very sweet manner showed his contempt for their historical naïveté. This was the Abbé Ferdinando Galiani, who had learned from Machiavelli and Vico to distrust human fallibility and to look at things as they are and not as they should be. He preferred the ministers of state and princes who did nothing to those who wanted to do good for mankind. He admired pure and simple Machiavellists, who adhered to Machiavelli in private but never stated so in public. He believed that the essence of politics consists in winning and being paid for it, and in the awareness that people are governed by illusions and not by truth. He gave as a summary of his philosophy: "Not to believe anything, about anything, on anything, for anything." (*Antologia del Galiani,* Nicolini.) He was a second Lucian, and he did not advance panaceas for the ills of humanity. Like his great predecessor, his books are read only by the few.

MACHIAVELLI
AND THE RISORGIMENTO

---

1 *Machiavelli's reduced stature*

The same reason that made the German philosophers and historians study Machiavelli at the beginning of the nineteenth century, and raised the discussion of his ideas to a higher level, produced the opposite result in Italy. During the Italian Risorgimento, writers seemed fascinated by Machiavelli as a prophet of Italy's independence, but they did not see beyond that. The moral problem his ideas evoked was considered with displeasure, hostility and silence. Machiavelli became provincialized, and Italian criticism gained very little from a study of his works. When at the end of the century Villari started his researches, he clarified many points about the personal life of Machiavelli but made very little progress in the study of his thought, beyond the timid ideas of Macaulay. In 1869 and in the preceding and following years, the fourth centenary of Machiavelli's birth was celebrated with inane speeches by literary men and "patriots", to the general boredom (so it was credibly reported at the time) of those attending. The only exception to this picture was a study by Francesco Nitti* published in 1870, which only reached the year 1512 of Machiavelli's life and never went beyond a first volume. Its modest merits were overshadowed by the sparkle of Villari's more superficial biography.

---

* See. G. De Matteis, *Uno storico della Rinascenza, Francesco Nitti, 1851–1905*, Taranto, 1937.

2 Cuoco

The name of Vincenzo Cuoco (1770–1823) should occupy an important place in the history of Machiavellianism of the nineteenth century for several reasons. He was the first writer to attempt to fuse the political concepts of Machiavelli with the philosophic teachings of Vico. His works were read by Mazzini, Gioberti, Foscolo and Manzoni; through them he might therefore have been expected to exert an influence on all currents of the Risorgimento. Cuoco was also the first writer to assert Italian "nationalism", and in a sense he occupied in Italy the position that Fichte held in Germany. However, he was not read in Italy in the way Fichte was in Germany. As Vecchietti has written: "The complex thought that Cuoco had developed in those years of Napoleonic history had only a weak echo in the Italian Risorgimento."[369]

Although there were a few readers of high calibre who listened to Cuoco and studied his writings, his books and articles fell into oblivion and were revived only after the nationalistic and idealistic movement of the twentieth century—for which we have Giovanni Gentile to thank. Cuoco belongs more to the twentieth century than his own. He interpreted Vico rather than Machiavelli to his contemporaries, and the two concepts he attempted to put forward were never fused.

As a reaction to the French Revolution Cuoco, like Burke, but with a more popular and less conservative emotion than the Englishman, insisted on the natural and traditional elements of associated life which all people develop on their own account, independently of each other. A political concept is not good in itself but only insofar as it is a spontaneous reaction to the customs, traditions and usages of a people. An idea can be called wrong simply because it is foreign. A revolution is "active" when it stems from the needs of the people; it is "passive" when it comes from without or is imposed on people for love of abstract ideas, no matter how noble, that are not felt by the people themselves. In other words, sentiments count for more than laws.

Cuoco affirms the nationalism of his century; the difficulties of life in small countries; the innate necessity of states to grow or perish; the eternal conflict between states and the impossibility of perpetual peace; the need for a national militia; and the need for education to be in the hands of the state, which provides for the instruction of all social classes in line with the needs of the state. Like Fichte, he is a protectionist, not so much for economic as for moral and national reasons. He also developed one of Machiavelli's theses on the harm caused the state by relations with foreigners.

Of utmost significance is Cuoco's belief in the *relative* importance of constitutions. They are not good or bad in themselves, but only insofar as they can or cannot be adapted to people of a country. He writes to his friend Russo:

> Constitutions are like clothes: each individual must have his own, which if given to someone else will not fit. All clothes, no matter how made, can be fitted to a man no matter what type of figure he has, but if you want to make some clothes for all men, although modelled on the statue carved by Polyclitus, you will always find that the majority are too tall, too short, too thin, too fat and cannot wear them.[370]

We can imagine what Cuoco would have thought of those who believe that the Anglo-Saxon democratic system, or the Russian autocratic one, can be applicable to all people! If these systems were imposed on people with different traditions who had never heard of the Magna Carta or of the institution of Mir—the ancient communist systems of Russia—they would suffer greatly as a result.

Cuoco's works are filled with realistic maxims, inspired by the purest essence of Machiavellian thought.

> All that men cultivate, navigate, erect, all the good things of this earth are the work of strong men; the lazy ones, the imbeciles are but playthings of events. Nor can they say: these goods are mine,

because *mine* is only what can be protected. Nor can they say: I possess this virtue, because the few and frail virtues they possess are reduced to anarchy, misery, hunger. Remember that the first builders of cities were warriors who, bestowing their own courage on their followers, have founded cities and have sown the seeds of all social virtues.

Inasmuch as wars are inevitable, all progress towards happiness made by humanity is dependent upon the various ways men have engaged in warfare.[371]

Like Machiavelli, Cuoco was a naturalist in politics; today these maxims could pass for those of Kipling or Treitschke. But he strengthened Machiavelli with Vico, basing the power of arms on the instruction and conviction of people. He is a naturalist in the sense that for him life is superior to reason. This is seen in his justification of people even when they err:

Constitutions must be made for men as they are and as they will eternally be—full of vice, full of errors. It is just as conceivable that they want to give up their customs and traditions to follow institutions that I believe are arbitrary and variable, as for a shoemaker to expect to shorten a man's foot because he made a shoe too small for him.[372]

Instinct, traditions, and the nature of man count for more than his intellect. Politics is built around these obscure and profound forces; it is not based on the superficial and brilliant veneer of reason. This in essence is the teaching of Cuoco.

What is extraordinary about him is his capacity to judge events and men objectively, even those with whom he was involved during his political activity. His *Saggio Storico sulla Rivoluzione Napoletana,* in which revolution he participated and on the failure of which he was forced to go into exile in 1801, is a tribute to the Neapolitan "patriots". He sees them as idealistic individuals but denounces their abstract theories and intellectualism. He seems to say, fine people but they have the brains of a rabbit. Such an objective attitude, which raises him above his partisan convictions, is a rare quality everywhere, especially in Italy.

3 Leopardi

Another exception during the Risorgimento, in addition to Cuoco, is Giacomo Leopardi (1798–1837), who interpreted Machiavelli's thought in a completely personal way, somewhat as Gracian had done. He considered Machiavellianism applicable to a philosophy of human society founded on egoism. He also considered Machiavelli "the founder of modern and profound politics" (*Zibaldone*, I, 1180). He wanted to write a treatise on Machiavelli, a sort of moral *Galateo* (id. II, 1276, and also 1309, 1310, the Machiavelli of society). He realized that Machiavelli had spoken the truth. He makes him talk to Xenophon in this way:

> My book [*The Prince*] is in man's opinion valued above yours [*Cyropedia*] only because I say frankly what things are true, what are done, what will always be done, and what should be done, and others say just the opposite, although they know and see, no less than I do, that things are as I say.

And still making Machiavelli speak, Leopardi reveals his own convictions:

> What remains for me to desire for the good of men especially of the youth is that the lesson I taught Princes be applied to private everyday life, adding what is necessary. And thus we would finally have a Code of Conduct, a true set of regulations on how to live in society.[373]

This is an original and profound thought, but completely one-sided and ironical in essence. Leopardi's work remains outside European philosophical speculation and Machiavellian controversy. It was known and published only many years after Leopardi's death.

4 Balbo

The perplexity of judging Machiavelli is particularly evident in the Catholic liberals who are forced to condemn him because of his moral principles, and to exalt him as a patriot. Cesare Balbo (1798–1853) was a realist in foreign affairs. (His suggestion to allow Austria to spread to the Balkans in order to restrict her in Italy was very clever.) But he considers *The Prince* an "infamous book", "putrefaction" and "filthiness"; he admits the "sanctity of its aims" but finds its "means to be most wicked" (*Lettere di politica e di letteratura,* Firenze, 1855, 408–415) and in his *Speranze d'Italia* (ed. Utet, 66) he deplores the "elegantly indifferent mind" of Machiavelli.

Besides morality, there was another angle of opposition between Machiavelli and the Catholics. Machiavelli held that the papacy was a disintegrating force in the Italian nation, while Balbo, Cantù, and Manzoni maintained that the papacy exercised a national function by preventing the absorption of Italy by the German Empire:

> The counterbalance of the papal power was of great benefit to Italy, bestowed by Divine Providence, in preventing among other disorders of the Middle Ages the resurgence of tyranny on the part of the old Roman Empire.[374]

Even the idea of the unity of Italy was not pleasing to these Catholics or Guelphs. In the *Studi o Pensieri sulla Storia d'Italia,* written between 1840–41, Balbo opposed the idea of the unity of Italy in one single state. He considered the papacy to be one of the "future" glories of Italy and maintained that because of its geographical configuration, Italy was destined to remain divided into various states.

The only thing that Balbo liked about Machiavelli was his style, but even here he was superficial:

> Machiavelli is not pedantic. . . . He is clear, natural, places substantive, verb and accusative case in regular order, and never tires of

so doing, in the manner of all those who write to be understood as much as possible; he writes as do men of action, political men throughout the world, as very few do in Italy.[375]

The "leit-motif" of liberal Catholic criticism is: praise for Machiavelli the writer and for his idea of ridding Italy of foreigners; repugnance for his subjugating morality to politics and for his opposition to the national mission of the papacy.

5 Gioberti

A strange case offered by Vincenzo Gioberti (1801–52), who was torn between Catholicism and idealism. He was attracted to the one by family heritage and to the other as a new instrument of the mind; he put both to the service of the national idea. Very few years elapse between his *Primato Morale e civile degli Italiani* (1843) and the *Del Rinnovamento civile d'Italia* (1851), and his opinion of Machiavelli kept changing with the times. In the first, Machiavelli is a corrupter of Italy:

> Machiavelli, civil servant of a Republic, considers the Pope a non-essential element of Italian civilization, indeed even an impediment not to say a scourge. He aspires to a united, strong and national Italy but animated by pagan spirits and founded principally on steel, as in the times of Camillo and Scipio. Having divested the national personality of Italy of its religious principle and of the dignity which Italy acquired from the Christian monarchy [Papacy] is not in my opinion the least of the reasons why Italian spirits have been weakening for many centuries.[376]

Naturally the problem of the papacy is found in the Gioberti of the *Primato*:

> He errs who attributes the civil disunion of Italy to the Popes when instead the papacy deserves credit for the unity of Italy—as far as the times permitted. The contrary opinion, made popular by Machiavelli, is a corollary of the errors of this great writer.[377]

But in the *Rinnovamento*, Gioberti is more in favour of Machiavelli:

A disarmed Rome is useless in itself—damaging to Italy, weakening the military forces and the defence of the peninsula. But defended by foreign armies Rome becomes an enemy of national autonomy, of which it should be the bulwark. The malady of the temporal power of the papacy is as old as Machiavelli's denunciation of it.[378]

Many more quotations could be added if not actually multiplied. In five years, Gioberti, when the political situation changed (there had been the disaster of the war against Austria of 1848–49), kept altering his opinion of Machiavelli. How many people in Italy were aware of this fickleness? The cultured classes read Gioberti with less enthusiasm but with the same approval. Then Machiavelli became:

For method [he is] the Galileo of politics, and by introducing an amplified and stimulating element of inductive and deductive reasoning, he embraced Dante's idea of national unity and perfected it, appealing to an Italian prince to incarnate it and make it a reality. One of his characteristics is moderation.[379]

Gioberti is richer in images and in big words than in ideas. This image of Galileo is also used by him for Leopardi! (*Primato,* II, 198.) He also refers to Machiavelli elsewhere as a Sadducee. As we can see, he used historical comparisons at random.

6 Manzoni

Everything should have disposed Manzoni against Machiavelli. Yet the probity of the man and the fairness of the scholar were so great that to him we are indebted for one of the more accurate and truthful evaluations of his thought. This is not a fertile evaluation, not even where it is in contrast with Machiavelli, but it is striking for its impartiality.

Manzoni also tried to refute Machiavelli on historical grounds, showing that the coalition of the Longobards and Romans which Machiavelli described in his *Florentine Histories* had really been an inhuman and painful separation between conquerors and slaves. In his view the Pope's appeal to the Franks for help against the Longobards had not interrupted the formation of a national state, but had actually put an end to the oppression of the Longobards. Manzoni was defending the papacy (*Discorso su alcuni punti della storia longobardica,* 1822) with an historical progress. Moreover Manzoni used it with philological finesse.

Manzoni's refutation of the view of writers who uphold a morality "founded on the principle of utility" is purely rational and dialectical. This is contained in an appendix to his *Osservazioni sulla morale cattolica*. A note is devoted to Machiavelli in this appendix that is a marvel of impartiality and clarity:

> Among writers who employ utility as a supreme standard of their judgment in political matters, to Machiavelli fell the dubious honour of giving his name to such a doctrine and to its application in more than one language. The words derived from that name, like "Machiavellian", were destined to mean exclusively the use of perfidy and, on need, of cruelty, in order to attain the utility of one, of several or of many. The judgment implicit in those words is true only in part. Machiavelli did not desire injustice.... He wanted utility, and he wanted it either with justice or with injustice, according to the needs of the various cases. But none can doubt that his spirit was not inclined to prefer the first.

7 Mazzini

The bewilderment of Italian "patriots" when confronted with Machiavelli's thought is seen even better in the case of a fanatic, Guiseppe Mazzini (1805–72). Because of his sermonizing temperament ("life is a mission", "the science of governing is more simple ... if one starts out with a few principles based on ideas of religion and of duty", "men must be convinced that each must live not for himself but for others"), he was bound to be at cross purposes with Machiavelli, although he was forced to reckon with him in his desire for national unity. Mazzini is not very consistent in calling him an expression of the corruption of his time and yet turning to him for support in his unitary thesis. He never fails to couple his name with that of Dante and Petrarch:

> Italy must be one [not federated], bounded by the Alps and the sea. This idea of a united Italy was the dream of Dante, Petrarch and Machiavelli.[379a]

At the same time he always considers Machiavelli (an old idea) as the "expression of his time, which was of corruption and decadence".[380]

Sometimes Mazzini, to whom fog seemed as clear as sunlight, found a reason to doubt:

> Those voices which seemed in agreement, as regards facts, raised doubts in the soul. The thought of Dante and of Machiavelli [the thought of the two men was profoundly different and even at variance—G.P.] became as nebulous as chaotic forms, visions, individual appearances, different in customs, and habits, rivals and enemies, which the formulas of those political writers called to our mind.[381]

This is pure rhetoric, with no attempt to reach the meaning of Machiavelli's thought. We can say that with Mazzini the knowledge of Machiavelli takes a backward step.

8 De Sanctis

Francesco De Sanctis (1818–83) as a youth felt enthusiasm for the Risorgimento, which in old age turned to disillusion. His *Storia della letteratura italiana* is a moral rather than a literary book. In his desire to urge Italians to become a serious and modern people, capable of competition and of international victory, he loses sight of literary values. Did he succeed in his aims? It is up to conscientious Italians to answer.

The chapter on Machiavelli is one of the most important in the book, a key chapter to an understanding of the structure of the work and of the aims of De Sanctis. Unlike other writers of his time, De Sanctis wanted to put an end once and for all to a consideration of Machiavelli merely as a patriot:

> It is a real insult to place the greatness of that man in his Italian Utopia [unity of Italy], today an accomplished fact.

In his conclusion, he shows Machiavelli to be the inaugurator of modern activism. In the Hegelian trilogy that De Sanctis adopted, Machiavelli represents the end of the Middle Ages and the beginning of the modern era which is no longer ascetic but a life of work:

> Worthy of note is the completely *modern* idea [italics mine] that the end of man is work, and that the greatest enemy of civilization is idleness; a principle that has demolished convents and has destroyed from the roots the feudal system founded on the idea that the idleness of the few was made possible by the work of the many.

If Marx had read De Sanctis he would have understood Machiavelli, and his estimation of him would not have contained senseless remarks.

9   Guiseppe Ferrari

Giuseppe Ferrari (1812–76) belongs in a sphere of his own. He is a type Italy often produces known as near-geniuses because they possess the fleeting sparks but not the lasting flame of a genius. He studied as none before or after him—except for Meinecke—the history of the *raison d'état* and the theories of Italian political writers. When he came to Machiavelli, he saw him in a curious light and clashed with him as an adversary of his Italian "federalism":

He expects to destroy with his chimerical unity the federation which devoured the Goths, the Longobards, the greatest kings, the most warlike nations.[382]

But in other respects, something penetrating and brilliant came from his pen:

A new Titan, Machiavelli, proposed to dethrone God and to replace him with Satan in the government of the multitudes. He even complains that Christ had humanized States, preached humility, directed men's gaze away from the earth to the Heavens, put an end to bloody sacrifices, circus of gladiators, heroic massacres, decimation of armies.[383]

10   The Romantics

In this period Machiavelli stirred imaginations and became a character in historical novels. Even today he continues to furnish background material for works of imagination. We see him appear in *The Romance of Leonardo da Vinci* (1902, 1928) of Dmitri S. Merezhkovsky (1865–1941) and in a short novel of Somerset Maugham (1874–1966), *Now and Then.* (In my opinion Maugham would have done better not to have written it.) Prezzolini wrote a fictionalized life *Machiavelli, The Florentine* (1928) for the purpose of saying certain things which during Fascism he could not express openly, and also to write a book that would be liked by the public in general. But perhaps the first writer to use Machiavelli in an historical novel, was that windbag Francesco D. Guerrazzi (1804–73) who begins *L'Assedio di Firenze* (1836) by having Luigi Alamanni report on the "last words" of Machiavelli. They are prolonged for three full pages, like the tenors in Italian operas who take so long to die, all the while singing one aria after another. Machiavelli appears also in *Nicolò de' Lapi* (1841) of Massimo D'Azeglio 1798–1866, with a few less declamations, and above all in the *Marietta de' Ricci* (1840) of Agostino Ademollo (1799–1841), which is still consulted for its historical notes rather than for its merits as a novel. It is a display of erudition.

Some writers who have used Machiavelli, like George Eliot (1819–80) in her *Romola* (1862–63), follow his text closely and have him speak as he wrote. In more recent times the dramatic possibilities of the figure of Machiavelli compared to certain living people have tempted many writers in various countries. See Oxilia, *Machiavelli nel teatro,* "Cultura", 1933, XII, 912–22; the voluminous *The Secretary of Machiavelli* by Daniel McCarthy, *Philadelphia* (1841); a drama by Franklin Pierce Norton, *Machiavelli,* New York (1915); W. H. Foodward's *Elena* (1919); Lemist Esler's *The Gray Fox* (1930); and *Maquiavelo,* a drama in verse by Ramon Caralt Sanromá, Barcelona (1940).

VII

MACHIAVELLI
OUR CONTEMPORARY

1 Machiavelli in the twentieth century

The most significant contributions to the development and understanding of Machiavelli after the *Risorgimento* were made by Croce and the Italian idealistic philosophical school of thought, and by the realistic political philosophy of Pareto and Mosca. Breaking away from their contemporaries, these writers reverted to an older tradition; having nothing in common with Villari or Ferrari, they date back to Cuoco and Galiani. Vilfredo Pareto (1848–1923) and Gaetano Mosca (1858–1941) contemporaneously, but independently of each other, formulated a purely political development of Machiavelli's thought: that states are never governed by one man or by the people (they are never "pure" monarchies or "pure" democracies), but are governed by aristocracies—that is, by the ruling classes. Without these, the dictator or monarch alone could not really exercise power. On the other hand democracies—that is, the government of the majority—are always lead by a small group of people. Therefore in this regard monarchies and democracies come to the same thing. To see the difference between various governments the character of the ruling classes must be studied—whether priests, warriors, lawyers, farmers, demagogues, adventurers, lower middle classes, veterans, merchants, bankers, etc. They reveal the political reality of that state better than a study of constitutions. This theory puts an end to all sterile academic discussions of the abstract goodness of this or that system. Is a democracy preferable? Is a dictatorship justified? Pareto, above all, was inclined to show by means of Machiavellian irony the rise and fall of the bellicose vitality of these classes. He saw that political classes become consumed with, and corrupted by, power. Like Machiavelli, he believed that the virtue of a people or of a hero makes its appearance and then vanishes, and has no relation to moral problems of good and evil.

With some reservations I would say that the best of Georges Sorel (1847–1922) finds a place in this group of thinkers. He indicated by name those forces of the moral imagination that bring about profound changes in society, through the agency of dedicated minorities. For the modern mechanical socialism of Marx, who foresaw an inevitable future communistic society which would bring about the end of conflicts in the world, Sorel substituted a hope in the future of labour unions. He conceived of them as one of those dedicated minorities which through myth would destroy the corrupted society of the middle classes (see his *Reflections on Violence*, 1908, English translation, 1914). This was a power that Machiavelli had never reckoned with, but which can very well fit in his system of politics as force. Sorel lived long enough to be disillusioned, and then put his faith in other myths which have disillusioned others who lived beyond him. The concept of myth remains a key to understanding social movements. Sorel's concept, of which he was so fond, that all societies are born and renewed only through recourse to violence, can also be called Machiavellian and certainly Machiavelli would have agreed with him on this point.

Alongside these extensions of Machiavelli's thought, true and original annexed territories still stand. Worthy of note are other efforts to crystallize Machiavelli. One, connected with the nationalistic movement of the new century in Italy, is the juridical and rigid one of Prof. Francesco Ercole. Here we have a Machiavelli seen through the eyes of Ercole who hoped to reassert the power of the state through Fascism, after the period of anarchy following the First World War. The other is connected with the interpretation of the Renaissance by Giovanni Gentile, for whom Machiavelli's thought is one of the proofs of the re-evaluation of man in that historical moment in contrast with the Middle Ages. Both exalt the Machiavelli of *virtù* at the expense of the Machiavelli of fortune, and the Machiavelli of nationalistic hopes over

Machiavelli the pessimist of humanity. Both interpretations absorb the problem of the necessity of evil in political action within the ethics of a state.

There are also two exceptional works, both in German, which deserve a place among the flowering of studies of Machiavelli in our century. One is the history of the *raison d'état* of F. Meinecke, *Machiavellianism; the doctrine of raison d'état and its place in modern history,* translated by Douglas Scott, with an introduction by W. Stark (Yale University Press, 1957, p. 438) which depicts humanity in the clutches of Machiavelli's concept of politics from which it unsuccessfully attempts to free itself. Meinecke was the first to note a stylistic break in *The Prince,* but not everyone is in agreement with him about this. The other is an original interpretation of Machiavelli by von Muralt, who pictures Machiavelli as a religious and national reformer who could have been for Italians—if they had been like the Germans—what Luther (1483–1545) was for Germany and Zwingli (1483–1531) for Switzerland.

Among the large number of books on Machiavelli's doctrines in the twentieth century, the dubious honour of adapting them to the needs of the Communist Party in Italy fell to Antonio Gramsci. He was the most original writer and unquestionably the most ethical figure of Italian communism. Perhaps his disciples did him a disservice in publishing, after his death which occurred in prison where he was serving a term for his opposition to Fascism, his *Note sul Machiavelli, sulla politica e sullo stato moderno* (Einaudi, 1949, p. 361). Their thought is not fully developed, so they do not bear detailed discussion, but Gramsci's idea of Machiavelli, to whom he turned with obvious sympathy, was that *The Prince* is not a systematic treatise, but a unified work advocating an anti-feudal revolution by the peasant masses of Italy. Machiavelli's attempt to create the myth of a commander capable of leading the masses from the countryside into the political life of the city of Florence is, according to Gramsci, a work of political poetry. He saw it as a "political manifesto" aimed at a "political party" in formation, that is, the people forming the revolutionary class of the time, "the citizen democracy which expresses in its inner being Savonarola and Pier Soderini and not Castruccio and Valentino".

This last quotation is enough to show that Gramsci has turned Machiavelli's thought upside down. He has created a Machiavelli who is a replica of Gramsci himself. Gramsci was the son of peasants and always advocated an Italian revolution in which the peasant masses (of the south) would be allied to the working masses (of the north). Never did Machiavelli's thought undergo such a travesty: Machiavelli admired and idealized the Castruccios and the Valentinos as much as he hated the Savonarolas and scorned the Soderinis! It is true that Machiavelli dedicated many years of his life to forming a militia from the countryside of Florence, which was to substitute the mercenary troops of the Commune, but if Gramsci had read the correspondence between Machiavelli and the Signoria about this matter he would have learned that both the Signoria and Machiavelli feared that the arms given to these "peasants" might serve for a local revolt. It was therefore decided to have the arms used only for drills and then removed to a place of safety; and the conscription was limited only to those districts considered loyal to the Republic.

Machiavelli was, and always remained, a representative of aristocratic urban political thought of central Italy. Nothing could have been further from his mind than the idea of a social revolution modelled on the Russian one four centuries later. Naturally no one can stop Gramsci from identifying his party with the mythical figure of *The Prince*. In fact, we have seen that the word "prince" in Machiavelli can mean many authorities, from the tyrant to the sovereign people, but always impersonated by a single man.

It is a political technique to want to transform the cult of Machiavelli for great historical personalities into a "collective" form. Nothing of this exists in Machiavelli's thought. I might even add that nothing of this exists in the history of Russian communism, which has developed and flourished because of such great personalities as Lenin, Stalin, Khrushchev.

2 Machiavelli in Russia

At first Russia did not have many productive contacts with Machiavelli's thought. Count Peter Andreivich Tolstoi (1645–1742) was called the Russian Machiavelli and supposedly translated *The Political Counsels of Nicolò Machiavelli,* but no trace of his book is found in libraries. In the *Moskovski Telegraph* of 1828 appeared an article about a French translation of the works of Machiavelli which had been published in France three years earlier. A certain S. Rotoski had amused readers of the *European News* of 1819 with samples of the wit in Machiavelli's works. The first translation of one of Machiavelli's books, *The Art of War,* published in a collection of military books and considered a technical book, did not appear until 1839 (*Voiennoie Iskusstvo,* translated by M. Bogdanovich). At that time Russia was still a province in the far reaches of Europe, late in receiving news. The Russian nobility, who then read French and German and knew some Italian, should have had opportunities to know about Machiavelli, but no trace can be found. Books on Machiavelli were not to appear until 1880 (A. Alekzev) and 1909 (Toporz-Radrevskaro)—not significant contributions. In 1869 *The Prince* and the *Discourses* appeared together in one volume, translated by N. Kuronchina, and *The Prince* appeared alone translated by F. Zatriev. In 1910 C. Rochovin translated *The Prince.*

It does not seem that Machiavelli's thought penetrated the Russian spirit to any appreciable degree. When Alexander Valentinovich Amfiteatrof (1862–1923), an Italianized Russian resident of Italy, made an excellent translation of *Mandragola,* he bemoaned the scarcity of translations which would have supplied him with traditional background material. He felt he was working on virgin soil, but perhaps his research had not been very extensive. In any case, his is an important testimony (1910). How little Machiavelli counted in Russian literature is seen by the fleeting mention of his name, along with those of Locke, Hobbes and Bayle, in the classical work on the influence of European literature

(Aleksiei Veselovskii, *Zapadnoi Vlianie v novoii ruskoii literatur,* Moskva, 1910, 48, 62). And in the more recent history of Russian philosophy by V. V. Zenkovsky (1953), Machiavelli is not even mentioned.

The only Russian writer who seemed to have an affinity with Machiavelli's spirit was Dostoyevsky but he probably only knew his name, which he never mentions in his works, and had no knowledge of him, not even through the works of De Maistre. In the *Brothers Karamazov* one chapter which has become famous but which was omitted in the first French translation, spread the fame of the Russian writer abroad. It is entitled "The Grand Inquisitor" and poses the problem, in a completely Machiavellian way, of the moral responsibility of the leader of people. Men, being "weak, evil, contemptible and rebellious", must be taught that "liberty and bread for everyone are things that do not go hand in hand". Therefore in order to have bread, they must forego liberty and allow themselves to be guided by types like the Jesuits who, in order to "make them (the majority) happy" will accept for themselves "a state of unhappiness". That is, they will risk losing their souls, as Machiavelli had said, for the good of the fatherland. There will be a few thousand of these selected souls "who will take upon themselves the burden of knowing good and evil" to the end that others, the ignorant majority, may live their life in tranquillity.

In this period many works on the history of political doctrines appeared—for example, Kacenovschii, D.I., *Vzgliad na istoriiu polit. nauk v Evropie,* (1859), and B. Cicerin, *Historia polit. ucenii,* (1869) which include Machiavelli in their exposition—and he is dealt with at length in a detached manner. I imagine this also holds true of books on the history of philosophy and of the Renaissance. They repeated what they read in English, French or German books on the subject. Cicerin, for example (1828–1890), a disciple of Kant and Hegel, had liberal tendencies and Belinsky (1811–48) followed the German thought of "power is law". But they did not realize how they could have made use of Machiavelli for their doctrines.

It was only after 1900, when the influence of Marx's thought was beginning to be felt, that Machiavelli appeared in a new light. Actually Marx and Engels did not pay much attention to him; indeed Marx at times used the word Machiavellian in the accepted stereotyped meaning of the term (*Briefwechsel,* M.E. IV, 541 *Gesammelte Werke,* B.I., 6.II, 318; IV, 297). We know that Marx had read Machiavelli in the Ziegler translation (B.I., Abt.II, 136). At one time he had called the *Florentine Histories* a masterpiece (B. 2,III, Abt. 229); at another he made the obvious remark that San Cuccù in *Mandragola* seemed a very good pun. However, all these new books caused Communists to consider Machiavelli as a precursor of Marx. It is strange that Marx did not grasp the full import of Ciompi's speech in the *Florentine Histories:*

> But if you note the behaviour of men, you will see that all who have amassed great wealth or have attained great positions of power have done so by means of fraud or force. They try to give the appearance of honesty to the things they have usurped either by deception or violence, in order to conceal the iniquity of their acquisition. Virtuous men are always poor. Only the unfaithful and audacious are ever able to free themselves of servitude; only the greedy and the dishonest can escape from poverty.[384]

But what Marx failed to note, the Communists who came after him saw clearly. As early as 1906 M. Pokrovschi, one of the first apostles in Russia of historical materialism, wrote:

> Three hundred years after the events, the Italian writer Machiavelli explained the changes in the political structure of his native city Florence brought about by economic factors and precisely by the class struggle. At first landed gentry fought against merchant citizens, then the leaders of commerce and industry contended with the artisan and labour masses. That is how he describes in it in his *Florentine Histories.* The Florentine manufacturers furnished goods (especially silk) to all commercial Europe. Florentine bankers supplied money to all European kingdoms. Many things which are accepted now that we live in a capitalistic society, but completely unknown to feudal Europe, came for the first time from Florence: foreign exchange, insurance, public revenue, statistics. . . .[385]

The precocious Florentine economic maturity also gives evidence of a precocious maturity in the thought of a Florentine writer. But seen after the discovery of America and of the water route to India, with the change of world commerce towards the Atlantic, Italy loses her economic pre-eminence and disappears from the political scene. Florence declines. Machiavelli was a witness to this decadence.[386]

Machiavelli then becomes a sign of economic times and of the capitalistic transformation of Italy. This is not a completely new concept. Previously Baldelli and De Sanctis stated that Machiavelli represented a movement in contrast to the Middle Ages, but here it is specified and expressed in Marxist terminology.

Another writer N. I. Tkaciev, who was republished during Soviet times, remarks:

Machiavelli completely abandoned medieval mysticism. He saw the good and the right not in abstract principles but in what is expedient—the evil and the unjust in what is futile. Having postulated that "the health of the people is the supreme law", Machiavelli did not overlook any means to attain that end. The concept of the true and of the right leads him to the simple calculation of the advantageous and of the efficient; he denies the natural right of the scholastics, their mystic morality, and without long circumlocutions reduces right to force. That is why all his efforts were directed towards making Italy first of all a strong united kingdom. In this way, Machiavelli interpreted the substance of law and in this regard he can be called a true realist.[387]

From one of the laboratories of official Russian Marxism there came a study of Machiavelli's idea of dictatorship, an idea which naturally has to be in agreement with that of Marx in order to be approved. This is a very long work and starts out with the hypothesis that "Machiavelli's doctrine is closely related with fundamental facts of his epoch. . . . He is the most powerful political writer of the Renaissance—an epoch that marks the beginning of the change from Feudalism to Capitalism in Western Europe."[388] And the author, Maximovich continues in that vein, giving evidence of a great knowledge of Machiavelli's works and also of the literature concerning Machiavelli. When coming to the concept of dictatorship in Machiavelli, he starts out with the "right, scientific" definition given by Lenin after the experience of the October Revolution: "Dictatorship, through the very meaning of the word, is unlimited illegal violence based on force. It is distinguished by an absence of any idea of compromise or balance."[389]

For a Machiavellian example of dictatorship he turns to the *Discourses,* where Machiavelli compares the conduct of Brutus in Rome with that of Soderini in Florence:

> He who becomes a tyrant and does not kill Brutus, and he who creates a free state and does not kill the children of Brutus, will only last a short time.
>
> Pier Soderini was wrong when he thought that with patience and goodness he could put an end to the desire of the sons of Brutus to change the government.[390]

For Maximovich a dictatorship is what Machiavelli called "assuming extraordinary authority". According to Maximovich, Machiavelli did "nothing more than design the idea of a middle-class dictatorship", although it was a different one from that of Mussolini.

> Machiavelli's idea of a dictatorship is when a state has only one leader whom he calls "the new prince". The general characteristics, typical of every dictatorship, are here mixed with the typical ones of middle-class dictatorship, and explain many oscillations in an appreciation of him by subsequent political writers.[391]

With a penetrating analysis, Maximovich shows that the concept of the revolutionary dictatorship of Lenin is in agreement with Machiavelli's teachings:

> First of all the new head [of state] must be politically active. He must foresee events and go forward to meet them—and not wait for them to take place, or he wastes time that can be favourable to the threat of a reaction, like a person who allows a sickness to develop which ends up by becoming incurable. First of all, conditions vary; at times desperate boldness is necessary, at times the contrary, that is

the greatest caution and reflection. Much depends on the power of the prince. If he is endowed with courage, it is better for him to make use of audacity. In the domain of war, offensive strategy is preferable. Even in other fields, if conditions are favourable he must pursue a resolute, bold policy.[392]

And he quotes the examples of Pope Julius II and Ferdinand the Catholic, in an analysis of chapters 21 and 25 of *The Prince*.

The study concludes with these words:

The political theory of Machiavelli is rather rough and primitive, his philosophical and social concepts smack somewhat of rationalism; they are enclosed within the framework of the teaching that human nature is immutable and that there is a circular social motion [Vico's theory of cycles, taken up again by Spengler]; but this must not prevent us from appreciating its value, that is of being the first formulation of the theory of middle-class dictatorship.[393]

It should not surprise anyone that in modern Russia everything is seen through the eyes of Marx, Lenin and later Stalin. In the big *Soviet Encyclopaedia* Machiavelli is treated fairly well, but the strange thing is that when we come to the bibliography, in addition to the existing Russian translations, nothing else is listed except passages from the works of Marx and Engels, whose few and superficial words can only be interpreted as a sort of official "benediction". That Marx called *Florentine Histories* a masterpiece is enough to justify the tone of the article.

A similar line is followed by other works of consultation; for example in the *Encyclopaedia of Government and Law* edited by N. Stuchka (vol. II, 806–11) although this gives evidence of a deeper knowledge than the other encyclopaedias already mentioned. It maintains that Machiavelli's idea of absolutism of the state comes from the capitalistic industrial conscience.

With uncertainty and confusion of thought Leon Trotsky, one of the last heroes of the revolution and of Russian political assassination, in his *Life of Stalin* approached the problem of Machiavellianism. His thoughts on the revival of Machiavellianism in the twentieth century are interesting:

Once again new times have brought into being a new morality. Strangely, the pendulum of history has returned once more, under many aspects, to the era of the Renaissance—indeed it even surpasses it in the extension and profundity of its cruelty and bestiality. Here we meet again the political *condottiere,* and the struggle for power is on a grandoise scale. . . . Once upon a time, the laws of political mechanism which Machiavelli struggled to formulate were considered the acme of cynicism. For Machiavelli, the struggle for power was like solving a chess problem. Moral issues did not exist for him any more than for an accountant. His task consisted in determining which politics were most suitable for a special need, and in explaining its application in a most crude and stark manner on the basis of experiences that had taken place in the political crucibles of two continents. This manner of approaching a problem is explained not only by the task itself but by the character of the epoch in which the task was set. It depends essentially on the development of feudalism and is in agreement with the decisive struggle for power between the two masters of the time—the dying feudalism and the middle-class society which was emerging.[394]

Trotsky continues by noting that in the nineteenth century (marked by parliamentarism, liberalism, reformism) Machiavelli was no longer in fashion and there came into being a new and superior morality. But for some unknown reason, the twentieth century, which was prepared for by the nineteenth, returns to the morality of the Renaissance:

This backward return to the most cruel Machiavellianism seems incomprehensible to those who only yesterday were cradled in the faith that human history moves according to a cultural and materialistic progress. . . . This is not true. . . . But in any case, no matter what you think of it, no era of the past has ever been as cruel, without feeling, or as cynical as ours.

According to Trotsky, what is the reason for this? It is that we are living, as in the Renaissance, in a period halfway between two worlds, the middle-class capitalistic one which is dying, and the new world of socialism that must take its place. There are many things to be said about this vague judgment of Trotsky—because if cruelty in human relations is necessary each time human societies are in *rapid* transition (I am adding *rapid,* because human societies are always in transition and one is always dying and being replaced by a new one) it is hard to see how those who are bringing about this transformation can be blamed. This theory presupposes that it is only possible to act in a cruel way.

In a certain sense Trotsky, being one of the actors, and also a victim of the times, is speaking about himself when he says that in our epoch the "cruellest Machiavellianism" has returned. This is a confession rather than a judgment. But as an "historic judgment" it is completely right. Our epoch has been as Machiavellian as the others of humanity—with the difference that it has had less recourse to hypocrisy. Statesmen, even the most innocuous and middle-class ones (like Salandra, a mediocre person whose only words worth remembering were "sacred egoism", when in 1915 he declared war on the old ally Austria and initiated the policy of back-stabbing) feel justified to tell a formal lie and make no excuses for acting in opposition to Christian morality for what they consider to be the good of their country.

It was not possible for me to consult translations of some of Machiavelli's works by L. B. Kamenev (1883–1936), *Socineniia* ... *Kniaz, Mandragola i melkie proizvedernia,* Mosca-Leningrad, (1933). Kamenev will be remembered as one of the first Russian socialists and Bolshevists, who up to 1936 held important positions in the Party and in the government. He was ambassador to Rome and, among other things, published the works of Lenin. In 1936 he was arrested, found guilty and condemned to death for having plotted with Trotsky the assassination of Stalin. As Freyer, the Italian ambassador in Russia at that time noted, among other accusations he was charged with having translated Machiavelli! I imagine that since then it has not been possible to study, translate or comment upon Machiavelli. ... Maybe even Gramsci, if he were alive, would be sorry he had devoted some time to Machiavelli, all of which goes to show how politics can belittle a subject and deviate a mind.

Some other details may be found in Jan Malarczyk, *Političeskoe učenie Makiavelli v russkoj dorevoljucionnoj i sovetskoj istoriografii* (The Political Doctrine of Machiavelli in Russia in the Historiography of Pre-revolutionary and Soviet Russia), in "Annales Universitatis Mariae Curie-Sklodowska", Lublin, vol. VI, I, Sectio G, 1959 (published in 1960), p. 26.

3 Machiavelli in America

America, being of more recent formation, does not interpret history in the European manner. American education is still impregnated with the abstract thought of the eighteenth century; from Benjamin Franklin to John Dewey there is very little difference in this regard. Optimistic and deaf to theoretic considerations, Americans considered Machiavelli almost always with a sort of shocked curiosity. Their Protestant formation, their English inheritance of contempt for Machiavelli, their jealous inferiority complex with respect to Europe (from whose ability in diplomatic intrigue, called Machiavellian, they always expected to be cheated in making peace treaties even when they were the victors), their social need to cover the expediency of their political action with a veneer of dignity and respectability—all these elements, with a few exceptions, made them refractory to an understanding of political realism.

Naturally this has not prevented American politicians from acting in the same way as politicians of all times and all countries. Historians can cite such American actions as liquidating entire populations (the Indians), conquering territory with force (Texas), abandoning friends who had helped them (the French), taking advantage of countries torn with internal strife (separating Panama from Colombia), attacking Spanish Florida, waging war on Mexico and, although not really wanting one, ending up by creating an empire in the Atlantic and Pacific. Like other states, while doing these things they were always invoking God, moral law and justice.

The contribution of such a country to Machiavellianism—which consists primarily of a theoretic consciousness of inherent and inescapable iniquity in political action—must needs be negative. In fact, no important work on the development of Machiavellianism has been written in the United States. The greatest number of American books and articles on Machiavelli are in opposition to him and spiteful. Even Americans by adoption, who were educated in Europe, tried to kill Machiavelli once and for all, perhaps in deference to the country that had given them such a warm welcome (Borgese, Cassirer, Salvemini). In recent years, many works on Machiavelli were translated but most of them were either semi-serious or used Machiavelli's era as background material (Lupo, Kirk, Prezzolini) and those with intellectual fibre were overlooked (until recently, when Meinecke was translated).

Translations of Machiavelli's works, which appeared in increasing numbers and which were always more faithfully translated with the passing of the years, had no discernible influence on public opinion. The articles in the encyclopaedias are a good example of this. It can be said that in the old encyclopaedias (for example, in the article on Machiavelli in the *New American Cyclopedia,* of G. Ripley and Charles A. Dana in 1857) Machiavelli received kinder treatment than in more recent compilations. In the *Encyclopaedia of Social Sciences,* published between 1930 and 1935, the article on Machiavelli was written by an Italian, Gaetano Mosca, as though there weren't any competent Americans to do it and it minimized Machiavelli's thought. The *Catholic Encyclopaedia* also turned to an Italian, Mons. Benigni. All of these articles fall short of expectations, the old encyclopaedias in matters of accuracy, and the new ones in lack of thoroughness.

I see that works of authors influenced by Hegel, Stahl, Bluntschli are called Machiavellian, although these authors never even so much as mention the Florentine. They are Elisha Mulford, 1833–85, *The Nation* (1870); John W. Burgess, 1844–1931, *The Foundations of Political Science* (1933); Mestel W. Willoughby, 1867–1945, *Prussian Political Philosophy* (1918). These political writers are good scholars of German thought, but at times they transform the thought into theology, like Mulford, or at other times, like Willoughby, without much insight they compare German thought with American policy which serves the interest and welfare of individuals. It seems to me these political writers get indigestion rather than nutrition from Machiavelli. Certainly the moral problem of politics remains alien to them.

The political men of the American Revolution knew Machiavelli better than those of modern times, because at that time classical culture and knowledge of the Italian language were more widespread. But a thorough knowledge of Machiavelli was possessed only by John Adams, 1735–1826. Benjamin Franklin supposedly imitated Machiavelli's ideas in his political pamphlet directed against the English, *Rules for reducing a great empire to a small one: presented to a late minister when he entered upon his administration* (written in 1774, *Works* IV, 387). Here he ironically lists, as ways to lose the colonies, all the policies adopted by the English government in America, but the satirical intonation of the booklet is not Machiavellian. Its origin is clearly that of the ironic pamphlets of Swift. Franklin knew Italian and was in correspondence with many Italians of his time, but he never mentions Machiavelli in his works. (See Antonio Pace, *Franklin and Machiavelli*, "Symposium", May 1947.)

Instead John Adams made use of Machiavelli, of his *Florentine Histories* and of the examples of politics in Florence for his book, *Defense of the Constitution of Governments of the United States* (1787–8). The catalogue of the books in his library lists Machiavelli's *Florentine Histories* (ed. Aldo 1546) in Italian and his *Works* translated into English by Ellis Farneworth (in 4 volumes, second edition, 1775). For his quotations he made use of the last mentioned. Adams' point of departure is the same as that of Machiavelli, *the evil nature of man*. Not only does he quote Machiavelli on this point, but adds a note of his own:

> So great is the depravity of the human heart, that ministers, who only can know it, are in charity to mankind bound to keep it a secret. . . .[395]

He also takes from Machiavelli the concept that only necessity makes men good. There is no other mention of the moral problem. For the rest he uses Machiavelli as his authority to support his view of the superiority of a mixed government—as other political writers had done before him—(which however dates back to Aristotle) and he is one of the few who paid attention to the *Discorso sulla riforma dello Stato di Firenze*. For the technical aspect of this mixed government which seemed ideal to him, in many other passages he makes use of Machiavelli's facts and ideas from the *Discourses*. It is characteristic of his Anglo-Saxon temperament that he never mentions *The Prince*. He limits his Machiavellianism to a consideration of Machiavelli as a truthful and distinguished advocate of the ability of the balanced forces of a constitutional state to correct human bestiality.

As a curiosity, I will mention the first work of Machiavelli published in an American, not English, edition. It is *The Art of War. In Seven Books. To Which is Added: Some anecdotes relating the life of Machiavelli collected from various authors; and hints relative to warfare by a gentleman of the State of New York*, published in Albany, N.Y. (1815) by H. C. Southwick. This is a republication of the English translation of Farneworth (London, 1762) which was based on a French version of Tétard, (1743).

Miss Shields, who listed American translations of Italian works, *Italian Translations in America* (1931), believes that Machiavelli had a considerable vogue in America for the simple fact that there are about fifty-three editions or revisions of his works (up to 1930). Actually these figures are misleading because as we have noted, in the last century the knowledge of the Italian language was much more general among the cultured classes than today, and in the case of America we must keep in mind the English editions which were imported.

An American from the south made a resumé rather than a translation of the Discourses, *Machiavel's Political Discourses upon the First Decade of Livy. Interspersed with various reflections*, by Robert Wickliffe, Jr., Louisville, Kentucky (1840). Wickliffe admired Machiavelli. In writing about Montesquieu, he said:

For many of his profoundest ideas and most comprehensive views, upon this, as well as upon many other subjects, he is indebted to an author whose fate has been as hard with posterity as it certainly was with his contemporaries, and whose example affords another proof that after-ages are frequently as unjust, as our own is generally neglectful of sterling talent and well-earned fame. In the *Discourses* ... Machiavelli ... unfolded with a masterly hand the principles and policy by which the grandeur of the Roman Republic was reared, and has thrown out with lavish prodigality some of the profoundest maxims of political wisdom that are recorded in the annals of government or the writings of constitutional lawyers. It is not our purpose at present to notice all his works, or to rescue his character from the obloquy under which is has for centuries suffered. This generous task has been performed by many wise and eminent men, from the time of Lord Bacon down to the present; and the day perhaps is not distant, when his character will be as fully understood and his fame as freely acknowledged in other countries, as they are already in his own.

Robert Wickliffe, Jr. (1815?–1850), from a well-to-do family of Kentucky, already possessed a sufficient Italian culture, as is proved by this adaptation of Machiavelli, when he was named Chargé d'Affaires of the United States at Turin, where he remained for five years in a most interesting period of Italian history (1843–48). The reports to his government show him to be an attentive observer of economic and political events. Nor did he miss the important books of the Risorgimento, like those of Balbo, Gioberti and D'Azeglio and he followed with interest the political conflicts in the court of Charles Albert. He realized that "affairs in Italy are taking a drastic turn and are heading for a solution" (7 Sept. 1947.) Naturally his sympathies are with the liberals but he also judges impartially the reactionaries. He tried to steer the commerce of Piedmont directly to the United States without passing through London. He was a man of rare intelligence. (See F. Livingston, *Biographical sketches of eminent Americans,* 1852; and Howard R. Marraro, *An American Diplomat views the dawn of liberalism in Piedmont,* in *Journal of Central European Affairs,* July 1946.)

It is understandable that some of the few voices raised in America to uphold the greatness of Machiavelli come from Americans who lived in Italy, some of whom like Wickliffe were diplomatic or consular representatives in the period of the formation of Italian unity, and were well aware of the change taking place. Another of these was Charles Edward Lester (1815–90), Consul at Genoa from 1842 to 1847 who translated D'Azeglio, Alfieri and among Italian political writers Cebá and Machiavelli. He was popular above all for his *Life of Vespucci* reprinted eleven times between 1846 and 1903. He translated Machiavelli's *Florentine Histories* in 1845. He saw them through the idealism of the Risorgimento and under the clear influence of Sismondi:

> These *Histories* are the annals of a brave and free people, whose laws, whose arts, and whose literature, made their capital the university of the world. Since the dismemberment of the republics of antiquity, no period of human history is gemmed with so much that is beautiful and glowing in human achievement. Every spot in Florence is hallowed with the recollection of some heroic deed in the defence of liberty; and every spot, too, has been bathed in the blood of civil faction.[396]

Another follower of Machiavelli of the same time was G. W. Greene (1811–83), from a rich and famous American family, lecturer, historian, friend of Lafayette and Longfellow, and for many years Consul at Rome. In an essay on Machiavelli, *Historical Studies* (1850) he skirts around the morality of *The Prince,* maintaining that this was "a work of youth" and "imperfect" and that it was later corrected and completed [by the Discourses? by the Florentine Histories?]. *The Prince,* he says, "contains important truths but also dangerous errors". He avoids the issue by praising some secondary doctrines of Machiavelli, like his criticism of the *condottieri.* His attitude is common to many Anglo-Saxons of that time who were attracted to Machiavelli's lucid and simple style and may even have sensed the truth of his assertions, but who wanted to avoid at all costs taking a definite stand. (On Greene, see G. Prezzolini, *Come gli Americani scoprirono l'Italia,* 1934). This probably explains why the name of Machiavelli is almost absent from the works of a famous but mediocre Italianophile, William Dean Howells (1837–1920). Favourable reports of Machiavelli (for example *Portfolio*, "Vindication of Machiavelli", 1809, 220–233) are more to be found in old issues of magazines rather than in modern ones.

We are more likely to find in the pages of the work of some American jurist, like John Jay (1745–1829) words that are reminiscent of Machiavelli rather than in American statesmen of today:

> I do not expect that mankind will, before the millennium, be what they ought to be; and therefore, in my opinion, every political theory which does not regard them as being what *they are*, will probably prove delusive.[397]

Modern statesmen from Wilson and Franklin Roosevelt to Truman and Eisenhower have gambled the safety and the independence of their country for universal peace and collective security as stakes. They all believed that men could be led by reason and none of them would have written (even in a personal letter) what John Jay wrote:

> As to the position, that "the people always mean well", or, in other words, that they always mean to say and to do what they believe to be right and just,—it may be popular, but it cannot be true. The word *people*, you know, applies to all the individual inhabitants of a country, collectively considered. That portion of them who individually mean well, never was, nor until millennium will be, considerable.[398]

In order to meet a genuine Machiavellian spirit, we must leave aside the professional of political science and turn to writers with no academic ties. Among these, for example, there is a satirical author who wrote in imitation of *The Prince* an amusing booklet called *The Boss*, with a sub-title, *Essay on the art of governing an American city*, containing instructions for a political dominator of a city in the United States. It was published under the pseudonym of Henry Champernowne in 1894. Although regularly quoted as a classic in all bibliographies dealing with municipal politics or political corruption in the United States, it is unfortunately no longer published. It possesses the brevity, succulence, spirit and style of one of Machiavelli's minor works. The author, whose real name is David McGregor Means (1847–1931) has very few other books to his credit. *The Boss* imitates the method and disconnected construction of *The Prince,* even the Dedication, and it is clear that it is modelled on *The Prince* (and on Aristotle):

TO THE BOSS OF THE CITY OF NEW YORK
Dedication

Those who court the favour of bosses generally present them with whatever they possess that is more rare, curious, or valuable, such as fast horses, fighting cocks or dogs, choice liquors and cigars, certificates of stocks, or even money, according to the dignity and taste of the personage whom they seek to profit.

For my part, my anxiety to present myself to the notice of your honour with the best proof of my devotion has not enabled me to discover, among all that I possess, anything that I account so valuable as a knowledge of the proper conduct for a boss who would maintain himself successfully; a knowledge acquired by a long experience of modern affairs and a diligent study of the past. The observations which I have made with all the reflection and accuracy of which I am capable are contained in the small treatise now addressed to you. And although I have not the vanity to deem it worthy of your acceptance, yet I am persuaded that your goodness will not refuse the offering. . . .

Still more presumptuous would it be were I to offer these reflections in place of that celebrated treatise of the great Nicolò Machiavelli, to the study of which you undoubtedly give your days and night. Nothing that I can contribute could ever supersede his wisdom; but where he has confined himself to sketching the outlines, it is possible for another to complete his work by filling them in. Moreover, as I shall make clear hereafter, the aims of a boss ought not to be altogether the same as those of a prince, nor are the methods to be used in guiding a democracy like those suitable for a principality. Hence, while I nowhere contradict Machiavelli, nor even venture to differ with him, I have felt it necessary to extend and adapt his plan in order to make it applicable to the present times. But I have tried to make these extensions in conformity with the original design, so that, although the workmanship may be inferior, the whole may appear harmonious.[399]

In this little booklet Means deals with systems used by bosses of American cities in order to attain their political ends, of relations with the electoral masses who because of their large number cannot reach an understanding with each other over the choice of a candidate—a task that requires more time than they can devote to it and with the political underlings whose activities must be prevented from becoming too powerful and betraying or threatening the authority of the boss, and of the whole technique of political struggle created by democracy in America, made up of cities of mixed races, interests, customs and religion. The maxims by the author of *The Boss* are always clear and have the realistic colouring of those of Machiavelli. At the end there is an *Appeal to the Boss* to provide the city with a good government, and this too corresponds not only to the letter but also to the spirit of *The Prince.*

But was this work of Means written in a serious vein, or ironically? I believe it is a satire, and for that reason Means must be excluded from the number of the real and true Machiavellians. However, in order to write this book Means became so immersed in the spirit of Machiavelli that he interprets it better than some pseudo-followers or timid apologists of the Florentine; for instance it is superior to the work of the Germanophile Frank Preston Stearns (1846–1917). In an essay, *Politics and Metaphysics* (1915) which had a second edition, Stearns had the courage to write that "the aim of his treatise, *The Prince,* is restricted and its details are petty; broad general views are lacking"! Let us hear what is lacking. According to Stearns, Machiavelli should have dealt with "the suppression of crimes, the progress of knowledge, the reduction of poverty". Just like that. He even compares Machiavelli with Pietro Aretino. He finds that "a tone *lightly* pessimistic" dominates Machiavelli's work, and finally decides that "*The Prince* is substantially a picture of the politics of his times".

We can find some Machiavellian phrases in some of the few surviving American writers whose thinking is non-conformist, like Albert Jay Nock (1872–1945), or H. L. Mencken (1880–1956). However, they are not real Machiavellists but rather irreverent critics of America as well as realists and men of wit. Some aspects of Machiavellianism were bound to rub off on them, although being individualists, they detest that omnipotent state which Machiavelli champions.

It is interesting to note that the first American translation of the complete works of Machiavelli came in 1882 from an American of German origin, Charles E. Detmold, former teacher in a military school of Hanover. In the preface, Detmold is favourable to Machiavelli but in that annoying manner characteristic of that period in Europe, especially of a follower of Villari:

> His morality must be judged by that prevailing at the time of his writing, and the principles of conduct laid down by him in *The Prince* are rather the reflex of the perversity of the period in which he lived, than of his own mind . . . Machiavelli was neither devil nor saint, but simply a most gifted, honest man and patriot who was not afraid to write, in the most terse and lucid manner, what he honestly thought calculated to advance the interests of his country, which he had so much at heart.[400]

The most curious application of Machiavellian thought in America was that of the political and social science writer, James Burnham, in *The Machiavellians, Defenders of Freedom*, 1943. He participated in 1929 in the leftist political circle of the Protestant minister, A. J. Muste, who concerned himself with the labour movement. Burnham emerged at that time along with other writers who became famous in different ways, like Louis Budenz and Sidney Hook. Burnham at that time wrote under the pseudonym of John West. *The Managerial Revolution* (1941) became a best-seller and made him famous throughout the world. In this book he maintained that a new class, that of technicians or managers, was about to seize the reins of modern social forces. Two years later he realized that this fortunate and in part correct concept would be strengthened if supported by the authority of Pareto, whose work Arthur Livingston had already called to the attention of America and had translated into English. In the manner of most neophytes, when Burnham suddenly discovered Machiavelli he became a rabid disciple of his doctrines. These he interpreted as the superiority of so-called "scientific politics", thus making Machiavellianism completely unrecognizable. His history of the Machiavellians can be likened to a head which is Machiavelli and a tail which is Pareto, with no body in between. He did not realize he was confusing the "science of politics" of Machiavelli—who excluded sentiment and morality from the study of the force that is the State—with "scientific politics" which was to be an active politics founded on reason and science. This is an absurdity which would certainly have elicited sarcastic remarks from that same Pareto whom Burnham wanted America to admire. The process of thought by which we know politics is not the one with which it is carried on. There is the same difference as that between a woman who gives birth but is ignorant of anatomy, and a doctor, incapable of giving birth, who has complete knowledge of procreative physiology. To be active in politics requires strong feelings and the use of myths which science is bound to consider unreasonable and without foundation.

Professor Hans Morgenthau of Chicago University produced works of value that are rational and solid, in harmony with Machiavelli—that is, with realistic politics—especially his *In Defence of the National Interest* (1951). Was the case of George F. Kennan during the fifties in America perhaps symptomatic of a dislike for realism in politics on the part of Americans? When Kennan denounced utopianism and other errors consequent to that viewpoint of American foreign policy in his book, *American Diplomacy* (1951), he lost his position of eminence in the State Department. Was it perhaps because he dared state that politics has no connection with morality?

In recent years better translations of Machiavelli than that of Detmold have appeared in America, like *The Prince* (1946) of Allan H. Gilbert, and *The Discourses,* translated by the English

Jesuit, Leslie J. Walker, with an introduction and notes by the translator (New Haven, Yale University Press, 1950).

Some letters were cleverly translated by Arthur Livingston in an edition entrusted to, of all people, Carlo Sforza. At that time, 1940, Sforza's name carried great weight in American publishing circles, but he was certainly never Machiavellian and in fact boasted of being an apostle of Mazzini. Allan Gilbert, in 1961, published an excellent translation, *The Letters of Machiavelli, a Selection,* New York, Capricorn Books.

4 Machiavelli, our contemporary

Today we find Machiavelli everywhere. Political forces are more stark than ever before, and the power of states has increased. From the moment the democracies instituted compulsory education, states have penetrated people's minds, having already taken possession of their bodies through the draft—another "democratic" application of Machiavellianism. Wars have extended to whole populations; women, children and the aged are called upon to sacrifice their lives for their country, as in the times of Carthage and Rome. The actual participation of all people in defeat is further confirmed by famines and general epidemics in certain areas. On the other hand, victory is sanctified by trials which pronounce the defeated guilty, and the winners worthy of becoming moral educators.

As they do with morality, states subjugate or attempt to subjugate religions to their needs. Those who refuse to comply become martyrs, but religion as a family and traditional rite has found it increasingly difficult to survive unless it is thought to be in agreement with the policies of the state or believed to strengthen the state directly or indirectly. Compulsory education extends beyond its own field to reach adults through powerful technical means, like radio and television. While the tentacles of political power of some states are not as far-reaching as others, this is only because of calculated policy; it is a question of expediency, not of principle. Diplomatic amenities of the old aristocracies have been completely discarded. Countries accuse each other of being traitors, liars, bloody butchers, and assassins in the very halls and assembly rooms where universal peace was to be established.

Everyone realizes that only by the use of force can ends be gained. Workers, creating a monopoly of manpower, unite in order to make their strength felt. As soon as they have reached an equilibrium with opposing forces, they seek to surmount and overwhelm them. The colonial populations in all lands and of all colours are in revolt against their masters and seek vengeance for century-old grievances of slavery and thraldom. They know the value of force and, when they cannot organize, resort to assassinations and guerrilla warfare. Wars are no longer declared; all countries now take precautionary measures against sudden attacks. Indeed wars have now become chronic. At times they are disguised as police operations on the part of those who defend themselves, and as liberal insurrections on the part of those who attack. Populations throughout the world are now more or less militarized. Industrial techniques have become a tool of the state. We are forced to go around with pockets bulging with identification cards, security numbers, passports, visas, licences, and ration cards. At certain critical times, they are our only means of sustaining life.

The great individuals of whom Machiavelli was an admirer and apostle appear today in more dramatic and miraculous fashion. Springing forth from the anonymous levels of humanity and achieving success by means of a power that can only create the expectation of miracles, Lenin, Mussolini, Hitler, Stalin, Tito, Ataturk, Peron, and Mao all established order with incredible speed, inciting great fervour and enthusiasm in the masses. The legends that follow in the wake of their deaths are almost fabulous. Moreover, great personalities like Roosevelt and Churchill, not so mysterious in their origins, do not seem less endowed with demonic power than the others. Populations are now much larger, states more powerful, arms more destructive, and techniques more perfected. Yet nothing prevents the appearance of these revolutionary apparitions. Often the results of their actions are different from and opposed to their original intentions. England lost her empire, despite Churchill's oratory ("I did not become Prime Minister to preside over the liquidation of Her Majesty's Empire"); Germany was split in two, instead of gaining *lebensraum* or vital space; Russia, whose programme was to free the workers, has subjected them to a life of slavery, and so it goes. Even in this regard Machiavellianism dominates the contemporary world.

Contemporary conflicts can be understood better if we consider them as conflicts between nations and not between ideologies. There are also minor conflicts of ideologies, religions, habits and traditions, but they are masks used to conceal the principal conflict which is at present between two great states, the United States and Russia, who take advantage of the tendencies and traditions of various people and individuals to try to impose on them their "way of life" and urge them to join their cause.

At this moment, the United States is allied with Fascist Portugal, has a treaty with Communist Yugoslavia, an arrangement with Spain, and has ties with many states in Latin America whose governments sprang from military juntas and whose elections are not democratic. Russia on her part made a treaty of friendship with Hitler's Germany in order to be permitted to occupy part of Poland, and is in conflict with Communist China. Everything is acceptable to the state that wants to win.

The war against Communism in itself is a contradiction of the principles of the United States, which advocates freedom of choice of government. If the United States is in conflict with Communism, it is only insofar as it is an instrument of a foreign power. The political conflict is often carried on behind a smokescreen of noble expressions in order to persuade the masses to tread the path towards a goal set by the leaders.

I wish I could help the United States, my country of adoption, to face the reality of politics, but I can't imagine why I would succeed where others have failed. A voice that tried to make itself heard in America in the late thirties fell on deaf ears when the journalist, Edgar Ansel Mowrer, who had become converted to realistic politics, urged Americans to open their eyes to the Machiavellian policies of other countries. The government of the United States will, I am sure, continue to be Machiavellian under the cover of sanctimonious intentions and humanitarian proposals. As long as this succeeds, I suppose I should be the first to be happy about it.

As for world problems, readers know by now that Machiavelli does not make prophecies or offer panaceas. History is improvisation, and unexpected events can lead us no one knows where. New forces can spring forth; indeed they are already showing signs of emerging. Organisms that seem strong in appearance may have within them the germs of destruction and disintegration. Machiavelli's pessimism does not allow for illusions about the basic tenets of human conduct: conflicts will never end—that is the only sure thing. Individuals, willingly or unwillingly, will be swept along in their wake. There will be no place for neutrals nor mercy for those who are indifferent. Fairly soon no corner of the world will be free for those who want to escape, like the convents or monasteries of the Middle Ages or the South Sea Islands of a few years back.

At the beginning of this century, several Utopias were envisioned in optimistic terms promising eras of abundance with peace guaranteed by the progress of science. Today Utopias are still promised and described, but the humanity of the future is pictured in anguish and despair. Humans are fashioned by machines, disciplined like robots, dressed uniformly like an army, and hardened in spirit. Today artificial satellites, revolving around the earth, are depicted as enemy fortresses—a grim picture—and thus war is even extended to other worlds.

SOURCES

Bibliographical Note

When I embarked on this book originally, I intended to add a bibliography. Later, when I saw the notes I had collected, I realized it would double the size of the volume and make it a book difficult to handle. Thus I have left in what are accidental mentions of books and articles, and for the rest refer the reader to the following works, where he can find all the necessary bibliographical aids:

NORSA, A., *Il principio della forza nel pensiero politico di Niccolò Machiavelli, seguito da un contributo bibliografico,* Milano, Hoepli, 1938.

PREZZOLINI, G., *Repertorio Bibliografico,* vol. 4 (1902–32; 1932–42), New York, Vanni; a sequel to and completion of Norsa.

Studies in Philology has a bibliography on the Renaissance which includes Machiavelli.

Rinascita (Florence, 1952) also has a bibliography covering Machiavelli.

My citations from the works of Machiavelli generally refer to the edition of M. Casella and G. Mazzoni, *Tutte le Opere,* Florence, 1929. In view of the multiplicity of editions, I wished to limit the citations to as few sources as possible. In the case of Machiavelli's letters, when the key *Lett.* is used it refers to the Alvisi edition (Florence, 1883); the key *LL* refers to the Carabba edition. For secondary works, I have used the Rizzoli edition. For citations from the *Legations* (Machiavelli's diplomatic reports), I have used the four volumes edited by Passerini and Milanesi (Florence, 1875–77). If any reader is not satisfied with the sources, I hope he will write me in care of the publisher.—G.P.

The keys for Machiavelli's works listed in the notes below are as follows:

A. — *The Art of War*

Cap. — *Capitoli*

D. — *The Discourses*

FH — *Florentine Histories*

Leg. — *Legations*

Lett. — Letters (Alvisi)

LL. — Letters (Carabba)

P. — *The Prince*

I THE DOCTRINE

1. Lett. CXX, 229.
2. P. III, 8.
3. P. XX, 42.
4. FH VI, vii, 535.
5. FH II, xxi, 422.
6. D. I, xxv, 93.
7. Leg. I, 171.
8. Leg. III, 244.
9. Meinecke, op. cit. 45.
10. Leg. III, 265 (24 Jan. 1507).
11. Leg. III, 271.
12. A. Norsa, op. cit., p. 21.
13. P. XV, 30.
14. D. I, i, 57.
15. D. II, 137.
16. D. III, i, 193.
17. Leg. IV, 47.
18. D. II, xlix, 261.
19. D. III, i, 193.
20. FH, V, viii, 505.
21. D. II, xxx, 189.
22. D. I, ix, 73.
23. A. I, 269a.
24. D. III, iv, 446–47.
25. P. VII, 16.
26. D. II, xxiii, 175.
27. D. III, xxii, 232.
28. P. XVIII.
29. Leg. III, 282.
30. D. I, xxxiv, 102.
31. P. XVIII, 35.
32. D. I, xxvi, 94.
33. P. XV, 30.
34. D. I, 56.
35. D. I, xi, 78.
36. D. III, xliii, 257.
37. D. I, xxxvii, 105 *and* FH VII, xiv, 573.
38. FH IV, xiv, 480.
39. D. I, xxxvii, 105 *and* Lett. 880.
40. P. XVII, 33.

41. FH VI, xviii, 543.
42. Lett. 888.
43. D. I, xxvi, 94.
44. D. I, iii, 62.
45. Lett. 895.
46. Cap. "Of Fortune", 845.
47. D. II, i, 139.
48. Ercole, *Pensatori e Uomini d'azine*, 1935, 169.
49. P. XVII, 33.
50. D. I, x, 75a.
51. P. VIII, 18.
52. D. I, xxx, 98.
53. *Golden Ass*, V, 831.
54. D. II, 136.
55. D. I, xxvii, 95.
56. D. I, 56.
57. D. II, xxx, 188.
58. A. II, 302.
59. A. VII, 367.
60. P. XIV, 30.
61. *Clizia* (drama), prologue, 661.
62. D. I, xii, 78.
63. Idem.
64. D. I, 12.
65. D. I, xii, 79.
66. FH I, xxiii, 397.
67. D. III, v, 448.
68. D. I, xii, 79.
69. D. III, xxii, 232.
70. D. I, xviii, 88.
71. P. XII, 24.
72. Leg. II, 162.
73. Leg. III, 456.
74. P. VI, 14.
75. FH V, xxxiii, 528.
76. A. II, 301.
77. P. XVIII, 35.
78. D. III, xxii, 233.
79. Leg. II, 403.
80. LL. I, 122.
81. D. III, 35.
82. Leg. IV, 311.
83. D. I, ix, 73.
84. P. XVII, 32.
85. D. I, ix, 72.
86. D. I, xvii, 86.
87. FH IV, i, 472.
88. D. I, xxix, 97.
89. *Golden Ass*, 106–14, 831.
90. P. XII, 25.
91. D. III, i, 193.
92. Cap. "Of Ambition", 109–120, 851.
93. D. III, xliii, 257.
94. D. II, ii, 141.
95. D. II, xxv, 181.
96. D. I, i, 58.
97. D. I, iii, 63.
98. Idem.
99. D. I, vi, 68.
100. D. II, xii, 155.
101. FH IV, xxxiii, 498.
102. FH IV, i, 472.
103. D. I, xviii, 87.
104. D. I, vii, 68–69.
105. FH II, xxxiv, 434.
106. D. II, xxix, 240.
107. D. III, viii, 214.
108. D. III, title of ch. xliv, 258.
109. P. III, 82.
110. P. III, 8–9.
111. P. XXI, 44.
112. LL. II, 61.
113. P. XXV, 49.
114. D. I, lv, 128.
115. D. I, xxvi, 94.

116. *Epigram* I.
117. LL. II, 61.
118. *Life of Castruccio*, 748.
119. P. XX, 42.
120. *De Natura Galli.*, 731.
121. P. VII, 15.
122. D. II, i, 138.
123. D. I, xi, 77.
124. D. II, 189.
125. Idem.
126. Cap. "Of Fortune", 847, v. 126.
127. Lett. 879.
128. FH II, xxx, 429.
129. Cap. "Of Fortune", 486, v. 40–43.
130. P. VI, 13.
131. P. XXVI, 51.
132. P. VI, 13.
133. Idem.
134. P. VI, 23 *and* 24.
135. Leg. III, 369.
136. D. I, x, 76.
137. D. I, ii, 62.
138. D. I, ii, 60.

139. P. III, 6.
140. Leg. II, 77.
141. D. III, xliii, 257.
142. Idem.
143. P. III, 9.
144. D. III, xlvi, 256.
145. A. IV, 327.
146. LL. II, 138.
147. A. I, 266.
148. Croce, *Critica* (1930), 331.
149. P. I, i, 5.
150. D. I, 120.
151. P. XIX, 92.
152. A. VII, 367.
153. Cap. "Of Ingratitude", 844.
154. D. I, v, 65.
155. D. I, vi, 67.
156. A. IV, 323.
157. LL. II, 20–21.
158. D. I, iv, 126.
159. D. I, xii, 78.
160. P. XXVI, 50.
161. LL. II, 20–21.
162. Lett. 901.
163. LL. CXVI, 221.

II MACHIAVELLI'S PRECURSORS

164. Plato, *Politics*, 293b.
165. Plato, *The Republic*, IV, 459d.
166. Plato, *Laws*, V, 735e.
167. Plato, *Gorgias*, 492.
168. D. I, xxxvii, 105–6.
169. Euripides, *The Phoenician Women*, I, i, 524.
170. Thucydides, Book V, 85.
171. D. III, xxvi, 237b.
172. D. II, i, 137.

173. D. II, i, 136.
174. Lattanzio, *De dig. inst.*, V, xvii.
175. D. I, v, 384.
176. Cicero, *De Off.*, I, 11.
177. P., xviii, 34.
178. St. Augustine, *De Civ.*, IV, 4.
179. Idem, *De. Civ.*, II, 21.
180. Ercole, *La Politica di Machiavelli*, 1926, 337.

181. A. H. Gilbert, 234.
182. Alberti, *Familia*, ed. Pellegrini, 246.
183. *Familia*, 237–8.

184. *Familia*, 11.
185. *Familia*, 128–29.
186. *Familia*, 79.
187. FH VII, vi, 566.

III HIS WORK

188. Leg. II, 253 ff.
189. D. II, xxiii, 176 *and* II, xxiv, 180.
190. D. II, xxiii, 176.
191. *Annals of Italy*, verses 34–36.
192. Letters in translation of Allan Gilbert, 1961, 142–43.
193. P., concluding lines.
194. D. III, xlii, 257 *and* i, 138; *also* P. II, 5.
195. Gaspary, *Hist. of Italian Literature*, II, 241.
196. A. I, 270.
197. P. VIII, 18–19.
198. Dieux de Radier, cit. Luiso 241, n. 2.
199. Gervinus, *Historische Schriften*, 1871.

200. D. III, xiv, 222b.
201. Idem, 445a, 552a, 419b.
202. Idem, 241b.
203. Idem, 463b.
204. Idem, 1992.
205. Idem, 401a.
206. FH II, xxxviii, 440a.
207. FH VI, xxxviii, 560b.
208. D. I, xi, 60a.
209. Idem, 62a.
210. FH VI, xxiv, 549.
211. F. Chiappelli, *Studi sul linguaggio di Machiavelli*, 7.
212. FH I, v, 384.
213. Letters, Gilbert translation, 184–5.
214. Idem, 99.

IV HIS LIFE

215. *Golden Ass*, 819.
216. D. II, xxiv, 177a.
217. L. Guicciardini, *Unedited Work*, IX, 267.
218. D. I, 56a.
219. A. VII, 367.
220. Lett. II, 54 (1514).
221. Lett. 8 March 1498.
222. Leg. I, 4–33.
223. Leg. I, 87–246.
224. Leg. I, 246–357.

225. Leg. II, 15 (26 July 1502).
226. Leg. III, 103.
227. Leg. III, 110.
228. Leg. III, 185 *and* D. I., xxvii, 95.
229. Leg. III, 345–432.
230. Leg. III, 435–65.
231. Leg. IV, ii, 176.
232. Leg. IV, 131–76.
233. Leg. IV, 188–209.

234. *Reform of the State of Florence,* ed. Flora, II, 527.
235. Lett. 219–21 (Sept. 1512).
236. Lett. 117–24, 131–42.
237. P., concluding chapter.
238. Lett. 397 (15 Feb. 1515).

239. Gilbert translation, 230–31.
240. Idem. 205–6.
241. Lett. 437 (8 March 1524).
242. Gilbert translation, 228.
243. Ed. Rizzoli, II, 541–43.

V HIS FRIENDS AND CONTEMPORARIES

244. Arch Stor. Ital IV, ii, 394–395.
245. Savonarola, Sermon XIX, iii, 408.
246. Sermon I, iii, 56–59.
247. Sermon XXVI, ii, 389.
248. Sermon XXIX, ii, 442.

249. Vettori, *Summary of the History of Italy,* 300.
250. Vettori, *Trip to Germany,* 140–42.
251. *Annals of the Republic of Genoa,* Genoa, 1799, 163–64.
252. Guicciardini, *Ricordi.*

VI MACHIAVELLIANISM

253. Fontanini, *Dell 'Eloquenza italiana,* I, 207.
254. Pole, *Apologia.*
255. Idem, Apologia, I, 137.
256. Lett. IX, 84–85.
257. Nerli, III, 33 (1728 ed.)
258. Nardi, *Histories of Florence,* II, 72 (1858 ed.)
259. Varchi, *Florentine History,* I, 95 (1858 ed.)
260. Idem, IV, 25.
261. Varchi, I, 210–12 (1832 Milan ed.)
262. Cecchi, *Pellegrine,* intermedio primo, 10.
263. Doni, *Marmi,* ed. Laterza, 247.
264. Gelli, *Errore,* ed. Le Monnier, 43.

265. Magalotti, Letters, 2, 38.
266. Gilbert translation, letter to F. Vettori, 10 Dec. 1513.
267. Ferrari, *Il Corso,* V, 338.
268. D. I, x, 74a.
269. Muzio, *The Gentleman* (1571), 245.
270. Curcio, *Dal Rinascimento alla Riforma* (1934), 150.
271. Botero, *Della Ragion di Stato* (1640), 148.
272. Ibid.
273. Ibid. Libro II, 40 (1671 ed.)
274. Ibid. Libro II, 25.
275. Botero, *Discorsa della Neutralità,* 28.
276. Boccalini, *Ragguagli de Parnaso,* II, 13.
277. Boccalini, *Centuria,* II, 87.

278. Sarpi, *Opinione toccante il Governo della Republica Veneziana*, 2–3.
279. Ammirato, *Discorsi*, XII, pt. I.
280. Ammirato, ibid, XI, iv, 216.
281. M., *Reforming the State of Florence*, ed. Rizzoli, II, 358.

282. Ibid, 540.
283. Campanella, *Poesie*, Madr. 962.
284. Ibid, 27.
285. Campanella, *Atheismus triumphatus*.
286. Ibid, *Poesie*, son. xxxiii, 82.

MACHIAVELLI AND THE PHILOSOPHERS

287. Orsini, *Bacon and Machiavelli*, 36.
288. Descartes, *Works*, ed. Cousin (1824), IX, 388.
289. Hobbes, *Leviathan*, I, 13.
290. Ibid. II, 21.
291. FH III, 456b.
292. Spinoza, *Tract. Politicus*, VI, 7.
293. Ibid, 8.

294. St. Augustine, *De Civ.*, IX.
295. Pascal, *Pensées*, ed. Havet, 39.
296. Leibnitz, *Works*, ed. Foucher, IV, 328.
297. Leibnitz, *Textes Inédits*, II, 563.
298. Leibnitz, *Philos. Schriften*, IV, i, 398.
299. Ibid, VI, i, 63.

MACHIAVELLI IN FRANCE

300. Pintard, *Revue de littérature comparée* (1933), 385.
301. G. Naudé, *Naudéana*, 1701.
302. Naudé *Bibliographia politica* (1633) 108.

303. Voltaire, *Works*, xxx, 153 (ed. 1829).
304. Richelieu, *Maximes d'Estat*, pub. by Hanotaux, nn. 80, 110, 124, 125, 142.
305. de Muller, *Works*, VI, 344.

MACHIAVELLI IN ENGLAND

306. E. Greenlaw, *Modern Philology*, October 1909.
307. Hume, *Essays on the Study of History*.
308. Bolingbroke, *Works*, I, 313 (ed. Philadelphia, 1841).

309. Discorsi, cap. 58.
310. Milton, *Works*, XVIII, 183 (Commonplace Book).
311. Milton, *Works*, III, part 2, 471.
312. E. Young, *The Complaint* (Night VIII, 329–32).

313. Macaulay, *Essays*, I, 270–71.
314. Southey, *The Library*, Colloquy XIV, 353–59.
315. Browning, *Letters*, I, 302.

316. T. S. Eliot, *For Lancelot Andrewes*, "Machiavelli," 1928.
317. Ibid.

MACHIAVELLI IN SPAIN

318. Almirante, *Bibliografía militar de Espana* (1876), 774.
319. Dempf, *Christliche Staatsphilosophie in Spanien*, 96.
320. Rivadencira, *Tratado de la religión*, 459.
321. Mariana, *Obras*, II, 468.
322. Ibid, II, 482.
323. Ibid, II, 483.
324. Ibid, III, vi, 545a.

325. Barrientos, report of 1598, 13–14.
326. Ibid, 105.
327. Ibid, 110.
328. Ibid, 128.
329. Ibid, 247–48.
330. Andreu, *Tratados politicos*, 1941, pref. 12.
331. Gracian, *Primor*, XI.

MACHIAVELLI IN GERMANY

332. Schoppe, *Paedia politices* (ed. 1624), 15.
333. Althusius, *Politica methodice digesta* (rist. 1932), 970.
334. Bruckner, *Historia philosophiaé* (1744), 784.
335. Ibid, 791.
336. Herder, *Briefe zur Beförderung der Humanität* (1795).
337. Elkan, *Die Endeckung Machiavellis in Deutschland zu Beginn des 19en Jahrhunderts*, "Histor. Zeitschrift" (1918), 427–58.

338. Hegel, *Anhang an der "System der Sittlichkeit"*, 57.
339. D. III, xli, 256a.
340. Ibid, 55.
341. Fichte, *Nachgelassene Werke*, III, 427.
342. Ibid, XI, 423–24.
343. Hegel, *Kritik der Verfassung Deutschlands*, 138.
344. Hegel, *Werke*, XI, 509–10.
345. von Schlegel, *Sämmtliche Werke* (1846), II, 18–19.
346. Ranke, *Zur Kritik der neuren Geschichtschreiben* (1824).
347. Treitsch, *Politica*, 7–9.

PERIODIC REBIRTH OF MACHIAVELLI

348. Vico, *Scienza Nuova*, I, ii, elemento lxviii.
349. D. I, xxvii, 945; Leg. III, 185.

350. Leopardi, *Sopra un bassorilievo antico sepolcrale*, I, 27–28.

MACHIAVELLI AND THE ENCYCLOPAEDISTS

351. Faguet, *Dix-huitième siècle* (1890).
352. Bayle, *tome* X (ed. 1820) 19.
353. Ibid, 21.
354. Ibid, 24.
355. Ibid, 25.
356. Ibid, 26.
357. Voltaire, *Oeuvres compl.* (ed. 1877–85), 552.
358. Voltaire, *Correspondence*, XL, 511.
359. Voltaire, *tome* XVII, art. Bataillon.

360. *Oeuvres*, XXXIV, 446 (31 mars 1738).
361. Ibid, 20 mai 1738.
362. *Tome* XXXV, 224.
363. *Correspondence*, XXXV, 419.
364. Culcasi, *Gli influssi italiani nell'opera di Rousseau*, 73.
365. Rousseau, *Oeuvres compl.* (ed. Garnier), *Contract social*, 656.
366. Ibid, 669.
367. Meda, "Il Machiavelismo" in Riv. d'Italia, (1927), xxx, 224–36.
368. Verri, *Mémoires*, Paris, 1823 (Letter to Morellet, 1766).

MACHIAVELLI AND THE RISORGIMENTO

369. Vechietti, *Riv. Stor. Ital.* (1941), 349.
370. Cuoco, *Saggio Storico* (ed. Laterza), 218.
371. Cuoco, *Scritti vari*, I, 87–88.
372. Ibid, 219.
373. Leopardi, *Carte Napoletane-Novella* (ed. Gregoriana), 1157 & 1174.
374. Balbo, *Vita di Dante*, 1839.
375. Balbo, *Lettera Dell 'Educazione*, 6 Feb. 1847.
376. Gioberti, *Primato morale,* (ed. Utet), I, 52.

377. Ibid, 67.
378. Gioberti, *Rinnovamento* (ed. Laterza), I, 276.
379. Gioberti, *Risorgimento* (ed. Laterza), III, 84.
379a. Mazzini, *Del 'unità italiana*, III, 264.
380. Mazzini, *Scritti*, Daelli, VIII, 65–66.
381. Ibid, 206.
382. Ferrari, *Histoire de la raison d'État*, 264.
383. Ibid, 265

VII MACHIAVELLI, OUR CONTEMPORARY

384. FH III, xiii, 456.
385. Pokrovschi, *Economic Materialism*, Moscow, 1906, 4.
386. Ibid, 5.
387. TKaciev, *Izdrannie sociniena* (1932), I, 70–71.
388. Maximovich, *Istorik Marksism,* "Idea diktaturi v Machiavelli", 13, Marx and Engels Institute, Moscow, 1929.
389. Ibid, 68.
390. Ibid, 197b.
391. Ibid, 72.
392. Ibid, 80.
393. Ibid, 93.

394. Trotsky, *Life of Stalin,* preface, xii-xiii.
395. John Adams, Works, IV, 409–10.
396. C. E. Lester, *Florentine Histories of Machiavelli,* New York, 1845, I, viii.
397. John Jay, *Life,* II, 282 (letter to Vaughan, 31 Aug. 1797).
398. Ibid, letter to Judge Peters, 14 March 1815, p. 370.
399. Means, *The Boss,* dedication.
400. Detmold, *The Historical, Political and Diplomatic Writings of Machiavelli,* Boston, 1882, 4 vols., preface.

INDEX

INDEX

Accetto, Torquato 213
"accidents" 132–33. *See also* Fortune
action 65–67. *See also* idleness, *virtu*
Adams, John 315–16
Ademollo, Agostino 297
Alamanni, Luigi di Piero 125, 160,
   163, 172–73
Alberti, Leon Battista 104–105
Alexander VI, Pope 115, 146, 150
Alfieri, Vittorio 224
Algarotti, Francesco, Count 20, 276
Althusius, Johannes 256–57
Amfiteatroff, A. V. 305
Ammirato, Scipione 212
Anghiari, battle of 50
Annals of Italy, see *Decennali*
anti-machiavellianism, *see* Machia-
   vellianism: enemies
antiquity, M.'s admiration 38, 99,
   118–19
Aquinas, St. Thomas 275
Aristotle 47, 90–91, 93–95
Art of War 112, 124–27, 161, 178–79
Aubigné, Agrippa d' 227
Augustine, St. 100–1, 222
Azeglio, Massimo d' 296

Bacon, Francis 217–18, 239
Baglioni, Giampaolo 36, 152
Balbo, Cesare 290–91
Bandello, Matteo 178–79
Baretti, Giuseppe 225
Barrientos, B. Alamos de 247–50
Bayle, Pierre 178, 274–75
Bechi, Riccardo 146
Bellaci, Pandolfo 169
Boccaccio 67
Boccalini, Traiano 210–11, 265
Bodin, Jean 228
Bolingbroke (Henry St. John), Lord
   237
Borgia, Caesar (Duke Valentino) 27,
   68, 113–15, 147–50
Botero 209–12
Bozius, T. 193
Brandolini, Aurelius 103–4
Brignole Sale, A. 213
Browning, Robert 240
Brucioli, Antonio 177
Brucker, J. J. 257
Buonaccorsi, Biagio 139, 169
Buondelmonti, Zanobi 120, 125, 160,
   163

341

Burckhardt, Jakob 20, 33, 214
Burd, Arthur L. 240–41
Burnham, James 322
Busini, G. B. 188, 194–95
Byron 240

Campanella, Tommaso 95, 215–16, 256
Capitoli 135, 154, 160
Capponi, Gino di Neri 76, 115
Cardano, Gerolamo 178
Carneades 98–99
Casavecchia, Filippo 116, 139, 145
Castiglione, Baldassare 125
Cecchi, G. M. 199
Champernowne, H. 319–20
Christ, J. F. 257
Christian morality, M. and 17, 21, 31–32, 37–39, 52
Cicero 99–100
Clement VII (Giulio de' Medici), Pope 130, 145, 164
Clizia 121
Colonna, Fabrizio 125
common good 25–26, 52
Communism 66, 303–4, 307–13. *See also* Marx
"composite body" (state) 22–25
Condillac, Étienne Bonnot de 282
condottieri, *see* mercenaries
Conring 256
Corbinelli, Jacopo 226
Croce, Benedetto 30, 76, 79, 122–23, 266, 267, 268, 271, 301
Cromwell, Thomas 190–92
Cuoco, Vincenzo 286–88, 301

Dacres 33
Dante 68, 102–3, 135
Da Vinci, Leonardo 50, 173
Decatur, Stephen 76

Decennali 115, 151, 154
Degli Albizi, Luca 146
Della Palla, Battista 125
Dell'Occasione 71
Del Nero, Francesco 139
De Natura Gallorum 155
De Sanctis, Francesco 122, 394–95
Descartes 218
Description . . . Duke Valentine . . . Slaughtering Vitelli 113, 149
Detmold, C. E. 34, 322
De Valera, Eamon 266
Dialogue on Language 135–37
Diderot, Denis 280–81
Discourse on Calling the State of Florence to Arms 127
Discourse on the Law of Forming a Florentine Militia 127
Discourses 112, 116–17, 119–21, 124, 127, 158
Doni 199
Dostoevsky 306
dream of M. 129, 186

Eliot, George 297
Eliot, T. S. 241
Encyclopaedists 274–84
end (justifies the means) 25–56, 53–55
England, Machiavellianism in 190–92, 217–18, 219–20, 232–41
Ercole, Francesco 18–19, 33, 102–3, 302–3
Estienne, H. d' 227

Fabricius, Johann Albert 96
Ferrari, Giuseppe 20, 204, 265, 295–96
Fichte, J. G. 258–61
Florence, advice of M. 65, 77, 161
Florentine Histories 112, 124, 129–33, 146, 161, 164
force, *see* government: and force

form (and matter) 47–48, 93
"Fortune" 33, 66, 67–72, 132–33
France, Machiavellianism in 193–94, 218, 226–31, 274–84
Franklin, Benjamin 315
Frederick II (of Prussia) 260, 277–80
freedom of speech 64
Fregoso, Ottaviano 174
French, M.'s opinions 68, 74, 155

Galiani, F. 283–84, 301
Galileo (M. compared to), 20–21, 292
Gelli 199
Genteil, Giovanni 286, 302–3
Gentillet, I. 188, 193–94, 207, 227, 232, 256
Germans, M.'s opinions 153
Germany, Machiavellianism in 222–223, 254–64
Gervinus, G. G. 129, 131–32, 262
Giannotti, Donato 49, 200
Gilbert, A. H. 34, 118, 323
Gioberti, Vincenzo 20, 291–92
Giovio, Paolo 128, 202–3
Golden Ass (by M.) 134–35, 144, 160
good faith 27–29, 49
government: art of 26–29, 49, 82–84, 103–7; and force 27–29, 48–51; forms of 46–47, 65, 77–78, 94–95; origin 94, 236–37. See also prince (M.'s ideal), state
Gracian, Baltasar 251–53
Gramsci, Antonio 66, 303–4
Greene, G. W. 318
Guerrazzi, F. D. 296
Guicciardini, Francesco 64, 76, 129, 139, 162, 164, 165–66, 174–76, 183
Guicciardini, Luigi 144, 177

Hegel 258–61, 274
Helvétius 282

Herder 258, 259
history (theories) 30–31, 35, 39–40, 79–81, 84–85, 268–73
Hobbes 219–20
Houssaye, Amelot de la 230
human nature 17–18, 30–32, 59–60, 80–82
Hume 236–37

idleness 59–61, 61, 73
imitation, principle of 39–40, 77–79
individual (and the state) 25–26
Instruction for an Ambassador 163
Italy, Machiavellianism in 194–216, 224–25, 265–73, 285–97, 303–4
Jay, John 319
Jesuits 207–8
Joly, Maurice 265–66

Kamenev, L. B. 312
Keats, John 240

Laerzio, Diogene 129
Landor, Walter Savage 240
L'Andria 121
language 73–74
Legations 137
Leibnitz 128, 222–23
Leo X, Pope 118, 134
Leo XIII, Pope 58–59
Leopardi 289
Lester, C. E. 318
Letters (of M.) 137–40
liberty 63–5
Life of Castruccio Castracani 127–29, 161
Lincoln, Abraham 24
"lion and fox" 98, 172
Lipsius, J. 255
Livingston, Arthur 234

Livy 79
Lorenzo il Magnifico, *see* Medici, L. dei
Luther 254, 263

Macaulay 239, 285
Machiavelli, Niccolò: career 145–66; character 143–45, 178–79, 195, 195–97; personal life 139–40; 145–46, 149
Machiavelli, works 111–40; editions 120, 185–86, 204, 205–6, 218; style 18–20. *See also* individual works
Machiavellianism: applied 44–45, 73–75, 183–87, 311, 313, 324–27; disciples, *see* Alfieri, Bacon, Baretti, Barrientos, Bodin, Cuoco, Gracian, Houssaye, Macaulay, Machon, Mariana, Montesquieu, Mussolini, Naudé, Niphus, Poccianti, Richelieu, Sansovino, Setanti; *and see also* Althusius, Boccalini, Bolingbroke, Botero, Browning, Burd, Byron, Fichte, Gervinus, Herder, Hume, Landor, Nardi, Nerli, Ranke, Schlegel, Segni, Settalà, Shelley, Spinoza, Treitschke, Varchi, Wordsworth, Young; enemies 187–89, 205–208, 221–22, 278–80, *and see* Aubigné, Bayle, Bozius, Busini, Campanella, Diderot, Estienne, Frederick II, Gentillet, Giovio, Milton, Osorio, Paruta, Pole, Politi, Possevino, Raleigh, Spenser
Machiavelli, Piero 49 n
Machon, Louis 231
Malvezzi, Virgilio 213
Mandragola 121–24, 139, 161, 164, 199
Manzoni, Alessandro 292–93
Mariana, Juan de 243, 244–47
Marlowe, Christopher 233

Marx, Karl 122, 307; *see also* Communism
Masks (comedy of M.) 121, 151
Maugham, Somerset 296
Maximovich 308–9
Mayer, E. W. 32–33, 104, 263
Mazzini, Giuseppe 293–94
Means, D. M. ("Champernowne") 319–21
Medici, Catherine de' 185, 193, 227, 275
Medici, Cosimo de' 29, 106
Medici, Giuliano dei 116, 117, 118, 157
Medici, Giulio de' (Clement VII) 130, 145, 164
Medici, Lorenzo (il Magnifico) dei 104, 106–7, 116, 146
medico politico 22–25
Meinecke, F. 19, 92, 94, 100, 116, 263, 303
Mencken, H. L. 322
mercenaries 25, 48, 50, 126, 127, 146; *see also* militia
Merezhkovsky, D. 178, 296
Method of Dealing with the Rebels of Valdichiana 114–15
military training 49–51, 59–61
militia 48–51, 125–27, 152–53
Milton, John 237–38
minorities 75
Montesquieu 228–29
morality: political 17, 27–28, 36, 54–55, 56–57; private 17, 19, 29–30, 33–34
More, Thomas 213–14
Morellet, André 283
Morgenthau, Hans 323
Mosca, Gaetano 213, 301, 314
Mowrer, Edgar A. 327
Muralt, L. von 32, 264, 303
Mussolini 266
Muzio, Gerolamo 205–6

Nardi, Jacopo 160, 163, 195, 197
nationalism 55–57, 72–75, 79, 115, 146
"Nature" 31–32
Naudé, Gabriel 228
"Necessity" 62
Nerli, Filippo de' 195–96
neutrality 66
Niphus, A. 204–5
Nock, A. J. 322

On Dealing with the Valdichiana Rebels 114–15
"one man" (uomo unico). 48, 55–57 See also prince, M.'s ideal
Orti Oricellari 120, 160, 163
Osorio, Gerolamo 192
Ottevanti, G. L. 242

Papacy 41–42, 290–91, 293
Pareto, V. 20, 213, 301–2, 323
parties (political) 51–52
Paruta, Paolo 208
patriotism 51–52, 76, 81. See also nationalism, Risorgimento
"physician" (medico politico) 22–25
plagiarism 203–5
Plato 89, 90–91
Plutarch 97–98
Poccianti 200
Pokrovschi, M. 307–8
Pole, Reginald, Cardinal 188, 190–93
Politi, A. C. 192
politics, see government, state
Polybius 21, 93, 95–96
Portrait of Things in France 155
Portrait of Things of Germany 153
Possevino, Antonio 207–8, 256
Prezzolini, G. 296
prince, M.'s ideal 28–29, 34, 48, 55–57, 70, 148
Prince 112, 116–19, 124, 127, 145, 158–59 169, 170, 190, 191–92,

Protocols of Zion 266
Provisions for the Florentine Republic 127

raison d'état 19, 29, 209–13
Raleigh, Walter 235–36
Ranke, Leopold von 89, 90, 94, 117, 129, 262–63
"Redeemer" 56. See also prince, M.'s ideal
religion: and M. 37–39, 45–46; use to state 40–45, 74
Renaissance, and M. 61, 78–79
renovation (of state) 22–25, 55–59
Report on . . . Pistoia Factions 112–13
Ricci, Giuliano de' 137, 206
Richelieu 230–31
Risorgimento 285–96, 317
Rivadeneira, Pedro de 243
Roman Catholic Church 43, 188. See also religion
Romans (antiquity), M.'s opinions 36, 38, 52, 69, 72
Rosa, Salvator 209
Rousseau 281–82
Rucellai, Cosimo di 76, 120, 125
Russia, Machiavellianism in 305–13

Salazar, Diego de 242
San Casciano (M.s house) 158
Sansovino, F. 201
Sarpi, Paolo 211, 283
Savonarola 50, 56, 146, 169–71
Schlegel, Friedrich von 262
Schoppe, Gaspar 255–56
Segni, 195, 197
Setanti, Joaquim 250–51
Settalà, L. 213
Shakespeare 236
Shelley 240
Soderini, Pier 67, 69, 143, 145, 150, 156

Sophists, 91–92
Sorel, Georges 302
Spain, Machiavellianism in 242–53
speech, freedom of 64
Speech on the Reform of the State of Florence 161
Spenser, Edmund 233–34
Spengler 35
Spinoza 220–21
Summary of Matters of Lucca 128, 161
state: defined 18–19; ideal 90, 93, 213–16; and the individual 25–26, 51–52, 59–62; organic nature 22–25, 26; reasons of, *see raison d'état*; renovation 22–25, 26, 55–59. *See also* government
Stearns, F. P. 321
Strada, Famiano 213
Strozzi, Lorenzo di Filippo 126, 199
style (M.s) 18–20
Swiss, M.'s opinions 46, 52
Switzerland, Machiavellianism in 264

Tasso, Torquato 212
Tkaciev, N. I. 308
Tolstoi, P. A. 305
Treitschke 20, 263
Trotsky, Leon 310–12
tyrannicide 184, 244–45

United States, Machiavellianism in 313–24
"*uomo unico*," *see* "one man"

Urbino, Lorenzo d' 119, 145
utopianism 90, 93, 213–16

Valdichiana Rebels 114–15
Valentino, *see* Borgia, Caesar
Vanini, J. C. 221–22
Varchi, Benedetto 195, 197–98
verità effetuale 21
Vernacci, Giovanni 160
Verri, Pietro 283
Vespucci, Agostino 139
Vettori, Francesco 45, 116, 139, 158–159, 171–72
Vettori, Paolo 158
Vico, G. B. 266–73, 286
Villari, Pasquale 61, 79, 285
Vinci, Leonardo da 50, 173
virtù 32–36, 70
Vitelli, Paolo 113, 146
vivere civile 63
vivere libero 63
Voltaire 122, 228–29, 276–80

war 26–27, 125–26
Wickliffe, Robert 316–18
Words . . . on Providing Money 113–14, 150
Wordsworth, William 239

Young, Edward 238–39

Zuccolo, Ludovico 213